ALAN ROSENTHAL is professor of political science at Rutgers University, and director of the Center for State Legislative Research and Service at the Eagleton Institute of Politics. He holds a Ph.D. degree from Princeton University.

Pedagogues and Pov

Teacher Groups in School F

EDUCATION IN LARGE CITIES SER

Alan K. Campbell, *Series Editor*

Pedagogues and Power

Teacher Groups in School Politics

ALAN ROSENTHAL

SYRACUSE UNIVERSITY PRESS

Foreword

Improving the quality of public education in America's large central cities is one of the most important domestic problems facing this country. It is within the central cities that many of the disadvantaged groups are concentrated; and partly because of this concentration the largest cities, more than any other type of governmental unit, are facing complex and difficult fiscal and social problems.

The *Education in Large Cities Series* represents an attempt to isolate and analyze policies and policy-making in America's large-city educational systems. The volumes are based on findings of the Large City Education Systems Study, sponsored by the Carnegie Corporation of New York, and conducted by the Metropolitan Studies Program of the Maxwell Graduate School of Citizenship and Public Affairs, Syracuse University, over the past four years.

The central emphasis of the study was on the economics and politics of large-city education. Five large cities, New York, Chicago, Boston, San Francisco, and Atlanta, were selected to receive extensive examination. The economics portion of the study concerned the public financing of education and the interrelation between the inputs and outputs of large-city schools, while the political analysis ranged from the forces involved in acquiring federal funds for education to the role of teachers' organizations in making educational policy.

All of the findings reported, and those yet to be reported, make clear that America faces a crisis in its central city schools. The failure of these schools to provide adequate education for the disadvantaged has been amply documented. Not only do disadvantaged pupils start out in their education behind other pupils, but as they progress through the school system they fall even further behind.

The findings also make clear that America has devoted fewer resources to the education of its inner-city pupils than it has to its middle-income students. Not only is this a result of the weakness of central city tax bases, but of the manner in which state education aid formulas work. In other words, instead of matching resources to need, the pattern is exactly the opposite.

v

Since these studies were done by students of economics, political science, and administration rather than of education, the reports do not carry any new information about educational techniques. Nevertheless, the findings do show that thus far no major breakthroughs have occurred. Further, the findings make clear that the type of efforts which will have to be made will be costly. This emphasizes, again, the significance of the fiscal characteristics in the provision of educational services.

Although the significance of education to nearly all of the goals of American society hardly needs emphasizing, perhaps the failures do need it. It is these failures which the various reports of the study document. The final volume in the series will try to draw together the policy implications which grow out of these findings.

The statements made and views expressed are solely the responsibility of the authors, but any research effort of this magnitude involves literally hundreds of people. In addition to the members of the research staff, these include many others whose cooperation was crucial to the success of the project. The author's preface to each volume will give appropriate acknowledgement to those who helped with that particular volume, but it is necessary to mention here a few individuals and institutions vital to the entire undertaking.

Without the financial support of the Carnegie Corporation of New York, the Large City Education Systems Study would not have been possible. Equally crucial was the cooperation of the five city school systems in which the large-city study had a representative for nearly two years. In every case, the personnel of the system extended full cooperation and made every possible effort to assist the Study representatives in carrying out their assignments. Without implying their endorsement of the findings of this Study, thanks are extended to each superintendent and his staff: Atlanta, Mr. John W. Letson; Boston, Mr. William W. Ohrenberger; Chicago, Mr. Benjamin Willis; New York City, Mr. Calvin E. Gross and Mr. Bernard E. Donovan; and San Francisco, Mr. Harold Spears.

Holding the whole operation together, and smoothing the administrative path for all members of the staff, was the executive secretary of the Metropolitan Studies Program, Mrs. Jane Rood. Every member of the Study's staff, and particularly its director, is in her debt.

ALAN K. CAMPBELL, *Director*
Metropolitan Studies Program, Syracuse University

Preface

This study, one of several in the *Education in Large Cities Series,* deals with the role of teacher organizations in making educational policy. Today, there are many forces reshaping the educational scene. Some may well exhaust themselves, while others will continue to persist. Among the latter, the teachers movement holds promise of having great and enduring impact. It is still too early to tell whether teacher groups generally will work to accomplish major reform or rather serve to defend the status quo. Just how they employ newly acquired power remains to be seen.

The purpose of this book is to examine some of the most important political characteristics of contemporary teacher groups, yet the book is not a comprehensive history. While it makes reference to recent developments, it can hardly describe those important events which are occurring with increasing frequency. Rather, it concentrates on certain factors that account for the emergence, primarily during the period from 1961 through 1965, of teacher organizations as potent members of the educational community. Nor does the book represent an effort on the author's part to defend or condemn policies and practices of those involved in the politics of public education. It represents instead an attempt to describe how and explain why teacher participation and power develop in large cities. If it accomplishes this, those who read it should have a better understanding of the recent past and a clearer perspective of the immediate future.

Any author hopes to achieve as wide a readership as possible. I am no exception. What I have to say is addressed to all those concerned with school politics—many social scientists, school board members, superintendents and administrators, teacher leaders and rank-and-file, and others. Such an audience is both wide and diverse. My approach to teacher organizations cannot be equally suited to everyone. Training and experience as a political scientist have compelled me to examine and discuss certain aspects of the subject in particular ways. The types of questions asked, evidence offered, and methods of interpretation used will be most familiar to my own colleagues, to sociologists, and to researchers in education and administration. Nevertheless, practitioners as well as professors, participants as well as observers should have no difficulty in assessing the data and recognizing the major dimensions of teacher participation and power.

In a research endeavor such as this one, important choices have to be made. One involves the principal targets for exploitation. The Large City Education Systems Study, sponsored by the Carnegie Corporation and conducted by the Metropolitan Studies Program of Syracuse University, selected five large cities for examination. Nine teacher organizations exist in these cities and comprise the basic subject matter for my work. Four groups are affiliated with the American Federation of Teachers (AFT): the New York City United Federation of Teachers (UFT); the Boston Teachers Union (BTU); the Chicago Teachers Union (CTU); and the San Francisco Federation of Teachers (SFFT). Three are affiliated with the National Education Association (NEA): The Chicago Education Association (CEA); the San Francisco Classroom Teachers Association (SFCTA); and the Atlanta Teachers Association (ATA). Two are independent groups: the Boston Teachers Alliance (BTA) and the Teachers Association of San Francisco (TASF).

The teacher groups mentioned above are as varied in character as the cities in which they are located. It might have been desirable to explore each one thoroughly but this was impossible. Some restrictions were necessary. On the one hand, I might have surveyed all of the groups, attending to only a few aspects of their complex lives. On the other hand, I might have dealt with a few groups, focusing intensively on a larger number of aspects. Actually, I chose each strategy, according to the specific objective I was trying to achieve. With regard to several questions, this study covers all of the organizations in the five cities. With regard to others, it concentrates on groups in New York, Boston, and San Francisco and makes little or no reference to Chicago and Atlanta.

Decisions governing the selection of certain cities and the use of particular methods of investigation and analysis were shaped to some extent by the kinds of resources at my disposal and the availability of information from place to place. Even more important, the frame of reference which I brought to the subject determined the scope, analysis, and the types of conclusions reached. The approach adopted prompted me to ask questions about participation and power, as well as attitudes and behavior, and to conceive of teacher organizations as groups pressing their demands on local governments of public education.

Although I have been eclectic in exploring these problems, my overall strategy is based on concepts derived from the study of interest groups by contemporary political scientists. The professional literature treating interest groups in American politics is rich and varied. There is no point in discussing it here, except to mention how it meshes with my own purposes. Those who have been working in this area, like David B. Truman (*The Governmental Process,* 1958), Samuel J. Eldersveld ("American Interest Groups: A Survey of Research and Some Implications for Theory and Method," in Henry W. Ehrmann, *Interest Groups on Four Continents,* 1958), and Harry Eckstein (*Pressure Group Politics,* 1960), generally agree on what should be of greatest concern to investigators. First, they stress group effectiveness, access, or influence. Second, they point to the characteristics of groups and the attributes of governmental decision-making structures, both of which are believed to account for the influence exercised by an interest group.

These matters have received considerable and illuminating attention. Some researchers have examined the behavior and impact of political interest groups. Others have dwelt on internal characteristics and processes. Some have concentrated on one group's activities in many situations. Others have focused on the activities of several allied or competing groups in a single situation. My own aims correspond to some extent with those of political scientists who have studied interest groups previously, but they are not exactly the same. In order to assess and explain differential influence, I compare a number of similar groups, instead of treating only one or sharply contrasting types. My description of influence is not based on the resolution of a single issue in one place alone, but covers a range of issues in different community settings. My explanation of influence does not rest on any one type of factor, but it depends on several types.

The concepts I have developed and explored in this study of teacher groups in school politics posit the importance of four categories of interdependent variables: first, *organizational strength,* based largely on a group's internal characteristics; second, *organizational opportunities,* shaped mainly by the practices of public school government and the dispositions of public school teachers; third, *organizational behavior,* determined primarily by strength and opportunities; and fourth, *organizational influence,* related to the combination of factors mentioned above. No single research technique is equally well suited to examining each of these categories. Therefore, I have employed different techniques as they seemed useful and have described them wherever appropriate in chapters of the text.

The first chapter of this book serves as a general introduction to the contemporary teachers movement in the United States. It discusses the doctrinal positions of educational administration and of NEA and AFT as they pertain to teacher participation, organizational involvement, and conflict. It also advances several explanations of the new militancy and describes recent patterns of behavior. All of these themes are developed in succeeding chapters.

In Chapters II and III, critical elements of organizational strength are considered. The first of these two chapters deals briefly with the struggle for adherents between the two national organizations. It then concentrates on the bases of group membership in two large cities. The second examines the motivations of teacher group leaders in all five cities, delineates the dimensions of militancy, and analyzes how these dimensions depend on oganizational affiliation, educational conditions, and personal and situational factors.

Chapters IV and V focus on New York, Boston, and San Francisco. The first of these chapters examines three patterns of organizational behavior—conflict, accommodation, and maneuver. The second explains these patterns in terms of organizational opportunities, which are mainly shaped by the conduct of educational chieftains and the attitudes of rank-and-file teachers.

Chapter VI surveys the distribution of power among mayors, boards of education, school superintendents, and central-headquarters administrators. It reveals patterns ranging from a concentration to a dispersion of powers, depending upon the city and the policy domain under scrutiny. With the relative powers of educational dominants established, Chapter VII explores the organizational influence of teachers in New York, Boston, and San Francisco. It compares the influence of three groups on the resolution of position and style issues which confront them.

In conclusion, Chapter VIII reviews the most important dimensions and findings. Here I specify and evaluate the essential conceptual elements in the study of the role and influence of teacher groups in school politics.

I have recently reported on some aspects of this research in several journal articles. A section of Chapter I was published in similar form as "Administrator-Teacher Relations: Harmony or Conflict?" in the *Public Administration Review,* 27 (June, 1967), pp. 154–61. My treatment of the bases of group membership in New York and Boston, part of Chapter II, appeared in somewhat different form as "The Strength of Teacher Organizations: Factors Influencing Membership in Two Large Cities," in the *Sociology of Education,* 39 (Fall, 1966), pp. 359–80. Two other articles in which a few of my findings have been noted are: "New Voices in Public Education," *Teachers College Record,* 68 (October, 1966), pp. 13–20 and "Pedagogues and Power: A Descriptive Survey," *Urban Affairs Quarterly,* 2 (September, 1966), pp. 83–102.

Like other works in this series, my study depended heavily on the cooperation and assistance of many people.

The 185 teachers who responded to the leadership questionnaire and the number I interviewed personally must be regarded as my chief collaborators. School board members, superintendents, and administrators in New York, Boston, and San Francisco and officials of the National Education Association and the American Federation of Teachers also provided information essential to my purposes.

I am particularly grateful for the help given me by Alan Campbell and others who participated in the Large City Educations Systems project. Lawrence O'Connell and Robert Lee, studying Boston and San Francisco respectively, made gathering information in these cities both productive and enjoyable. They shared their knowledge and insights and taught me much of what I know about school politics. Marian Oberfest in New York, Thomas Fox in Chicago, and Thomas Lauth in Atlanta were also helpful. Without their efforts, it would have been far more difficult for me to pursue or achieve my survey objectives.

At different stages along the way, I received able research assistance from Richard Feld and Renee Glattstein and institutional support from the Urban Research Center at Hunter College of the City University of New York and the Eagleton Institute of Politics at Rutgers University.

I wish also to thank those who read all or parts of this manuscript, at a time when it was still possible to make improvements. Blanche Blank, Alan Campbell, Jamison Doig, Laurence Iannoccone, Robert Lee, Larry O'Connell, Marvin Schick, and Charles Tantillo offered advice I have tried to incorporate in the pages that follow.

Pat DeCandia typed and proofread one manuscript after another. I am grateful that she survived it all. Others at Eagleton—Edith Saks, Chickie Charwin, Susan Hetherington, and Christine Shaw—also helped, especially in the final stages.

A politician of my acquaintance once criticized professors at state universities for writing books on the people's time. Much of this book has been written on my wife's and my children's time. I appreciate their patience, but am thankful nonetheless to have a position which is protected by tenure.

To all these people I owe a large share of whatever credit this study deserves. As much as I might desire otherwise, the blame for errors or shortcomings is completely mine.

A.R.

Summer, 1968

Contents

Foreword   v

Preface   viii

I. The Contemporary Teachers Movement   1
  The Clash of Doctrine   2
    Participation in Educational Policy-Making   2
    The Character of Organizational Involvement   6
    Harmony or Conflict   9
  Mobilization and Struggle   13
    Some Explanations of the New Militancy   13
    The Consequences of Warfare   15
    The Changing Educational Scene   19

II. Group Membership   22
  The Struggle for Adherents   22
  Factors Influencing Membership   28
    Personal Factors   29
    School Factors   34
    Organizational Factors   41
  The Varying Bases of Membership   45

III. Leadership Motivations   48
  Dimensions of Militancy   49
  The Impact of Group Affiliation   58
  Educational Conditions and Their Effects   62
  Personal and Situational Factors and Their Effects   63
  The Determinants of Militancy   65

IV. Patterns of Behavior   71
  Conflict in New York City   73
  Accommodation in Boston   82
  Maneuver in San Francisco   87

V. Opportunities For Action 94

The Conduct of Educational Chieftains 96
Resistance and Combat 98
Benevolence, Diversion, and Delay 103

Teacher Communities and Problems of Representation 109
Rank-and-File Constraints 109
Competitive Pressures 116

Contrasts in Group Behavior 121

VI. Government of Education 123

Perceptions of Power 123
Distributions of Power 127
Relative Power 129

Independence from Mayoral Control 131
Separation of Powers 133
Sharing of Powers 135
Integration of Powers 137

Board, Superintendent, and Bureaucracy 140
Checks and Balances 143
Superintendent–Board Collaboration 146
Dominance of Laymen 148
Dominance of the Superintendent 151

VII. Organizational Influence 154

Efforts and Effects 155
Position Issues—Economic Welfare 156
Position Issues—Working Conditions 159
Style Issues 165

The Nature of Group Influence 171

VIII. Strength, Politics, and Power 174

Index 187

Tables

1. AFT Membership, by Size of City and Region, 1965 25
2. State Competition for Representation between NEA and
   AFT Groups, 1961–66 26
3. Representational Election Outcomes, by Size of City, 1961–66 27

4. Boston Teacher Alliance and Boston Teacher Union Membership, by Sex, 1963 and 1965   31

5. Boston Faculty Sex and Alliance and Union Membership, by Division, 1963 and 1965   32

6. Boston Faculty Sex and Female Membership in the Union, by Division, 1965   33

7. New York City and Boston Teacher Organization Membership, by Division and Year   35

8. Boston Teacher Alliance and Boston Teacher Union Membership by Division, with Sex Controlled, 1963 and 1965   36

9. New York City Size of Faculty and UFT Membership, by Division, 1962, 1963, and 1965   37

10. New York City Teaching Situation and UFT Membership, by Division, 1962, 1963, and 1965   38

11. Boston Administrators' Affiliations and Teacher Organization Membership, Elementary Schools, 1963 and 1965   40

12. New York City Strike Turnout and UFT Membership Growth, by Pre-Strike Membership   44

13. New York City Strike Turnout and UFT Membership— The Impact of the 1962 Strike on Subsequent Membership Strength   44

14. Teacher Organizations and Leadership Respondents   50

15. Participatory Objectives and Prescriptions for Organization Power, by Policy Domain   55

16. Participatory Objectives and Prescriptions for Establishment Power, by Policy Domain   57

17. Participatory Objectives and Tactical Orientations   58

18. The Strength of Relationships between Union Affiliation and Leadership Orientations   60

19. The Strength of Relationships between Dissatisfaction and Leadership Orientations   63

20. The Strength of Relationships between Personal and Situational Factors and Leadership Orientations   64

21. Organizational Affiliation and Leadership Militancy, with Other Factors Controlled   66

22. Educational Conditions, Personal and Situational Factors, and Leadership Militancy, with Group Affiliation Controlled   67

23. The Militancy of Teacher Leaders, by Organization, in Five
    Cities   72
24. Teacher and Leader Views of UFT Collective Bargaining
    Priorities, 1965   112
25. The Distribution of Educational Power   128
26. An Index of Relative Educational Power   131
27. Relative Independence from Mayoral Control   132
28. Relative Power of the Superintendency, Compared to the
    Board of Education   141
29. Relative Power of the Superintendency, Compared to the
    Administrative Bureaucracy   142
30. Relative Powerlessness of Teacher Organizations   155

I. The Contemporary Teachers Movement

Today, more than ever before, public education in the United States is in a state of ferment. The managers of the nation's school systems, try as they may, can scarcely escape the pressures besetting them. Confronted first by the civil rights revolution and then by black power movements, by demands for racial integration and by those for compensatory school programs and local control, they are being forced to respond to a world they never made and not of their own choosing. Members of local boards of education and professional administrators—the people who have had the most to say about running the public schools—now are under pressure to adopt new curricula, different methods of teaching, and altered patterns of school organization. Formerly, the leaderships of local education had only to rise to the occasion of raising greater funds for school improvement and expansion. Today they have to struggle with problems completely unanticipated a decade ago.

Another revolution is in progress, further complicating the already complicated lives of members of public school establishments. At the same time that they are being assailed by forces from outside their systems, they are being challenged from within. Classroom teachers have organized themselves and are seeking guarantees that they will not only be listened to on matters concerning school policy but that they shall be given an active part in determining policy. This is not to imply that relations among school boards, administrators, and teachers have been free from contention in the past. Periodically, teachers appealed to their superintendents, boards, and communities in order to achieve salary increases. Yet, for the most part, educational professionals—administrators and teachers—stood together in amicable hierarchy. The show of professional unity was notable indeed, but no more notable than the present reality of its withering away.

One thing has become crystal-clear. Public school teachers, once the docile handmaidens of public education, are no longer quiescent. Spearheaded by resolute state and local organizations and stimulated

1

by the competition between the National Education Association (NEA) and the American Federation of Teachers (AFT), the "teachers movement" is gaining strength nationwide, and particularly in large cities. The former widespread, if passive, consensus on the operating rules of the educational game has undergone erosion. Teachers, or at least their leaders, are beginning to envisage a full partnership in the educational enterprise. They are beginning to talk about rights, not privileges, and power, not consultation. Their actions indicate that they mean what they are saying, as they never meant it before.

THE CLASH OF DOCTRINE[1]

What roles should teachers play in shaping public school policy? Should they participate at all, in their individual capacities as faculty members, or by virtue of organizational affiliation? Should differences between teachers and their employers, if and when they exist, be settled in friendly fashion or by combat? These questions are major ones.

In order to appreciate the nature of the contemporary teachers movement, it would help to examine the positions of educational managers and educational employees on the matters of participation, collective power, and combat. To ascertain employee doctrines, we have relied upon the pronouncements of spokesmen for national teacher organizations. For the moment, let us assume that what NEA and AFT representatives say in Washington and Chicago both reflects and shapes the opinions of teachers across the country. Later, in Chapter III, we shall test this assumption by examining the views of teacher leaders in five large cities. To get at administrative doctrine, we have taken a more circuitous route, relying on, among other sources, a number of leading textbooks in the field of educational administration. It is useful to assume here that the beliefs of school superintendents and the prescriptive statements in the training literature bear close resemblance. Likely, the two are inextricably linked. The stuff in texts influences the ideas of practicing administrators and, in turn, the views and behavior of administrators help shape the textual lessons.

Participation in Educational Policy-Making

There was a time, decades ago, when few people thought very much, of even thought at all, of the idea that teachers might play a role in determining school policies. The doctrine of educational administration then stressed the "authority" of the superintendent, not "democracy"

---

[1] A version similar to this section appeared earlier as "Administrator-Teacher Relations: Harmony or Conflict?" *Public Administration Review*, XXVII (June, 1967), 154–61.

and "participation" as it does today. With regard to teachers and their spokesmen, except for the hardy souls promoting the cause of unionization, scarcely any addressed themselves to this question.

Until about the mid-1930's school administration was heavily influenced by concepts and practices associated with scientific management and efficiency. In the works of men like Franklin Bobbitt and Ellwood Cubberly the school administrator was pictured as the dominant educational figure—the man who knew all the answers and who could and should tell others what to do and how to do it. Cubberly, for instance, described the superintendency as the office "up to which and down from which authority, direction, and inspiration flow." Insofar as he had to deal with workers on the line, the superintendent, according to this same writer, was "the supervisor of instruction . . . and also the leader, adviser, inspirer, and friend of teachers." While administrators were obliged to manage their staffs in humane and understanding fashion, teachers were obligated to faithfully perform their productive functions. As loyal workers, they might even be trusted to advise and counsel their administrative leaders. But anything smacking of policy decision was deemed beyond both their rightful purview and their professional competence.[2]

Thanks to the human relations movement, an entirely different strain dominates the current literature on educational administration. Sophisticated methods of content analysis are unnecessary in order to discern the popularity and pervasiveness of democracy in contemporary doctrine. Commenting on this more recent element, W. W. Charters has observed that "hardly a textbook on school administration fails to invoke the distinction between autocratic and democratic leadership . . . ," the former disavowed and the latter enthusiastically applauded.[3] Internal democracy brings with it teacher participation. Therefore, administrators are now taught to engage their staffs in the formulation of policy, especially on matters which immediately affect teachers and their work.[4]

Although seldom clearly stated, administrative rationale for teacher involvement can readily be pieced together. "The liberating values of group action through participation," and so forth, means that teacher

[2] Quoted and discussed in Raymond E. Callahan and H. Warren Button, "Historical Change of the Role of the Man in the Organization: 1865–1950," in Daniel E. Griffiths, ed., *Behavioral Science and Educational Administration* (Chicago: National Society for the Study of Education, 1964), 73–92.

[3] "The Social Background of Teaching," in N. L. Gage, ed., *Handbook of Research on Teaching* (Chicago: Rand McNally, 1963), 781.

[4] There is some evidence on this point. In their study of the superintendency role, Neal Gross and associates found that of 105 Massachusetts superintendents interviewed all but three thought it desirable for teachers to participate in policy formulation. *Explorations in Role Analysis* (New York: Wiley, 1958), 362.

participation improves staff performance and facilitates administration. Techniques such as two-way communication, teacher committees, and cooperatively planned policies promote staff morale. The latter ingredient is vital to the success of instructional programs. In addition, the understanding and sense of joint responsibility engendered by participation helps to improve the execution of policy. That is to say, if teachers work on a problem, share in developing alternatives, and are in on making a choice, they will be more willing to carry out policies and adapt, if need be, to promulgated change. The State Department of Education in New York, for instance, advising that teachers have an opportunity to present proposals, advice, and views prior to policy adoption by school boards, put the point simply: "Participation of the staff in consideration of policy contributes to more acceptable decisions and their more effective implementation."[5] A final reason, one that is usually left vague, is that the cooperative approach promotes more effective administrative control of the educational enterprise. It permits administrators to artfully influence the behavior of their employees and it enables them, by means of cooptation, to discourage teacher tendencies toward anti-managerial orientations.

Since staff involvement is justified not only because of what it does for teachers, but more importantly in terms of how it aids administrators, one might guess that a line setting limits would be drawn somewhere. Indeed, it is. Implicitly noted in administrative doctrine is the following argument: responsibility for decisions is delegated by boards of education to school superintendents; it cannot satisfactorily be shared; thus, superintendents are obligated to make final decisions. One authority states the limitation in a rather backhanded way. Teachers should be made aware, he writes, that they are being consulted on vital educational matters and that "their ideas or proposals for action make a difference to *those who have the power to make final decisions.*"[6] Or, as another states in a similar vein, the staff must recognize its own subordinate role in the cooperative enterprise and "develop understanding and appreciation of the limits within which it has power of *final* decision."[7] The document issued by the New York education department, to which we have already referred, makes the same point. Teachers, as professionals, may have the right to influence school policies, but they have the cor-

---

[5] State Education Department, University of the State of New York, *School Board-Superintendent-Staff Relationships* (Albany: The Department, 1966), 5.

[6] Emphasis added. Roald F. Campbell *et al., Introduction to Educational Administration* (Boston: Allyn & Bacon, 1958), 214.

[7] Russell T. Gregg, "The Administrative Process," in Roald F. Campbell and Russell T. Gregg, eds., *Administrative Behavior in Education* (New York: Harper, 1957), 280. See also Edgar L. Morphet *et al., Educational Administration* (Englewood Cliffs: Prentice-Hall, 1959), 98–9.

responding responsibility to bear in mind that final authority for decision-making resides with their superiors.

One might expect that the views of teacher spokesmen on the staff's rightful role in policy-making would differ substantially from those of administrators. Until lately, however, differences were slight. A national organization like NEA took little cognizance of the local school scene. Its platforms repeatedly made mention of local teacher participation, but the Association's energies were almost entirely devoted to other matters. Standards and ethics, tasks of lobbying for federal funds, the conduct and dissemination of research, and the support of state affiliates commanded major attention.

Like its rival, AFT has long waved the banner of participation, doubtless in a more flamboyant manner. Throughout its life, the union showed little reluctance to express its dissatisfaction with the participatory rights actually accorded teachers. If administrators had surrendered some doctrinal ground, this meant little, for teachers were only permitted to take part in policy-making on the most inconsequential matters. Despite its firm opposition to hierarchy in the schools, the Federation's positive program appeared modest or ambiguous. AFT seemed to call not for equal power in making decisions but rather for some system of consultation which would ensure that administrators took seriously the views of their staffs.

Due to the impetus of events and changing conditions, about which we shall comment shortly, both national groups are more concerned today with claiming their rights than in fulfilling what management cites as their responsibilities. The right to exercise professional judgment, the right to a voice in selecting teaching materials and planning the curriculum, the right to some say on class size and non-teaching assignments, the right to a major voice in setting salaries and related welfare benefits—all are being claimed by leaders of the two national organizations. This boils down to an increasing demand by teachers for a larger share of authority and a greater role in educational decision-making. AFT's recent president, Charles Cogen, missed few occasions to mention the need for teachers to upgrade their status and dignity and not to settle for anything less than complete equality. In similar step, Richard Batchelder, a former president of NEA, told the 1966 convention of school administrators that teachers "have been taking seriously the things that superintendents have been saying to each other . . . about the right of teachers to participate in the formulation of policies which affect them."[8]

Both peak organizations deem teacher participation a matter of

[8] Remarks before the 98th annual meeting of the American Association of School Administrators (AASA), Atlantic City, N.J., February 15, 1966.

urgency. At its 1965 convention, NEA enacted a resolution insisting on the rights of local affiliates to participate with boards of education in the formulation of policies of common concern. These would include not only problems dealing with "welfare" or "working conditions" but rather the entire range of policies related to conditions under which teachers teach and children learn. As one staff member of the Association interpreted the scope: "The subject matter of negotiations, then, should be as broadly defined as the educational program itself."[9] The AFT's position as to the subjects on which teachers should have a say is no different. Class size, number of classes taught, curriculum, textbooks and supplies, hiring standards—in fact anything having to do with the operation of the school—are matters to which they should address their organizational power.

The Character of Organizational Involvement

School administrators used to deal with individual teachers, not teachers as they are collectively organized today. In consequence the doctrines of educational administration pay relatively little attention to formal, organized groups of teachers. Front-line pedagogues are simply individual professionals in the system's service. Their participation, when the question is discussed, derives from their status as faculty, not from their status as representatives of an organization. When groups themselves are accorded legitimacy, their prescribed role according to administrative doctrine is severely circumscribed. Only on matters concerning personal welfare, such as salaries and working conditions, is collective participation regarded as proper. On matters of educational programming, including curriculum development, personnel practices, and class size, teachers should participate through staff committees, not by virtue of organizational membership. One good example of this outlook is the view held by Calvin Gross, a former superintendent of schools in New York City. Although Gross had to coexist with one of the most powerful teacher groups on the educational scene, he stuck to the belief that staff involvement on issues other than salaries and working conditions should not be channeled through a bargaining organization.[10]

Both the National Education Association and the American Federation of Teachers naturally consider local organization and collective

[9] Jack H. Kleinmann, "Guidelines for Professional Negotiation," paper delivered at AASA meetings, February 15, 1966. On the matter of scope, see Myron Lieberman and Michael H. Moskow, *Collective Negotiations for Teachers* (Chicago: Rand McNally, 1966), Chapter VIII, and T. M. Stinnett *et al.*, *Professional Negotiation in Public Education* (New York: Macmillan, 1966), 154–55.

[10] Calvin Gross, "Ways to Deal with the New Teacher Militancy," *Phi Delta Kappan*, XLVI (December, 1964), 149.

action to be vital means for the achievement of those professional rights which teachers claim. The former group in the past gave scant attention to the job of energizing local associations. Instead, NEA allowed teachers pretty much to go it alone in their respective communities. In contrast, the Federation since earliest days put great stress on local organization as the only effective means of staff participation.[11]

The necessity for strong organization at national, state, and local levels is today agreed upon by both union and association spokesmen. Urbanization and consolidation have led to large, depersonalized school systems. Especially in such places, professional rights can be assured and exercised only through collective action. In the absence of permanent organization communications among teachers themselves, negotiations between employees and managers are exceedingly difficult, if not impossible. Organization provides the effective means for teachers to decide among themselves. It alone serves as a framework through which they can participate with administrators and board members on an equal basis. Staff participation through various committees of teacher representatives is no adequate substitute for broad-based organization. In the former relationship, an administration can overwhelm atomized employees; in the latter, a collective agent protects the rank-and-file. In short, unity implies power. So teachers must rely upon group representation to make their voices heeded by those above.

Organization means more to NEA and AFT than common membership or action in concert with colleagues. A wide difference exists between situations where teachers are not consulted at all and those in which their views are regularly solicited. Similarly, there is a distinction between cases where teachers collectively participate with no established guidelines and those in which formal ground rules govern negotiations between a majority representative and the school administration. Both national organizations today encourage formal relationships for their local affiliates.

As a member of the AFL, and later the AFL-CIO, the American Federation of Teachers has advocated collective bargaining arrangements for more than thirty years.[12] Not until much later, and evidently in response to the union challenge, did the National Education Association

---

[11] See *Organizing the Teaching Profession* (Glencoe, Ill.: Free Press, 1955), 103; also 90, 138.

[12] Michael H. Moskow points out that not until the UFT victory in 1961 did the American Federation of Teachers actively push collective bargaining for its local units. He cites a 1947 survey reporting that few union leaders, even where locals had a majority of teachers enrolled, sought bargaining rights. *Teachers and Unions* (Philadelphia: Industrial Research Unit, Wharton School of Finance and Commerce, University of Pennsylvania, 1966), 106–107.

begin to call for collective negotiations at the local level. Before 1961, NEA had little to say about group action. At its convention that year it took a step toward formulating policy on teacher–board of education relationships. In the following year, 1962, the Association launched a dramatic program for collective negotiations. The resolution adopted at the Denver convention, far more aggressive than any adopted previously, marked the official entry of NEA into the area of professional negotiation.

In certain respects, collective bargaining and professional negotiation differ. Notably, and quite predictably, the procedures of the two are dissimilar. The union's method naturally advocates that labor precedents and laws apply, and, in case of mediation and appeal as a result of a local impasse, that labor channels be used in the state. The Association denies any affinity with labor, which it claims is external to the teaching profession and little aware of the peculiar problems of educators. Obviously, then, NEA's method would remove negotiation procedures from labor laws and precedents and would resort to state educational agencies, rather than those of labor, to mediate or resolve conflicts which cannot be settled locally. In major respects, however, the two approaches are similar. Each national group is separately striving for the organizational advantages likely to be gained by contrasting procedural means. But each also is proposing important items in common: a direct, one-to-one relationship between teachers and the managers of local education and a written contract or policy defining the nature and conduct of the relationship.[13]

To achieve collective bargaining or professional negotiation, AFT and NEA further agree on what might have to be done. The relationship may have to be established through state legislation providing compulsory practices. As of now, there are laws providing for collective negotiations in public education in Alaska, California, Connecticut, Florida, Massachusetts, Michigan, New Hampshire, New Jersey, Oregon, Washington, and Wisconsin. In a number of other states, constitutional provisions or statutes permit or guarantee public employees the right to organize and bargain collectively. The Federation has urged its state affiliates to work for the adoption of statutes requiring boards to bargain with recognized agents in local school districts. The Association has been even more vigorous in urging its affiliates to push legislation requiring professional negotiation. Although it has been compelled to battle locally, NEA still prefers the state arena where associations generally are strong and federations usually are weak.[14]

[13] James P. Steffensen, *Teachers Negotiate with their School Boards* (Washington, D.C.: Office of Education, HEW, 1964), 55.
[14] Often urban combat works to the disadvantage of an NEA group. In Cleve-

There is agreement, too, that the relationship may have to be established by resort to persuasion or pressure. Thus, both national groups now advocate collective action, either for hastening the adoption of bargaining and negotiating procedures or for possible employment thereafter. There are differences, of course, between the Association's professional sanctions and the union's strikes. The former seems to risk less than the latter, since an unsuccessful strike attempt may cripple an organization. Yet, there are important similarities. Both weapons are coercive and, depending upon the specific conditions of their use by local groups, may be equally impressive to local educational authorities and equally severe in their impact upon local school systems.

Harmony or Conflict

It would be fruitless to proceed much further in attempting to distinguish collective bargaining from professional negotiation and strikes from sanctions. More important are the views of educational participants as to the existence of differences and the conflict of interests. Here, group doctrines contrast sharply with one another.

According to the tenets of educational administration, group activity, particularly when reinforced by formal arrangements, may foster unnecessary and harmful conflict. True to human relations precepts, administrative doctrine emphasizes the harmony of interests and the agreement on goals that supposedly exist among administrators and teachers. Start with these vital ingredients, add a pinch or two of consultation, and stir well with humane administration. Then few genuine misunderstandings need arise. If disagreement should occur, it may often be attributable not to the inadequacy of the recipe but to the willful intent on the parts of some to spoil the broth. Specifically, once employee organizations become viable political entities, then leaderships may develop a vested interest in seeking out and maintaining conflict situations.

But conflict, for administrators who already have their hands full, is not the path of wisdom and public service. When people think separately, make demands upon each other, and wage battle, public education stands to gain little and lose a lot. Satisfaction and justice within the

land, for example, no state laws applied. The AFL-CIO was economically and politically strong and supported the local teacher union. But groups predisposed to the local association remained neutral. As a result, pressures on the school board for one set of procedures rather than another were quite unequal. Donald H. Wollett, "The Importance of State Legislation," in Stanley M. Elam *et al.*, eds., *Readings on Collective Negotiations in Public Education* (Chicago: Rand McNally, 1967), 101. In Connecticut, by contrast, the educational association tangled with the federation of teachers at the state level and won every basic point of difference. Robbins Barstow, "Connecticut's Teacher Negotiation Law: An Early Analysis," in *ibid.*, 113–22.

system depend upon real cooperation. Consequently, reason among the likeminded, not pressure between adversaries, is the highway of educational progress. In sum, administration pleads: why fight when we are all bound together by ties of professionalism, common goals, and the mutual ability to settle minor differences sensibly?

Along rather similar lines, NEA speaks of shared interests and cooperation. Administrators and teachers alike are recruited into one inclusive organization. This leads to some problems, but as an Association official, arguing the case of administrative membership, said: ". . . the primary premise underlying the concept of education as a profession is that all of its practitioners, regardless of their individual role in the over-all process, have a common interest and objective."[15] And at the Association's 1966 convention the new Executive Secretary, noting commonality of goals, purposes, and expertise, declared: "I refuse to believe that the concept of professional unity is dead. . . ."[16]

All professionals are part of the same team, "children of light" trying to achieve the best for public education. Despite over-all unity, the peculiar position of the school superintendent has recently been recognized by NEA. The very nature of the superintendency forces him to respond not only to professional norms but also to non-professional pressures. He has to represent both teachers and the school board. Still, professional solidarity can be maintained. Even with formal negotiations, no breach between teachers and administration is necessary. Squarely in the middle, the superintendent should align himself with neither the board nor the teachers. He can serve as a statesman, a neutral catalyst providing objective information, a facilitating and harmonizing agent in the cooperative development of educational policies.

As mentioned earlier, NEA, like its rival, provides for the possible resort to force by means of professional sanctions. These may range from the mildest form, which alerts members to the existence of unsatisfactory conditions in a given school district or state, to stronger ones, which involve the withdrawal and withholding of teacher services in a district or state. Nevertheless, contemporary doctrine stresses consensus rather than conflict. The employment of sanctions should be an exceptional last resort. Given good faith in negotiations, the resolution of differences depends not on combat but on orderly methods of reaching mutually satisfactory results. In fact, if a professional negotiation agreement exists, chances are great that sanctions will rarely have to be invoked.

[15] Robbins Barstow, Jr., "Which Way New York City—Which Way the Profession?" *Phi Delta Kappan,* XLIII (December, 1961), 124.
[16] T. M. Stinnett, quoted in *American Teacher,* September 1966.

The Contemporary Teachers Movement / 11

Thus, basic assumptions which underlie AFT's approach to resolving issues are not accepted by the National Education Association. Unlike the Federation, it "is not so sure about the inevitable inherency, nature, and depth of conflict in the schools" and is reluctant to accept the concepts of power and opposed interests as being applicable to relationships within the educational fraternity.[17] An occasional fight may have to be waged. Sanctions may have to be invoked in order to win professional negotiation rights. Sometimes their employment may be necessary to persuade school boards and politicians of the merits of professional claims on community or state resources. But these will only be skirmishes, in no way disturbing the solidarity of the profession. The major battle, if there be one, is that which finds all true professionals unified in opposing "those forces which would pit one segment of the teaching profession against another."[18]

Without doubt, the sharpest division between the two national organizations is over questions concerning commonality of interests, the need for combat, and the uses of power. For a long time the Federation has talked in terms of "the two professions," stemming from the contrasting statuses of teachers and administrators. It excludes school superintendents from membership, whereas NEA both welcomes them and places them in top leadership positions. According to the union, the ban is because administrators have different ideas and responsibilities as a result of their dissimilar roles in the school organization. This means that they are managers, and as such are more closely aligned with school boards than with school teachers. This division between employers and employees is inevitable. To call attention to it is not to create it, but rather only to perceive what really exists.[19] Furthermore, there is the feeling that to build an organization around dissimilar interests would be extremely hazardous. Group cohesion ordinarily becomes weaker as group homogeneity declines. In other words, the more diverse an organization's membership, the more likely that the organization will fall prey to internal conflict and dissension.[20]

---

[17] Wesley A. Wildman and Charles R. Perry, "Group Conflict and School Organization," *Phi Delta Kappan*, XLVII (January, 1966), 246.

[18] Quoted from Batchelder's address before AASA, *loc. cit.*

[19] Robert E. Doherty and Walter E. Oberer, *Teachers, School Boards, and Collective Bargaining* (Ithaca, N.Y.: New York State School of Industrial and Labor Relations, Cornell University, 1967), 61.

[20] Harmon Zeigler, *The Political World of the High School Teacher* (Eugene, Oregon: The Center for the Advanced Study of Educational Administration, University of Oregon, 1966), 75. Dissension has begun to affect NEA groups. In Michigan, for instance, superintendents pulled out of the Michigan Education Association and there are prospects that superintendents and principals will move out of NEA groups in other places as well. Joseph H. Cronin, "School Boards

In its philosophical outlook, AFT has deviated little from its position of a half-century ago. At that time, in a pamphlet titled "A Call to Action," it condemned the structure of control in American education. "With few exceptions," the pamphlet reads, "American public schools are autocratically administered by officials chosen by and subservient to school boards representing business and politics."[21] Today the tone is less polemical and more tactical. Even so, the theme of brave and dedicated unionists being exploited by reactionary employers prevades AFT's literature.[22] The board and the superintendent remain the teacher's adversaries. Together, these members of the educational establishment are responsible for the lack of status, dignity, and equal rights accorded classroom teachers.

An action document, written by David Selden, the union's chief organizational strategist, who was elected president in 1968, illustrates AFT's hardheaded attitude toward management. First, school administrators are servants of the boards who employ them. In suggesting tactics for local bargaining campaigns, the document points out that if union representatives meet with the superintendent, they will invariably find him doing the school board's bidding and stalling on their carefully formulated proposals. Second, school boards likely will be deaf to teacher proposals. Union locals should not ask boards to adopt their programs, members are advised, but instead should demand negotiations. "This is important," Selden explains, "because either way you're pretty sure to get a negative response, and it is much better that refusal to negotiate —undemocratic procedure—be the issue than any specific program point."[23]

Conflict rather than harmony tells the story of school relationships according to AFT. In order for teachers to win status, achieve dignity, and attain a rightful role in decision-making through collective bargaining, a hard struggle must be waged to overcome the resistance of educational authorities. And even after gains have been made and proper procedures worked out, very real issues will continue to provide a basis for conflict between teachers and their employers. As the president of the union local which has made greatest progress said, if everyone had all the facts,

and Principals—Before and After Negotiations," *Phi Delta Kappan,* XLIX (November, 1967), 125.

[21] Quoted in *Organizing the Teaching Profession, op. cit.,* 10.

[22] Doherty and Oberer, *op. cit.,* 29. These authors point out that the monthly *American Teacher* and the new quarterly *Changing Education* (of which the front cover on the first issue carried an Osborn cartoon showing a supervisor sitting on top of the head of a bound and gagged teacher) exude "a sense of victimization that almost borders on the paranoiac."

[23] "Winning Collective Bargaining," AFT, 1962. A version of this document now appears in Elam, *op. cit.,* 333–49.

"there would be greater conflict than there is at the present time."[24] To AFT, nothing is very remarkable about all this. Like democratic politics generally, the educational game is often rough-and-ready, involving the push and pull of conflicting groups. The only way to win is by recognizing the inevitability of contention and seeking power by means of militant, hard-hitting organization.

MOBILIZATION AND STRUGGLE

Collective power, combat, and more effective participation in policy formulation are beginning to reshape the educational scene. Not only doctrinal positions, and their gradual or rapid evolutions, but also recent happenings signify the awakening of public school pedagogues in many cities and an increasing number of smaller communities as well.

Some Explanations of the New Militancy

A variety of factors seem to account for current developments in the contemporary teachers movement. Some explanations put stress on economic injustice and other unfavorable conditions of employment. Accordingly, the increase in group action of late has resulted from poor salaries and substandard conditions of work fostered by penurious school boards and communities. Whereas some years ago teachers had to reconcile themselves to economic bondage, today the labor market is different. With the growing competition among school systems, and particularly between city and suburban ones, qualified teachers are in greater demand. Recognizing their growing economic potency, teachers and their spokesmen have become more and more inclined to press their demands for a fair share of society's dividends.

Another point is frequently mentioned as a cause of the new militancy. Men are embarking upon careers in elementary and secondary teaching as never before. A decade ago men comprised about one-quarter of the nation's public school teacher staff; now they account for about one-third. Their numbers are growing gradually in elementary education, and in secondary schools, during the past ten years, the proportion of males has increased from about 46 per cent to approximately 54 per cent. Men, much more than women, the argument goes, are in the vanguard of teacher politics today. For they, unlike their female colleagues, cannot economically stand meager salaries or psychologically endure low status. In the past, men tended to leave teaching for higher paying jobs, but now they have stopped running and decided to fight.

Still other explanations emphasize the trend toward bigger school

[24] Albert Shanker, in "Teacher-Supervisory Relationships: a Symposium," *Changing Education*, I (Spring, 1966), 23.

systems with the resultant loss of identity by teachers. Increasing bureau-cratization, further centralization of decision-making, and a growing distance between classroom teachers and school executives all facilitate collective action by the rank and file. A labor relations expert has commented on this point:

> The informal give-and-take . . . between teachers and administrators, characteristic of small school districts, is being replaced by a formal, bureaucratic structure of the larger ones. . . . Teachers recognize that it would be impossible to restore the informal relationship; what might be possible . . . is to regain some of the authority they once employed by accommodating themselves to the changed structure.[25]

Irreversible change in the structure of public education requires, in short, that the bureaucratic strength of the administration be matched by the organizational strength of the teachers.

Some explanations account for teacher militancy by alluding to the new regulations governing public employment—first President Kennedy's executive order in 1962 and then a host of state and local regulations—which permit employees to organize. Others view it from a different angle, emphasizing the desperate efforts by the AFL-CIO to win white-collar, service, government, and professional workers to its ranks. In any event, more and more government workers have been joining labor unions, and they have become increasingly militant in their attitudes and dealings with their government employers.[26] Teachers constitute one such group, but policemen, firemen, garbage men, transit workers, postal employees, and social service workers are others.

Another explanation accounts for contemporary teacher behavior as a product of the times. One expert portrays the current mood as one of *"dissatisfaction with the status quo expressed in action more than words."*[27] Three NEA officials write: "The emergence of new nations as a result of the twilight of colonialism . . . and of paternalism is a part of the commitment of peoples throughout the world to a new status and dignity."[28] Teachers, too, are swept up in this movement. Their recent uprisings are also pictured as an outgrowth of the civil rights drive by Negroes in the United States. Yet, the loosening of colonial bonds and the rights of citizenship slowly being accorded Negro Americans

[25] Robert E. Doherty, "Teacher Participation in the Determination of School Policy," New York State School Boards Association, 8 (February, 1966), 2; also Lieberman and Moskow, *op. cit.*, 59.

[26] Rollin B. Posey, "The New Militancy of Public Employees," *Public Administration Review*, XXVIII (March/April 1968), 112.

[27] *Ibid.*, 115. Emphasis in original.

[28] Stinnett *el al.*, *op. cit.*, 5.

have not stemmed the tide. Expectations rise, demands for equality continue to be advanced, and deprived groups resort to more forceful action. Likewise, teachers have not been placated by initial gains, but only set their sights higher. Finally, as Wesley Wildman notes, recent trends in democratic administration have whetted the appetites of teachers and prompted them to push farther. "It appears at least conceivable," he writes, "that in some situations democratic administration of any enterprise may actually hasten the process of organization and power accumulation."[29] Seeing and experiencing the benefits of some democracy, teachers do not rest content. They aspire to and work toward greater democracy in the public schools.

In one combination or another, these factors go far in explaining the heightened militancy of teachers around the country. No doubt underlying causes vary considerably from state to state and community to community, but whatever the fabric of causation may be in a particular locale, an essential and proximate ingredient of the rise of collective action as been the heated rivalry between NEA and AFT and their affiliates at state and local levels. These groups, more than any other immediate stimulus, awakened American teachers. Their words and their actions have been necessary, as Robert Doherty explains so cogently:

> Matters about which there seemed to be little interest can become issues of vital concern in the heat of a representation campaign, and teachers can easily come to believe that the denial to elementary teachers of a daily fifteen-minute rest period, for example, is a festering sore in the hide of teacher dignity when actually it is a benefit that occurs to very few until one of the competing organizations introduces it into the campaign.[30]

It is probably fair to say that were it not for the recent challenge to NEA hegemony by the American Federation of Teachers, neither the Association nor many local groups would be stirring as they are today.

The Consequences of Warfare

Perhaps few people would agree as to the specific time when warfare started. But if any period seems critical it is that of 1960–62. The major impetus of group competition and teacher militancy was the rapid ascendancy of the United Federation of Teachers in New York City. Charles Cogen, AFT's past-president, is not guilty of exaggeration when

---

[29] "Implications of Teacher Bargaining for School Administration," *Phi Delta Kappan,* XLVI (December, 1964), 154.

[30] *Loc. cit.* Doherty and Oberer argue that this growing competition "might be as important a cause of organizational activity as all the other reasons combined." *Op. cit.,* 32.

he states: "By winning our two strikes, in 1960 and 1962 in New York City, we set a pattern of teacher militancy for decades to come."[31] Sandwiched between these two strikes was the union's collective bargaining victory over an NEA-sponsored coalition. Since then the battle for membership, electoral support, representation, and benefits has been proceeding at a furious pace. Despite contradictory claims of partisans in the struggle, neither side is far out ahead or near to victory. Yet there can be little doubt that, since winning in the nation's largest city, the Federation has become a competitor whom NEA must regard most seriously.

Because of the union threat, the National Education Association probably will never be the same again. State and local associations, especially in the industrialized states of the nation, are becoming much more aggressive in confronting school boards and administrators.[32] One indication of this is the increased number of work stoppages by NEA-affiliated groups. According to the U.S. Bureau of Labor Statistics, during the two decades from 1946 through 1965, twenty-two work stoppages involving 16,450 teachers were conducted by NEA groups. But in 1966 alone, as many as eleven involving 31,200 teachers were held by local and state education associations.

National leaders and staff talk differently now than before about teacher participation and collective action. And policies such as professional negotiation and sanctions—if mentioned in previous years—have become major, and increasingly stronger, components of NEA doctrine since 1962. From our perspective, just as important as advocacy of pressure tactics is the Association's new commitment to local activity. For some time the Federation devoted its chief resources to strengthening affiliates at the local level. Meanwhile, NEA's main operations were national or through strong state affiliates. Today, however, the association pays major attention to local education associations as well. Since 1962 the national office has concentrated larger and larger resources on services to urban groups and has helped some 65 urban associations to hire professional staffs.[33] And quite recently, NEA has undertaken a massive, two-year self-study, a project prompted to some extent by the sense of urgency, if not panic, among younger members, and particularly those in larger cities where unions have been forging ahead.

[31] "The President's Column," *American Teacher,* April 1968.

[32] On the militant response of the New York State Teachers Association, see Michael D. Usdan, "New York State's Educational Conference Board: A Coalition in Transition," *Phi Delta Kappan,* XLIX (February, 1968), 330.

[33] In 1961–62, NEA's Urban Project expended only $28,037. Expenditures increased tremendously in successive years—$203,900 in 1962–63, $613,000 in 1963–64, and $884,663 in 1964–65. Cited in Moskow, *op. cit.,* 104.

Nor does it appear that competition for teacher allegiance, and the heightened militancy which ensues, will abate in the near future.[34] Even if a *modus vivendi* were reached, it is unlikely that the contemporary teachers movement could soon be thwarted. Docility among pedagogues may have become a relic of the past, for the signs of the present signify that the current armies manning the battlements of elementary and secondary education will remain in "a state of ferment bordering on rebellion."[35] The vast majority of American teachers surely favor strong organizations which employ either the device of professional negotiation or collective bargaining. An NEA survey in 1965 of a nationwide sample of classroom teachers, in fact, found that almost nine in ten supported some type of group action. Another poll found that half of the sample believed strikes were justified under extreme circumstances, such as low teacher salaries. By 1968, the NEA poll showed that over two-thirds of the teachers surveyed considered strikes acceptable.[36] The climate of opinion is favorable. Teacher dispositions are turning toward action. As a consequence, the incidence of combat between teacher groups and educational authorities is on the rise.

It is not our intention to detail the variety of pressures teacher organizations have resorted to in order to win negotiating agreements or substantive demands. Moskow has described instances of the use of milder tactics: campaigns in school board or municipal elections; criticism of school authorities; packing public meetings of the board of education; picketing; and the refusal to participate in extracurricular activities. He has also noted the employment of stronger tactics: slowdowns; investigations; professional holidays; work stoppages; strikes; mass resignations; the withholding of salary agreements; and recommendations that no new teachers accept assignments in a state or local school system.[37] Nor can we be very precise about how much combat has ensued lately. Estimates differ, but all point to a rapid increase of instances in which teachers threaten or actually take action against educational or other public authorities to gain some end.

[34] There has been some talk on each side of a merger of the two organizations. The principal stumbling block seems to be AFT's affiliation with organized labor, which many Federation leaders are unwilling to dissolve. However, David Selden, elected president of AFT in the summer of 1968, has promised to press hard for a merger with NEA.

[35] These words are quoted from Allen M. West, Assistant Executive Secretary for Field Operations and Urban Services, NEA. "What's Bugging Teachers?" *Saturday Review* (October 16, 1965), 88.

[36] About three and one-half times as many preferred professional negotiation to collective bargaining. "Teacher Opinion Poll," *NEA Journal,* 54 (September, 1965), 23–4. See also Doherty and Oberer, *op. cit.,* 37.

[37] *Op. cit.,* 196–208.

A few examples should illustrate the character of NEA and AFT activities in recent battle. Revolt broke out in Utah during 1963 and 1964 and resulted in NEA sanctions until the state, to some extent at least, met demands for adequate financing of the schools. Trouble in Oklahoma started about the same time when the governor vetoed legislation to raise teachers' salaries. Struggle between politicians and teachers led thereafter to NEA's invoking sanctions which lasted until the situation was remedied by the legislature and electorate of Oklahoma. By 1966 the Kentucky Education Association was calling a one-day walkout to press its demand for higher salaries and greater support for education by the state. The Massachusetts Teachers Association simultaneously was imposing sanctions against the public school system of Nantucket. Recently, NEA imposed national sanctions on Florida and, for the first time, invoked sanctions against a city school system, the target being Baltimore. In 1968 the Florida Education Association called a strike that lasted three weeks.

Nor was AFT dormant. During the past few years, a union local struck twice in Pawtucket, Rhode Island, gaining salary increases; another struck the school system in Perth Amboy, New Jersey, in order to bring about a collective bargaining election; and strikes either occurred or were threatened in New York, Chicago, and Philadelphia, forcing school authorities to comply substantially with teacher demands. In New Orleans AFT waged a collective bargaining drive by launching a three-day strike. Union members struck for four days in Plainview, Long Island, in defiance of state law and a specific order from the New York Commissioner of Education. They also struck in Baltimore and in Woodbridge, New Jersey. In September, 1967, union locals launched strikes in a number of cities, involving about 100,000 teachers and crippling school systems for several weeks in both New York City and Detroit.

Occasionally, local associations and unions in the same places have embarked upon similar hard-hitting campaigns. In Jersey City, for instance, both the NEA and AFT locals, objecting to a cut by the mayor in the education budget, advocated striking at approximately the same time. Michigan teachers boycotted about 100 schools in several Detroit suburbs and Flint, and the Michigan Education Association and the Michigan Federation of Teachers lent support. In Baltimore, too, both the Association and union have been vying to see who can protest a deplorable educational situation most forcefully. Common conditions and competition, it seems, engender like responses.

Frequently, one local group, usually the union, pushes the other toward more militant activity than would have occurred otherwise. With teacher organizations competing for followings, the combativeness of teacher unions and the fruits combativeness has borne, generates greater militancy among local education associations. A graphic example, demonstrating how a contest for rank-and-file allegiance and representational victory impels one group to match or outdo the other, is provided by events in Newark, New Jersey. In this city the teachers association held a strike, not as an action of last resort, but rather to show that it could act as forcefully as its rival, the teachers union, which had struck several months before. More and more local associations are resorting to strikes, causing NEA to depart from its traditional stance in 1967 and agree to support local chapters when they decided a strike was necessary. It may well be, as an education reporter for the *New York Times* wrote, that open warfare promises "to become a routine in school bargaining tactics and . . . a weapon in the intra-profession rivalry between affiliates of the National Education Association and the American Federation of Teachers."[38]

The Changing Educational Scene

One result of all this is that the educational establishment in the United States is on the defensive. Many members, who are beginning to feel the shoe pinch, now realize that the disturbing implications of teacher militancy can no longer be evaded. At a former time the question was *whether* school authorities would negotiate with their personnel. Now it is *how* they will negotiate and on *what kinds* of matters.

Naturally, school administrators have become gravely concerned about their own role, as parties in disputes begin to take sides. The American Association of School Administrators (AASA) is on record as pledging "to resist any effort to displace the superintendent and his authority in matters affecting the interest and welfare of school personnel."[39] But many administrators realize that they cannot prevent some form of negotiations by teachers. Their problem now is how best to cope with these new circumstances. Faced with a Hobson's choice, most would encourage the development of local associations, which they much prefer to unions, and state laws "with which we can live." One of AASA's resolutions, adopted at its 1966 convention, clearly demonstrates where school administrators stand. Declaring that efforts to superimpose a pattern of staff relations borrowed from another segment of society should be resisted vigorously, it goes on to support local education associations as suitable to preserve unity, promote harmony, and serve the cause of education.

[38] Leonard Buder, *New York Times,* April 3, 1966.
[39] *Resolutions, Platform, Constitution, Bylaws, Ethics* (Washington, D.C.: The Association, 1965), 11.

On their parts, local school boards, which constitute the other pillar of local educational establishments, have collectively resisted any erosion of their own prerogatives. Particularly disillusioned because NEA was embracing the same tactics as teacher unions, the National School Boards Association has tried to stand firm, even while administrators paid lip service to the negotiating rights of teachers. Its policy, if not the practice of constituent boards, declared that it would be irresponsible for school boards to enter into compromise agreements based on negotiation or collective bargaining, resort to mediation or arbitration, or yield to threats of reprisal.[40] At its annual convention in 1966, however, NSBA relented somewhat. It deleted the policy section referred to above and substituted a statement calling for a method of "utilizing the knowledge and experience of professional personnel in the formation of education policies." A former NSBA president expressed it this way:

> It is time for teachers to decide whether they are calling for joint *responsibility* with boards of education—or whether they are saying we have joint *concerns* with boards of education, and we want our opinions to be heard and our counsel to be carefully considered before decisions are reached by the board. If it is the latter, school boards can give this their support.[41]

Admitting on the one hand what had become inevitable, the association of boards of education continued on the other to limit teacher participation and remained on record in opposition to strikes, sanctions, and boycotts.

If recent developments are harbingers of the educational scene ahead, we may expect some important changes in the relationships among key participants.[42] Certainly, there will be a diminution of managerial prerogative and flexibility. One union official predicts: "The day is gone forever when school boards and administrators will run the schools single-handed."[43] Another comments on the likely future as follows:

> Power is never given to anyone. Power is taken, and it is taken from someone. Teachers, as one of society's powerless groups, are now starting to take power from supervisors and school boards. This is causing and will continue to cause a realignment of power relationships.[44]

[40] Cited in Steffensen, *op. cit.*, 2.

[41] Quoted in Harold Webb, "The National School Boards Association and Collective Negotiations," in Elam, *op. cit.*, 199–200. Emphasis in original.

[42] Usdan notes that "traditional educational alliances between teacher associations, school board associations, and administrators groups are becoming more difficult to maintain." As a result, in New York State, for example, a powerful educational coalition is disintegrating. *Op. cit.*, 330.

[43] Quoted in *Washington Post*, January 16, 1967.

[44] Shanker, *loc. cit.*

Such realignments, when they occur, will naturally vary from city to city and town to town. But wherever they take place, chances are that boards, superintendents, principals, and teachers will begin to adopt new roles and participate differently than before in the governments of public education.

II. Group Membership

In discussing the contemporary teachers movement to this point, we have identified several ideological strands and some emergent patterns of behavior. All of them point toward the increasing influence of teacher organizations. More specifically, organizational influence depends upon strength. In this chapter we shall examine one of the factors which relates to strength. This factor is group membership.

There is little argument over the contention that an important basis of organizational strength is the number of teachers who are members. Numbers are usually impressive. Other things being equal, we would naturally expect that large membership groups will do better in pressing their claims on school or civic officials than on small membership groups. It may also be, as Lieberman and Moskow allege, that membership size is linked to militancy—the larger a group becomes, the more likely that some of its members will be willing to take aggressive action to achieve organizational ends.[1] Larger groups, moreover, should have advantages over smaller competitors in elections to choose exclusive agents for school employees, and agency status strengthens any organization. Size appears to be relevant even after representation has been achieved, although then members may be easier to recruit. "Every additional member counts," one officer of the United Federation of Teachers said. "The more members, the more strength we'll have—the more strength, the better the final agreement."[2] Up to some point—and the precise point is likely to vary from place to place—numbers are extremely important if a teacher organization hopes to gain power and influence educational policy.

THE STRUGGLE FOR ADHERENTS

Simple comparison between the memberships of the National Education Association and the American Federation of Teachers fails to do

[1] Myron Lieberman and Michael H. Moskow, *Collective Negotiations for Teachers* (Chicago: Rand McNally, 1966), 58–9.

[2] *United Teacher* (a publication of UFT), January, 1962. Several years later, the theme was the same: "The success of the UFT in representing the teachers has been in ratio to how many teachers are in the Union and how actively they have participated." *Ibid.,* October 8, 1965.

justice to the actual situation today. In terms of over-all size, AFT is not a match for its larger competitor. In fact, the Association has about eight times as many members as the union. Founded in 1857, NEA has grown steadily to the present day. At the turn of the century, it had 2,300 members, by 1920 about 52,000, a decade later 216,000, and now about 1,000,000. Presently, the Association has affiliates in all 50 states, a state membership of more than 1.6 million, and about 9,000 affiliated local associations. By contrast, AFT is still a pygmy. Since 1961, largely due to its success in New York, the Federation has more than doubled its membership. Yet it can now claim only about 135,000 teachers, 25 state federations, and 560 locals.[3]

But a comparison of contemporary membership rolls can be misleading. A better way to examine the contest between the two groups is to focus on the challenge from the teachers union. Although about nine of ten teachers in the United States belong to an educational association, few people would seriously contend that the Federation has posed, and is posing, little challenge to NEA in winning the loyalties of rank-and-file teachers. It would seem, therefore, that union membership has significance belied by a simple ratio of its numbers compared to those of NEA.

Some indirect support for this view is furnished by teacher voting in fifteen recent election contests across the nation, for which we have group membership figures and election results. With unions and associations battling for representational status, the former inevitably received more votes from unaffiliated teachers than did the latter. More important here, while unions apparently won the votes of all their members, associations in ten out of 15 elections received votes from fewer teachers than those who actually held membership. Large numbers of association members, in other words, did not bother to support their own groups. In New York City, for example, a coalition of NEA groups had a membership of approximately 30,000, while UFT had about 5,200. Yet the Teachers Bargaining Organization received only 9,770 votes as opposed to the union's 20,045 in the election. In Philadelphia, to cite another example, the local association had about 5,200 members while the AFT affiliate had only 2,000. But the union won the representation election by a good margain.[4]

[3] AFT members are ordinarily required to join local, state, and national organizations simultaneously. Therefore national membership is the sum of local affiliations. In the case of NEA, national totals do not reflect membership in local districts. Usually a teacher does not have to join NEA in order to belong to a state or local association. Thus totals vary, depending upon whether one is examining NEA, state association, or local group affiliations.

[4] Lieberman and Moskow, *op. cit.*, 41, and Robert E. Doherty and Walter E. Oberer, *Teachers, School Boards, and Collective Bargaining* (Ithaca, N.Y.: New

It may be, of course, that the membership base of the American Federation of Teachers is extremely limited and consequently the challenge to NEA hegemony is limited as well. Officials of the Association argue that most union members are located in the large cities of the country. Outside these urban areas, professional associations still have greatest appeal. On their parts, union leaders contend that the base of AFT is steadily broadening and non-metropolitan locals are now accounting for almost one-third the total increase in organizational membership.

There can be little doubt that the American Federation of Teachers got its start in the big cities. The first union was formed in Chicago in 1897. During the following two decades, 20 groups in ten different states organized into locals affiliated with labor. A number were short-lived. Finally, in 1916 a national union was formed by eight charter locals and AFT came into existence. In the ensuing years, its strength was confined primarily to those geographic regions where organized labor was strongest—in urban areas, especially in those states forming a line running from New York City across to Chicago. Thirty years ago, according to one estimate, four of five AFT members were located in 17 cities of the nation.[5]

By 1966, although its base had widened somewhat, the Federation could still accurately be characterized as a large-city phenomenon.[6] Approximately two-fifths of its members came from New York City, Chicago, and Detroit. And about half were from ten large cities which, in addition to the three already mentioned, included Philadelphia, Minneapolis, San Francisco, Boston, Cleveland, St. Louis, and Los Angeles.

The large-city bias of the union can also be discerned from a slightly different perspective. In those districts with a public-school enrollment of 100,000 or more, union locals were strong in about one-third, medium in another third, and weak in still another third. In districts where enrollments were lower, ranging from 25,000 to 99,999, the situation was quite dissimilar. Union locals were strong in less than 10 per cent and weak in about 70 per cent of the cases. Nor does this pattern result because southern school districts are smaller than northern ones and are also the districts in which it has been extremely difficult for AFT to

York State School of Industrial and Labor Relations, Cornell University, 1967), 27.

[5] David Mesirow, "The AFT's Role in the Thirties," *Changing Education,* I (Summer, 1966), 30.

[6] This analysis of AFT membership is based upon figures as of November, 1965, made available to the author by the Federation, with the understanding that the membership of individual locals, drawn from these data, would not be revealed. Similar figures were made available by NEA.

organize since the decision to desegregate its locals. In northern districts only, as Table 1 shows, unions are likelier to be stronger in larger than

TABLE 1
AFT MEMBERSHIP, BY SIZE OF CITY AND REGION, IN NUMBERS, 1965

Membership Strength†	Size of City*					
	Larger		Medium		Smaller	
	North	South	North	South	North	South
Weak	0	6	16	15	22	23
Medium	7	0	9	1	13	0
Strong	6	1	4	0	5	0
Totals	13	7	29	16	40	23

* "Larger" include districts whose pupil enrollments are 100,000 or more; "medium" those with from 50,000 to 99,999; and "smaller" those with from 25,000 to 49,999. These are strata 1, 2, and 3, as classified in Research Division, NEA, *Twenty-Second Biennial Salary Survey of Public-School Employees, 1964–65: Individual School Systems,* Research Report 1965-R6 (Washington, D.C.: The Association, 1965).

† "Weak" districts are those with memberships of 5 per cent or less; "medium" with 6 per cent to 20 per cent; and "strong" with 21 per cent or more.

in medium-size or smaller cities.[7] Thus far, at any rate, AFT membership has been concentrated in the larger cities of the North.

More than membership is at stake, however. Of vital concern also is the non-member support each type of group can attract. This factor assumes greatest import in the context of a representational election to choose between an NEA and AFT local to serve as negotiating or bargaining agent for the entire teaching staff of a school system. If we look at elections contested by affiliates of both groups during the period from early 1961 through the end of 1966, it will be possible to add some further observations on the distribution of union strength.[8]

All told, 114 contests have taken place during this period. Over 80 per cent have occurred in six states, where specific provision has been made, either by legislation or administrative ruling, for representational elections. In two states, New York and Illinois, unions have come out ahead. In two, Connecticut and Wisconsin, educational associations have emerged as victors in large majorities of the contests. And in still another two, Massachusetts and Michigan, the balance sheet has been about

[7] It should be noted that while Northern school districts generally follow city lines, Southern ones are coterminous with county lines.

[8] Results are reported in the *American Teacher*, February, 1967, and Michael H. Moskow, *Teachers and Unions* (Philadelphia: Industrial Research Unit, Wharton School of Finance and Commerce, University of Pennsylvania, 1966), 108–13.

equal. Table 2 summarizes information for states in which five or more elections have been fought out by the two organizations. The impact of New York City and Chicago on the fortunes of AFT can easily be seen.

TABLE 2
STATE COMPETITION FOR REPRESENTATION BETWEEN NEA AND AFT
GROUPS, 1961–66

State*	Number of Elections Won		Percentage of Total Votes Received	
	NEA	AFT	NEA	AFT
Connecticut	15	2	66	34
Illinois	1	7	07	93
Massachusetts	7	6	49	51
Michigan	21	17	48	52
New York	3	5	36	64
Wisconsin	7	4	59	41

* Only states where five or more elections held.

Depending upon one's inclination in these matters, argument can be waged for the greater success of the Association or the greater success of the Federation. Naturally, NEA makes the former case, AFT the latter. In terms of the numbers of contested elections won during the six-year period, the Association holds a commanding lead. It has triumphed in 70, or just over three-fifths, of those which have been held. In terms of total votes, however, the tables are turned. Of about 116,000 ballots cast in various elections across the country nearly three-fifths have gone to union locals. In terms of numbers of teachers represented as a result of such contests, the Federation does even better. Its locals have won the right to bargain for more than three times as many teachers as NEA affiliates.

Electoral support for the two organizations is differentially distributed according to city size. Just as AFT membership varies in this regard, so does union representational achievement. Thus, unions have prospered electorally in the larger cities, but have done less well in medium-sized and smaller places. The percentages of elections won, votes cast, and teachers represented as a consequence are shown in Table 3.[9] In large cities, AFT locals have won ten of 18 contests, received about two-thirds of the vote, and become agents for almost 90 per cent of the total teachers. In medium and smaller cities, AFT locals have fared poorly, winning only 34 out of 96 of the contests, receiving slightly less

[9] Because there have been relatively few elections, cities are classified differently than in Table 1, above.

TABLE 3
Representational Election Outcomes, by Size of City, 1961–66

Size of City*	Number and % of Elections Won		Number and % of Votes Cast		Number and % of Teachers Represented	
	NEA	AFT	NEA	AFT	NEA	AFT
Larger	8 (44)	10 (56)	32,603 (37)	54,652 (63)	16,470 (13)	112,919 (87)
Medium	13 (65)	7 (35)	6,229 (54)	5,358 (46)	8,268 (66)	4,179 (34)
Smaller	49 (64)	27 (36)	9,794 (57)	7,422 (43)	13,011 (67)	6,485 (33)
Totals	70 (61)	44 (39)	48,626 (42)	67,432 (58)	37,749 (23)	123,583 (77)

* "Larger" includes cities with 1,000 classroom teachers or more; "medium" with 500 to 999 teachers; and "smaller" with fewer than 499 teachers.

than half the electoral vote, and gaining the right to represent only one-third of the teachers in bargaining with school authorities. Once again, the restricted base of the American Federation of Teachers becomes apparent. Whether we take into consideration membership or electoral support, the pattern is essentially the same. AFT has held the advantage in larger cities, NEA has had the edge in smaller communities.

FACTORS INFLUENCING MEMBERSHIP[10]

Traditionally, public school teachers have been portrayed as inflexible, conservative, and status-conscious. It is remarkable, therefore, that unions have been so successful in recruiting teacher members, particularly in large cities. Since our study focuses on organizations in several large cities, it would be useful at this point to inquire into the bases of group membership. Why do teachers join one group rather than the other or refuse to join at all? For this task, we have concentrated on membership in three organizations in two cities—New York's United Federation of Teachers (UFT), and the Boston Teachers Union (BTU) and Boston Teachers Alliance (BTA). The former two are unions affiliated with AFT; the latter, BTA, is independent.

Chapter I advanced several reasonable explanations of the new militancy. We would expect that factors affecting militancy, such as increasing numbers of male teachers and the trend toward bigger and more impersonal school systems, might also be associated with organizational membership. Surely, there are many other factors that help determine the decision on affiliation. A teacher's race, religion, family background, and political dispositions undoubtedly shape his attitudes toward the union movement and whether or not he chooses to participate. Here we shall examine the impact of several factors, some of which are related to the attributes of teachers, others to the school contexts in which they work, and a few to the nature of teacher organizations.

In exploring these correlates of group membership, it is necessary to describe just how we have proceeded. Instead of surveying a sample of teachers to elicit their reasons for affiliation retrospectively, we have tried to assess factors influencing organizational development by relying mainly on aggregate data for a brief span of time.[11] As a consequence,

[10] This section is based on methods and findings reported in my article, "The Strength of Teacher Organizations: Factors Influencing Membership in Two Large Cities," *Sociology of Education*, 39 (Fall, 1966), 359–80.

[11] Aggregate data of the kinds used here contrast with information that is customarily provided by the sample survey. Despite some inherent limitations, aggregate data make comparison possible on a wider scale. Their most notable advantage in studying teacher-group membership is that they allow us to see

the principal (but not exclusive) units of analysis are schools, not teachers. What concerns us is group membership by different types of schools at different stages in an organization's growth. In New York City, all academic and vocational high schools and a stratified probability sample of elementary and junior high schools have been examined in early 1962, mid-1963, and mid-1965; periods of UFT's childhood, adolescence, and maturity. In Boston the entire universe of schools (except for a few special ones) has been studied in mid-1963 and mid-1965; periods of BTU's significant development.[12]

Organizational membership, by individual school, was obtained through the collection of aggregate data. Since membership at several points in time was deemed important, it was not possible to rely on the records of teacher organizations themselves, for they only keep lists of current members on a school-by-school basis. Instead, group-membership figures are based on the numbers of teachers in each school who have their membership dues deducted from their salaries, as recorded by check-off figures on the payrolls of the departments of education in New York and Boston.[13] In addition, information on such variables as the sexual composition and teaching experience of faculties, the racial composition of pupil bodies, the size of schools, and absences on the day of a UFT strike, have been gathered from payrolls, other records, and official reports. On the basis of these data, we shall investigate the relationships between the personal characteristics of teachers, the environments of schools, and the activities of organizations.

Personal Factors

Social science research has recently focused considerable attention on the effects of an individual's attributes on his attitudes and behavior.

---

whether or not identical relationships hold for different places, or invariable associations pertain at different times.

[12] For New York City, all 59 academic high schools, all 29 vocational high schools, 64 junior highs (half of those operating during 1964–65), and 140 elementaries (about one-quarter of those operating during 1964–65), a total of 292 schools, are included. For Boston, 16 senior high schools, 16 junior high schools, and 56 elementary districts are included. In Boston no distinction is drawn between academic and vocational high schools. Data on individual elementary schools in Boston are not available. Districts, which are relatively homogeneous and under the administration of one principal, serve adequately.

[13] We must assume that check-off accurately reflects actual membership. The obvious problem is that some teachers choose not to have their dues deducted. Rather than publicly announce affiliation, they join covertly, remitting dues directly to the organization to which they belong. Nevertheless, there is reason to believe that overt and covert membership do not vary significantly by school. In any case, for present purposes, members who count most are those who make known their affiliations.

Personal characteristics have been shown to influence political participation, party affiliation, and voting behavior, as well as attitudes on a wide variety of matters. As far as teachers are concerned, a number of investigators have explored the impact of personal factors. Mason, for example, considered sex, age, and marital status in his survey of 7,150 beginning teachers. Zeigler paid particular attention to sex and teaching experience in a study based on interviews with 803 high school teachers in Oregon. Cole surveyed 331 New York City and 126 Perth Amboy, New Jersey, teachers and demonstrated the effects of non-teaching statuses such as sex, religion, and class of origin, on teacher support of group militancy. Even more relevant to our present purposes, Lowe, using responses to questionnaire items completed by 531 teachers in a suburban community, explored factors that distinguish teachers who join one group or another or remain unaffiliated.[14]

Undoubtedly, the most salient characteristic of all those considered is sex. The social role one is expected to play in life varies according to whether a person is male or female. As a result, attitudes and behaviors with regard to many issues vary as well. The values, aspirations, and satisfactions of men and women teachers differ.[15] Men appear to be more dissatisfied with their jobs and more motivated to take drastic action to improve their occupational positions.[16] In terms of affiliation, an investigation of one school district revealed that men were more likely to join the AFT local and women were more inclined to join the NEA association, but generally, male teachers were more likely than females to join no group at all.[17]

Information about individual teachers in Boston enables us to test the relationship between sex and affiliation. Table 4 presents membership figures, by sex, for both the Teachers Alliance and the Teachers Union in 1963 and 1965. In this city, at least, men are likelier joiners. One-third of the men but only one-quarter of the women in 1963, and half of the men but only one-third of the women in 1965, belonged to either BTA or BTU. The reason why male teachers were more apt to be organization members than were their female counterparts has to do with

---

[14] Ward S. Mason, *The Beginning Teacher: Status and Career Orientations* (Washington: U.S. Department of Health, Education, and Welfare, 1961); Harmon Zeigler, *The Political World of the High School Teacher* (Eugene, Oregon: The Center for the Advanced Study of Educational Administration, University of Oregon, 1966); Stephen Cole, "The Unionization of Teachers: Determinants of Rank-and-File Support," *Sociology of Education*, 41 (Winter, 1968), 66–87; and William T. Lowe, "Who Joins Which Teachers' Group?" *Teachers College Record*, LXVI (April, 1965), 614–19.

[15] Mason, *op. cit., passim.*

[16] Zeigler, *op. cit.,* 5; Cole, *op. cit.,* 80.

[17] Lowe, *op. cit.,* 615.

TABLE 4
BOSTON TEACHER ALLIANCE AND BOSTON TEACHER UNION MEMBERSHIP,
BY SEX, 1963 AND 1965

Organizational Affiliation	Male		Female	
	1963	1965	1963	1965
Percentage of total teachers belonging to BTA	09	08	12	16
Percentage of total teachers belonging to BTU	25	43	13	19
Percentage of total teachers with group affiliation	34	51	25	35

the peculiar drawing power of the Teachers Union. Table 4 indicates that while females divided their allegiances rather evenly between the two groups, men chose overwhelmingly to affiliate with BTU. In 1963, men were almost three times as likely to belong to the Union, and two years later the ratio had increased to approximately five to one.

Using aggregate data, which focus on schools rather than individuals as basic units, we can see how personal factors help shape social climates and in turn affect membership. What matters here is not so much individual sex-status, but the kind of climate which exists in a particular school. We may hypothesize that the greater the male composition of a school faculty the easier it is for a union to recruit members.

In New York City junior high schools men comprise about half the total teaching staff, and schools vary from about 30 to 70 in percentage male. At this level during 1962, 1963, and 1965, the more men on a faculty the greater was the membership strength of the union. Indirect evidence from New York's high schools tends to corroborate the association. Although exact figures on the sexual composition of faculties are not available, we know that faculties in girls' high schools are primarily female, while those in coeducational and boys' high schools are either evenly divided by sex or largely male. The number of cases in the girls' subgroup is quite small, but the findings which emerge follow the anticipated pattern. For the three years, 57 per cent, 46 per cent, and 76 per cent of coeducational and boys' high schools had "large" UFT memberships. Only one of ten girls' highs ranked similarly.

Our hypothesis about male climate and union membership is further supported by aggregate data from Boston schools. Table 5 depicts positive associations between male faculty composition and Union strength, at each divisional level and for 1963 and 1965. It shows, however, much less of a patterned relationship between faculty sex and Alliance strength. It should be noted that this table, like Tables 9, 10,

TABLE 5

BOSTON FACULTY SEX AND ALLIANCE AND UNION MEMBERSHIP, BY
DIVISION, 1963 AND 1965

| | Differences Between Percentages of Schools with "High" and "Low" Male Percentages Ranking "High" in Organizational Membership* | | | |
| | BTA | | BTU | |
Division	1963	1965	1963	1965
Elementary (N = 56)	+07	+11	+21	+37
Junior high (N = 16)	+13	−10	+07	+02
Senior high (N = 16)	−02	−17	+55	+75

* A plus sign indicates a greater percentage of high-male schools ranking high in membership; a minus sign indicates the opposite. Schools with high-male percentages are elementaries with 30 per cent or more men, junior highs with 50 per cent or more men, and senior highs with 40 per cent or more men.

and 12 which follow, is a summary presentation of separate cross-tabulations for various divisions and several years.[18] Each entry represents the difference between the percentage of schools with predominantly male climates ranking high in organizational membership and the percentage with predominantly female climates ranking high. For example, the first entry in the first row for the 56 elementary districts reports a difference of +07, reflecting the fact that in 1963 whereas 63 per cent of high-male schools had more than 10 per cent BTA membership, only 56 per cent of low-male schools had comparable BTA membership. Reading across, 56 per cent of high-male and 45 per cent of low-male schools had a large BTA membership in 1965, as is signified by the difference of +11 in the table. Similarly, BTU differences of +21 in 1963 and +37 in 1965 are based on memberships of 63 per cent and 67 per cent in high-male schools and 42 per cent and 30 per cent in low-male schools in the two years.

If the presence of male teachers on a faculty affects a school's climate sufficiently to encourage union membership, it follows that where males

[18] In cross-tabulation of aggregate data on organizational membership and other factors, as in Tables 5, 9, 10, and 12, we have dichotomized each variable and analyzed for the several school divisions. Where appropriate, breaking points for independent variables are explained in notes to the tables. For membership, the dependent variable, breaking points between "high" and "low" vary by organization, division, and year. High UFT membership schools are categorized as follows: elementary: 1962—1 per cent and over, 1963—20 per cent and over, 1965—40 per cent and over; junior high: 1962—20 per cent and over, 1963—60 per cent and over, 1965—70 per cent and over; academic high: 1962—20 per cent and over, 1963—50 per cent and over, 1965—70 per cent and over; vocational high: 1962—5 per cent and over, 1963—40 per cent and over, 1965—60 per cent and over. For both BTA and BTU, within all divisions, high membership schools are 10 per cent and over in 1963, and 20 per cent and over in 1965.

make up a sizable part of a faculty not only men but women also will be more inclined than otherwise to enter a union. Once again, use of individual data from Boston serves to demonstrate that this is true. On the basis of the average male percentage of teachers for the years 1963 and 1965 combined, we have dichotomized schools into those ranking high and those ranking low, and then calculated percentages of female teachers in each group who belonged to the Union in 1965. Findings appear in Table 6. In schools with substantial numbers of men, the percentages of women teachers belonging to BTU were noticeably higher than in schools where only a few men taught.

TABLE 6
BOSTON FACULTY SEX AND FEMALE MEMBERSHIP IN THE UNION BY DIVISION, 1965

Division	Percentage of Female Teachers in BTU	
	High-Male Schools*	Low-Male Schools
Elementary	22 (N = 7)	13 (N = 49)
Junior and senior high	28 (N = 23)	10 (N = 6)

* For junior and senior highs, schools with 40 per cent or more men are ranked high; for elementaries, schools with 30 per cent or more men are ranked high. Schools which are entirely male have been eliminated from analysis.

On the basis of evidence from New York City and Boston, there can be little doubt that men are more apt to join a union than women and that teachers, including females, in male climates are more apt to join than those in more female climates. One reason for the relative lag in unionization of the elementary schools is the low density of men teachers. But since the percentages of teachers who are men has been rising during the past decades, especially in the secondary schools, the increased drawing power of unions and their gains in membership are quite understandable.

Another personal factor worth consideration is age. Generally, age and teaching experience go hand in hand. The median age for people embarking upon a teaching career is about 24 years.[19] Thus, younger people tend to be new to teaching, while older ones have served in the classroom for some years. There is reason to believe that younger teachers offer the best recruiting prospects for unions. They are persons who have served their probationary periods, are still groping, and who desire the kinds of change and improvement that unions promise. But the longer a person teaches the better the chance he has accommodated to the status quo.

For the veteran, who has probably devised personal adjustive strategies,

[19] Mason, *op. cit.*, 4.

a union offers few advantages. As Cole points out, older teachers, on maximum salary and approaching retirement, have less to gain from changed conditions. They have fewer years left in which to benefit from whatever changes might be made. Perhaps they have too much at stake to risk even joining a group that appears oriented against management. In addition, older teachers are likely to be more security-minded than their younger colleagues, having begun teaching during a period when jobs were scarce and finding it harder to move to positions in other school systems.[20]

Lowe discovered that although length of service did seem to be associated with joining some organization it did not relate to membership in the NEA group as opposed to the AFT local.[21] Our impression from conversations with UFT leaders is that in the group's formative years experienced teachers constituted the hard-core membership. By 1963 the union appeared to have principal attraction among the younger teachers in the school system. And today, with UFT an established and entirely legitimate agency in the field of local education, significant differences in membership by teaching experience or age seem unlikely. No doubt some of the older teachers remain holdouts, but they comprise a distinct minority in the system.

In the case of Boston, we have information about teaching experience in the elementary division. Here the Teachers Union recruits more successfully in schools with larger proportions of relatively inexperienced teachers. Examination of aggregate data is suggestive, at least for 1965. In those schools where half of the teachers had twenty-one years or more general experience, BTU had high membership in only one-quarter. On the other hand, where fewer than half had served as long, BTU was strong in nearly half of the schools. For the Alliance, membership strength ran in the opposite direction. These data are incomplete and far from compelling, especially since male elementary teachers tend to be located in schools where average seniority is low. Still, we might venture that unions, especially in periods of their most substantial growth, are likely to have greater appeal in schools whose contexts are partly shaped by newer teachers.

School Factors

Until recently, social surveys had dwelt largely on the effects of a person's own background or attitudes upon his behavior. Little attention was given the effects of social context on a person. Our consideration of sex differences illustrates how important the contextual situation

[20] Cole, *op. cit.*, 82–3.
[21] *Op. cit.*, 615–16.

might be. Personal factors, no doubt, shape an individual's frame of reference. School factors then play an independent or reinforcing role. It is natural to expect that the working environments in which teachers pursue their professional careers play a major part in determining the comparative drawing powers of various organizations.

In his study of a suburban district, Lowe found that elementary teachers were more likely to join the NEA group, whereas junior high teachers were more likely to join the AFT group.[22] Among teacher leaders in New York City there is widespread agreement that UFT strength, especially in the early years could be attributed to the peculiar susceptibility of junior high school teachers to union appeals. Historical and contemporary membership data from both New York and Boston support the contention that recruitment success varies markedly by division or level. As Table 7 shows, in each city during the base years

TABLE 7
New York City and Boston Teacher Organization Membership,
by Division and Year

| | Percentage of Total Teachers in Organization | | | | | | |
| | UFT | | | BTA | | BTU | |
Division	1962	1963	1965	1963	1965	1963	1965
Elementary	05	19	40	15	18	12	18
Junior high	26	57	74	14	13	24	43
Academic high	16	46	65	04	05	17	31
Vocational high*	07	42	62	—	—	—	—

* Boston trade high schools are included in the academic grouping.

unions recruited the largest percentages of teachers from the junior highs and the smallest percentages from the elementary schools.

By 1965, with UFT growing tremendously at every level, the gap between junior high and other schools had narrowed. But in the case of BTU membership the gap had actually widened. In each city and for each year the rank order of membership was junior highs first, high schools second, and elementaries third.

As has been mentioned previously, the fact that elementary teachers have consistently shown the least inclination to join unions can be accounted for in part by the low percentage of men teaching at this level. But this still does not explain away the association between division and union membership. Table 8, containing individual data on Boston teachers, clearly indicates that both men and women in junior high schools are more likely to be members of BTU than their colleagues in

[22] *Ibid.,* 616.

TABLE 8

BOSTON TEACHER ALLIANCE AND BOSTON TEACHER UNION MEMBERSHIP BY
DIVISION, WITH SEX CONTROLLED, 1963 AND 1965

Division and Year	Percentages of Total Teachers in BTA		Percentages of Total Teachers in BTU	
	Male	Female	Male	Female
Elementary				
1963	18	14	17	10
1965	18	19	33	14
Junior high				
1963	18	10	29	19
1965	13	12	47	38
Senior high				
1963	02	06	23	07
1965	02	10	43	13

other divisions. This is not true of BTA, however, which recruits best in elementary schools.[23] In New York City, moreover, UFT has done disproportionately well among junior high teachers, even though as many men were teaching in academic high schools.

Neither the sex nor the age of teachers can completely account for our findings. Evidently, there is something significantly different about the school contexts in which junior high teachers find themselves. Perhaps the controversial and marginal quality of these schools, the nature of the subject matter taught, and the unusual problems posed by adolescent pupils account for the special proclivity of teachers in the junior highs.

Another factor may also exert influence. The size of a school, or numbers of faculty and pupils, might have an effect on teacher attitudes and willingness to join a union.[24] In relatively small schools, such as elementaries where there are fewer than thirty on the staff, teachers may feel that they are visible to their principals and consequently can be singled out more easily for the application of subtle administrative sanctions. In larger schools, they may feel that, whatever the size of the administrative staffs, their joining an "anti-administration" organization will go unnoticed. Alternatively, of course, teachers in smaller schools, through individual and informal interaction, may succeed in obtaining much of what they want from superiors and consequently be less disposed to join a union group.

[23] High school teachers were especially hostile to BTA because of its previous campaign for a single salary schedule.

[24] Edwin M. Bridges, among others, points out that size is related to the increasing alienation of the worker. "Teacher Participation in Decision Making," *Administrator's Notebook*, 12 (May, 1964). See also Seymour Martin Lipset *et al.*, *Union Democracy* (New York: Anchor Books, 1962), 172–76.

Whatever the explanation, it appears that one contextual hypothesis worthy of test concerns the size of a school—the larger the faculty, the greater the proportion of union members. In New York City UFT has had greater success at every divisional level in attracting members from larger school faculties. Although differences are never overwhelming, the pattern is consistent, as illustrated in Table 9. In eleven of twelve comparisons large-faculty schools are greater in UFT strength.

TABLE 9

New York City Size of Faculty and UFT Membership, by Division, 1962, 1963, and 1965

| | Differences Between Percentages of Schools with "Large" and "Small" Faculties Ranking "High" in UFT Membership* | | |
Division	1962	1963	1965
Elementary (N = 140)	+27	+26	+12
Junior high (N = 64)	−06	+14	+17
Academic high (N = 57)†	+19	+15	+13
Vocational high (N = 29)	+24	+23	+23

* A plus sign indicates a greater percentage of large-faculty schools ranking high in membership; a minus sign indicates the opposite. Large-faculty schools are: elementary—40 teachers and over; junior high—80 teachers and over; academic high —140 teachers and over; vocational high—80 teachers and over.

† N = 58 for 1965.

Because at the elementary and junior high levels, larger schools are likelier to be difficult ones while smaller schools tend to be easier, we have controlled for "teaching situation" to see whether size really matters. It does. But teaching situation deserves special attention, particularly since so much has been said or written by American educators about the determinants of teacher morale. In his study, Lowe tried to find out whether or not job satisfaction was related to membership in teacher associations. He discovered that those who joined a local AFT group were more unhappy or disaffected than those who entered an NEA association or who remained unaffiliated.[25] Our belief is that a teacher's satisfaction hinges to some extent on the objective problems he encounters in the classroom and in the school. The nature of these problems may be indicated by means of either the types or the numbers of students who attend various schools.

Disadvantaged pupils in the "special service" schools confront the teacher with greater difficulties than do middle-class pupils in the "regular" schools of New York. This leads us to hypothesize that teachers serving in the special service schools will be more predisposed

[25] *Op. cit.,* 617.

to join a group critical of the educational status quo. In New York City the hypothesis appears to be confirmed. Over the years, UFT membership predictably has been proportionately greater in special service than in regular junior high and elementary schools. This is shown in Table 10.[26]

TABLE 10

New York City Teaching Situation and UFT Membership, by Division,
1962, 1963, and 1965

	Differences Between Percentages of Special Service and Regular Schools Ranking "High" in UFT Membership*		
Division	1962	1963	1965
Elementary (N = 140)	+25	+14	+06
Junior high (N = 64)	+26	+32	+21

* A plus sign indicates a greater percentage of special service schools ranking high in membership; a minus sign indicates the opposite.

Also evident is the fact that as UFT strength rose generally from 1962 to 1965 differences by teaching situation narrowed. In Boston the school department unofficially distinguishes three classes of elementary schools in terms of the quality of students: Group I, the most difficult; Group II, medium; and Group III, the best. Here, however, no meaningful relationship emerges.[27]

Another indicator of teaching situation relates to working conditions, in terms of the numbers of pupils taught. Working conditions may be denoted, at least roughly, by figures on class size, the percentage of "large" classes, or pupil-teacher ratios on a school-by-school basis. Especially in view of union bargaining demands for reductions in class size, it seems reasonable to hypothesize a relationship between heavy student load and union strength. Accordingly, a high proportion of large classes in a school adversely affects teacher morale, contributes to dissatisfaction with the educational status quo, and thereby encourages union membership.

[26] Men are more heavily represented on the staffs of special service schools. Nevertheless, controlling for faculty composition does not wash away differences in UFT strength by type of school.

[27] We also examined the relationship between the racial composition of pupil populations and union membership. As anticipated, because special service schools are likely to be attended by ghetto children, the association between non-white pupil population and UFT membership held within both the elementary and junior high divisions. The relationship for New York's high schools was exceedingly weak. In Boston, when other factors, such as the sexual composition of faculties, were taken into account, no racially related differences in the schools characterized either Union or Alliance strength. What apparently counts in the elementary and junior high schools of New York City matters less in the academic highs and vocational highs, and not at all in any of the public schools of Boston.

In New York, figures have been compiled on the percentages of classes with thirty-five or more pupils in elementary, junior high, and academic high schools for each of the three years. At the lower levels no association exists, probably because special service schools, having been allocated compensatory resources by educational authorities, evidence proportionately few large classes. For academic high schools, there is a slight relationship between the percentage of large classes on the one hand and UFT membership on the other. Controlling for the racial composition of student bodies does not diminish this relationship. In Boston, instead of class size, a ratio of numbers of pupils per teacher was adopted as the variable to reflect working conditions. In 1963 both BTA and BTU were strongest in schools where pupil loads were heavier. By 1965 this factor lost influence with regard to Alliance strength, but gained in power, at every level and particularly in the senior high schools, as an explanation of union membership strength. Nor was this association due to factors like percentage non-white or percentage male faculty members, both of which decreased as pupil-teacher ratios increased.

Despite variability in findings, we might venture that teaching situation has had dissimilar effects in the two cities under study. Of greatest relevance in New York with regard to elementary and junior high schools was the quality of students, indicated by type of school or racial composition. Especially during 1962 and 1963, special service schools with large minority-group populations contributed disproportionately to UFT strength. Academic highs, nearly all of which were racially integrated, did not fit this pattern. They varied in membership, if only slightly, according to the percentage of classes categorized "large." By way of contrast, Boston membership in either the Alliance or Union proved somewhat contrary to expectations on the variable connoting pupil characteristics. Here, what appeared to be more influential as an indicator of teaching situation and a stimulant to Union strength was the ratio of pupils to teachers, particularly in the senior high schools during 1965. Generally, where men were represented on faculties in substantial numbers, the ratio factor proved of little importance. Where schools were staffed primarily by women, however, the pupil-teacher ratio accounted notably for variation in BTU membership.

Still another school-related factor merits attention. What role do principals play in encouraging or discouraging group membership?[28]

[28] We have in mind here informal pressures and not the type of coercion union leaders attribute to administrators who "require" teachers to join an NEA group. For an examination of who coerces whom, see Michael H. Moskow, "Teacher Organizations: An Analysis of the Issues," in Stanley M. Elam *et al.*, eds., *Readings on Collective Negotiations in Public Education* (Chicago: Rand McNally, 1967), 237–40.

Increasing evidence points to the crucial role school principals play in leading their staffs.[29] If the attitudes and behavior of administrators have impact on the morale of teaching staffs, they may also affect the willingness of teachers to join organizations. Discovery of the contributions made by principals to organizational strength is a difficult task, but let us assume that the attitudes of administrators are reflected by their own group memberships. Then our hypothesis would state that, in schools where principals and/or assistant principals belong to a particular association, teachers will emulate their examples for one reason or another and will join in greater numbers than otherwise.

Among the principals and their assistants in the 56 elementary districts of Boston a number were members of the Alliance or the Union. Our analysis for 1963 and 1965 shows that schools where administrators belonged to BTA had comparatively high staff membership in that group. Where they belonged to BTU there was significant Union strength. In 1965, for instance, 47 elementaries were either without administrator membership or with mixed membership in both BTA and BTU. Only fourteen (30 per cent) ranked high in Union strength. Among nine schools where a principal and/or at least two assistant principals belonged to BTU, six (67 per cent) ranked high in Union strength.

Another way of exploring the impact of administrative membership is by the use of individual data, grouped totally and into two separate categories for 1963 and 1965. Table 11 reveals the relationship between administrators' affiliations and staff membership in teacher associations.

TABLE 11

BOSTON ADMINISTRATORS' AFFILIATIONS AND TEACHER ORGANIZATION MEMBERSHIP, ELEMENTARY SCHOOLS, 1963 AND 1965

	Percentage of Total Teachers in BTU		Percentage of Total Teachers in BTA	
	1963	1965	1963	1965
All schools	12	18	15	18
Mixed or no administrative affiliation	09	15	16	20
BTU administrative affiliation*	28	33	11	12

* This class includes schools where the principal and/or at least two assistant principals are members of BTU. In 1963, N = 7; in 1965, N = 8. One school that appears in 1963 does not appear in 1965; two in 1965 are not in the 1963 group.

[29] Neal Gross and Robert E. Herriott convincingly demonstrate that the professional leadership of principals is positively related to teachers' morale and performance. *Staff Leadership in Public Schools* (New York: John Wiley and Sons, 1965), 34–60.

In those schools where principals and assistants are BTU members, that group's strength is three times (1963) and twice (1965) as great as in schools where administrators have no effective affiliations. At the same time, Alliance membership is considerably lower in schools administered by BTU members than in the others. We know that the Union and the Alliance have competed on fairly equal terms at the elementary level, but in schools administered by principals or assistants affiliated with BTU the ratio of Union-to-Alliance strength has been almost three to one. Nor can this striking association be attributed to differences in the percentages of men on the faculties of the two categories of elementary schools. Although the BTU-principal schools had a higher proportion of male teachers than the others, the differences are too slight to explain away the effect of administrators' memberships. Moreover, even female teachers in these schools were more disposed to join the Union than their counterparts in elementaries where principals took no position by means of membership.

Organizational Factors

We have seen that organizational membership is linked to personal characteristics and the climates of individual schools. Membership relates also to the qualities of teacher organizations themselves. Organizational campaigning has as much to do with winning members as anything else. Information from Boston and New York casts some light on recruitment by teacher groups. In both places tremendous increases in membership followed militant union campaigns.

Late in 1962 the Boston Teachers Union launched a drive to win annual sick-leave benefits for the system's teachers. After its membership mobilized, a Union proposal was finally adopted. During these months of feverish organizational activity, BTU gained 224 members on check-off, an increase of about 118 per cent over the 190 members before the campaign began. Even the Boston Teachers Alliance, which took less of a lead in the sick-leave struggle, increased its membership, growing from 238 to 364, a gain of 53 per cent. Another drive, this time to win a duty-free lunch period for elementary teachers, was started by BTU before the summer of 1963 and was resumed the following fall. As a result, about 200 teachers joined, an increase of 33 per cent. During the same period BTA grew by 49 members, or only 13 per cent. Since these were the greatest membership strides made by the two groups in the period from 1962 through 1965, it seems fair to attribute them in large part to the effects of organizational activities.

UFT recruitment successes were also spurred by dramatic campaigns. The first occurred in April, 1959, when a city-wide work stoppage was called by the Teachers' Guild, a predecessor group. In May 1960, UFT called another work stoppage. Both walkouts were averted when city authorities finally made substantial concessions to the teachers. The first actual strike sponsored by the Union took place in November, 1960, and about 15 per cent of the teaching force participated. Because of the lack of dues check-off information for the period prior to January, 1962, it is impossible to determine whether these early campaigns led to significant membership growth. But in April, 1962, after it had won the collective bargaining election, UFT organized a strike that attracted several thousand new recruits. Before the strike check-off membership stood at 7,250. Within about a month it had jumped to 9,630, an increase of 33 per cent. Again in September, when, after a long period of hard bargaining, the union negotiated an initial contract, it grew by about 2,150 members, or 18 per cent. The following year a strike was cancelled at the last moment, a second contract agreed upon, and UFT gained almost 3,000 teachers on check-off, another 18 per cent. These increases, coming on the heels of the April, 1962, strike and the two contractual settlements, were the largest made by the union during the period from 1962 through 1965.

In both cities, therefore, strenuous campaigns, which went far in accomplishing organizational goals, were followed by quantum jumps in membership. Did the victories, in terms of rewards for teachers, or the campaigns themselves, regardless of their substantive accomplishments, have the greatest impact on membership growth? Undoubtedly, both counted. But in the case of UFT during 1962 we wish to emphasize the overriding significance of the campaign, its stimulation of teacher involvement, and its immediate and continuing impact on the recruitment of members.

If success in winning benefits for teachers were the only major factor, we would expect, *ceteris paribus,* recruitment gains within individual schools to have been about the same after the 1962 strike and contractual agreement. All teachers came out ahead, and, though some gained a trifle more than others, variations were slight. Yet schools varied noticeably in membership growth from 1962 to 1963—periods before and after the settlement. These differences cannot be explained satisfactorily by the contractual achievements of bargaining or by any of the personal or contextual variables discussed above, or by levels of early membership in various schools without considering one additional factor. Contrasting levels of teacher involvement, as indicated by participation in the UFT strike of April, 1962, must also be taken into account.[30]

[30] Data on strike turnout were collected from payroll and attendance records of the Board of Education for the 290 schools in the sample which were operating in

But first, it is necessary to point out the association between the pre-strike membership of UFT and actual strike participation by teachers in New York City's schools. In a study of the 1960 strike, Charles Winick, on the basis of interviews with sixty staff members in one junior high school, concluded that union membership itself did not seem to be related to intended strike turnout.[31] Our findings, although not strictly comparable since they are based on aggregate data for the later strike, suggest that union membership did make a difference. On a citywide basis, while approximately 20,000 teachers walked out, less than half that number belonged to UFT at the time. By division, membership was: 5 per cent of elementary teachers; 26 per cent of junior high teachers; 16 per cent of academic high teachers; and 7 per cent of vocational high teachers. Yet, at these respective levels, 27 per cent, 65 per cent, 62 per cent, and 54 per cent of the teachers stayed away from school for other than ordinary reasons. It may be presumed that all, or nearly all, members struck and a good many others besides. In those schools having memberships of 10 per cent or over, about eight in ten had high strike turnouts. But among those with lesser memberships, only about three in ten had high turnout rates.[32]

Even more significant, however, is the relationship between strike turnout and subsequent membership. Winick's study of attitudes toward the 1960 walkout posited that "no teacher had decided to join a union as the result of the imminent strike, although a number said that they had decided against joining a union. . . ."[33] Our findings for 1962 show that as a result of the strike the union's appeal increased notably. Whether prior membership strength in the schools was relatively high or low, the strike itself appears to have had a major effect on the organization's local growth. This is shown in Table 12. Healthy participation in UFT activity looms in importance as a stimulant to membership in both strong- and weak-union schools. But its major impact was felt in those schools with few members prior to the militant campaign. These places apparently possessed the potential for growth and needed only the kind of impetus the strike provided. If teachers were willing to risk participation in an illegal strike, it is understandable that their subsequent affiliation involved no greater commitment and consequently came comparatively easily.

In a post-strike assessment, UFT's president, Charles Cogen, declared

---

1962. On the basis of these records, we calculated the percentage of teachers in each school who stayed out because of the strike.

[31] "When Teachers Strike," *Teachers College Record*, 64 (April, 1963), 602.

[32] Strike turnout is also positively related to the personal and contextual variables previously discussed, particularly sex.

[33] *Op. cit.*

TABLE 12

NEW YORK CITY STRIKE TURNOUT AND UFT MEMBERSHIP GROWTH, BY
PRE-STRIKE MEMBERSHIP

	Differences Between Percentages of Schools with "High" and "Low" Strike Turnout Ranking "High" in UFT Membership Growth, 1962 to 1963*	
Division	High Pre-Strike Membership (1962)	Low Pre-Strike Membership (1962)
Elementary (N = 140)	+29	+29
Junior high (N = 64)	+16	+52
Academic and vocational high (N = 86)	+09	+55

* A plus sign indicates a greater percentage of high-turnout schools ranking high in growth; a minus sign indicates the opposite. Growth is the difference between the percentage of UFT members in 1962 and 1963 for each school. High growth schools are: elementary—10 per cent and over; junior high, academic and vocational high—30 per cent and over. High strike-turnout schools are: elementary—20 per cent and over; junior high—70 per cent and over; academic and vocational high—60 per cent and over.

that "our union will now grow to even larger numbers than before."[34] He was absolutely correct. The mobilizing effects of the strike were tremendous and lasting. This can be seen if we compare correlational coefficients between strike participation and membership strength for the period preceding the strike as well as the several years that followed. Table 13 reveals that within every division the association between strike turnout and 1963 membership is stronger than that between pre-strike membership and turnout. Teacher involvement in the strike explains a

TABLE 13

NEW YORK CITY STRIKE TURNOUT AND UFT MEMBERSHIP—THE IMPACT OF THE
1962 STRIKE ON SUBSEQUENT MEMBERSHIP STRENGTH. (CORRELATIONS)

Independent and Dependent Variables	Elementary	Junior High	Academic High	Vocational High
Pre-strike membership/ strike turnout	.35	.35	.41	.27
Strike turnout/1963 membership	.50	.56	.66	.80
Strike turnout/1965 membership	.49	.38	.67	.80
Pre-strike membership/ 1965 membership	.41	.44	.56	.24

[34] *United Teacher*, April-May, 1962.

greater part of subsequent UFT strength than prior membership explains teacher involvement. This is especially evident for the academic and vocational high schools. Union strength mattered in determining strike activity by teachers in each school, but strike activity mattered even more in its effects on levels of future school membership. Table 13 also reports correlation coefficients for membership by schools in 1962 and 1965. It can readily be seen that, except for the junior high schools, which seem to be in a class by themselves, strike turnout functions as a more effective predictor of contemporary union strength than does early membership.

Whatever our means of analysis, these data persuasively argue the importance of dramatic and militant activities in the recruitment of new members. Campaigns, whose manifest goals are the achievement of substantive benefits for teachers, have latent consequences for an organization. Gaining these benefits is certainly important. But a hard-hitting campaign to achieve them is also critical. At least as far as UFT strength is concerned, one good strike may have been worth several good settlements.

The Varying Bases of Membership

The aim of this comparative and longitudinal analysis of selected personal, school, and organizational factors has been to shed light on several significant bases of teacher-group membership.

Some findings emerge with great clarity. As anticipated, when we examine group membership by sex the results are remarkably consistent. Individual data from Boston, for all divisions and both points in time, demonstrate that male teachers are more likely to join a union than are females. Aggregate data from Boston and New York add still another dimension, showing as they do that the relative "maleness" of school climates also affects group-membership. A number of reasons could be advanced to explain why men are more apt to join unions and why schools which have large proportions of men on their staffs facilitate union membership.

Among the most important is that men more often see teaching as a lifetime career and have greater need of the benefits, particularly of the pecuniary sort, recently promised teachers by unions. Because they are much more likely than women both to carry weighty financial burdens and consider themselves relatively deprived, male teachers have the greater incentive to join organizations that evince militancy and the willingness to fight hard for monetary gains. Consequently, schools dominated by males are more likely to encourage aggressive behavior while those dominated by females tend to promote submissiveness.

Other consistent findings relate to the propensity of teachers in junior high schools to enter union ranks. In both cities, and for the several years, rates of membership are visibly higher within these particular schools. By way of conjecture, it seems that from a number of viewpoints junior highs may be considered educational middle-grounds, characterized by transition and instability. Students here are passing from childhood to adolescence, inevitably raising problems, not only for themselves and their parents, but also for their teachers. On top of these difficulties, junior high faculties encounter their own peculiar transitional problems. Located as they are in institutions that share the child-classroom orientations of elementary schools and the subject-departmental orientations of high schools, they find coherent identification especially challenging. To add still another disconcerting element to the unique mix, teachers in these schools have objective cause to feel insecure in their particular positions. Elementary and high schools, in one form or another, are firmly rooted in the educational terrain; the utility and legitimacy of junior highs have repeatedly been questioned by public school influentials, most recently by the board of education and school administration in New York City. As a result of these factors, the junior high teacher might reasonably be assumed to suffer the maladies of confused identification, insecurity of status, and depressed morale. Any one, or some combination of these factors could make him distinctively susceptible to the appeals of groups advocating or contributing to altered relationships in the educational system.

As we proceed, our findings take more protean form. Even the attribute of sex, which predictably relates to organizational membership, gives rise to dissimilarity. In New York the "maleness" of faculties is linked less to UFT membership in 1962 than in 1965, and less in 1965 than in 1963. In Boston this factor matters more in 1965 than in 1963. It may be that in the initial stages of organizational growth early recruits join unions for a variety of reasons unrelated to whether they are male or female or whether men or women set the tone in their individual schools. With growth proceeding apace and recruitment increasing in extent, sex-related attitudes and school climates become important. By the time an organization reaches maturity and membership becomes rather commonplace, things pretty well even out and male-female differences recede in prominence. When analysis focuses on specifics, approximately the same type of variability applies to division or level. Generally, differences between membership rates in elementary, junior high, and high schools seem greater in the early and middle phases of organizational growth than in the later stage.

With the data available, we have been able to examine administrative affiliation only in Boston elementary schools, and the impact of organizational activities during one brief period in New York City. Since school principals apparently do influence teachers' dispositions to join a group, it is appropriate to inquire into just how this comes about. We can imagine that a principal's manifest hostility towards a union will keep teachers from joining, but it may also foment staff rebellion and encourage membership. Conversely, administrative support for a union may make affiliation very convenient. Or it might have the opposite effect should benevolence create a climate in which teachers feel there is little to be gained from paying dues and belonging to a militant group.[35]

In view of evidence demonstrating the recruitment impact of city-wide campaigns, which are manifestly directed toward the achievement of policy goals, we can conclude that real-life happenings mean more to organizational growth than mere words. Yet, it is possible that what works quite well during an early or middle phase has lesser influence by the time a group is fully developed. It is possible, too, that in some cities strikes and strike threats are viable recruiting techniques, whereas in other cities moderate means must be employed to accomplish similar results.

[35] In San Francisco, for instance, union leaders claim a high membership in schools with both authoritarian and democratic principals. Important to recruitment is not only the style of the principal but also the vigor and skill of an organization's building representative or chapter chairman.

III. Leadership Motivations

The size of a group's membership is one element which determines organizational strength. Another is its motivations, and particularly those of organization leaders. The single aspect of motivations which we shall examine is militancy. Whereas a group's size is relatively easy to determine, militancy is a rather nebulous concept, lending itself to varying interpretations.

In light of efforts by local teachers to strengthen their organizations, achieve the right to negotiate or bargain, and win substantive benefits, it is not at all surprising that the *activities* of teacher organizations crowd other aspects of their lives from view. A strike here, a boycott there, and the imposition of sanctions elsewhere are events that command public notice. In consequence, popular conceptions and newspaper accounts of the new teacher militancy all stress behavioral features— aggressive activity, hard conflict, open warfare. There can be little argument about the relevance of action to any consideration of organizational militancy, but for the moment, our concern is with attitudes, not behavior.

To understand teacher militancy one must consider not only what teacher organizations actually do but also how they, or at least their leaders, perceive the educational world. Their views of the role they should play help to determine their conduct and the part they take in shaping educational policy. To what extent, and under what conditions, leadership views prove decisive are questions to which we shall return later. First, it is necessary to define the concept of militancy in terms of the orientations of teacher leaders.

In this analysis, our principal data are the evaluative and cognitive attitudes and the personal and situational characteristics of the leaders of nine teacher organizations in five large cities. For purposes of this study, leaders are defined as members of the governing bodies of local teacher organizations. These bodies, most often called "executive boards" but sometimes referred to as "boards of directors" or "trustees," are composed of officers and other representatives generally elected by the organization's membership. Included also are a few executive

48

secretaries or directors of several associations. Thus, only individuals holding certain nominal positions within the various groups have been classified as leaders. There is little doubt that these people serve together as the organization's cadre and share responsibility in both theory and fact for fashioning group policy.[1] They are the ones who man the command posts of the teacher organizations under study. In late 1965 and early 1966, structured questionnaires were distributed to 270 such persons in NEA, AFT, and unaffiliated or independent groups in New York, Boston, Chicago, San Francisco, and Atlanta. Completed questionnaires were returned by 185 leaders, over two-thirds of those solicited. The response rate by city and group is shown in Table 14.[2]

These 185 leaders provide the basis for the present exploration of militancy and later examination of group influence. At the outset, we shall try to clarify the concept of militancy by specifying the several dimensions of militant orientations, taking a cue here from the doctrinal positions already reviewed in Chapter I. Then we shall be in a position to identify a number of factors, such as the ones discussed in Chapter II in the context of group membership, which appear to be related to leaders' orientations. Finally, an assessment of the relative strengths of various factors will be made in an effort to isolate the main determinants of militant orientations.

Dimensions of Militancy

Earlier discussion of the doctrines of NEA and AFT has suggested the pertinence of ideas like participation, power, and combat to the contemporary teachers movement. To catch the central meaning of militancy, attention must be paid to each one of these ideas. No single one can adequately define what is meant by militant orientations. Nor do the three fit together in easy combination to reveal some unidimensional

[1] Policy proposals of this designated leadership must be ratified by another body of delegates and sometimes by the entire membership. In the case of UFT, policy initiative resides with the Administrative Committee, composed of officers, and a larger Executive Board, composed of officers and other representatives. New policy proposals are offered to the huge Delegate Assembly for ratification. In some instances, such as the calling of strikes, the entire membership votes in a referendum. Generally, the views of the nominal leaders prevail. In the interim, of course, these leaders make critical decisions within the permissive limits of policy.

[2] We make no claim that these respondents represent teacher leaders throughout the country. Had other cities or smaller communities been surveyed, our findings might have proved different. We suspect, however, that a number of them would hold. Even our working sample is open to question. Mail questionnaires inevitably raise doubts about the representativeness of those who respond. In this survey response rates vary considerably by group, as Table 14 shows. But a check of respondents, on the basis of sex at least, suggests that they are likely to accurately represent the orientations of entire leaderships.

TABLE 14
TEACHER ORGANIZATIONS AND LEADERSHIP RESPONDENTS

City	Organization and Affiliation	Number of Leaders	Number of Respondents	Percentage of Leaders Responding
New York	United Federation of Teachers (UFT), AFT	47	39	83
Boston	Boston Teachers Union (BTU), AFT	40	28	70
	Boston Teachers Alliance (BTA), Independent	17	8	47
Chicago	Chicago Teachers Union (CTU), AFT	40	18	45
	Chicago Education Association (CEA), NEA	32	19	59
San Francisco	San Francisco Federation of Teachers (SFFT), AFT	33	24	73
	San Francisco Classroom Teachers Association (SFCTA), NEA	26	22	85
	Teachers Association of San Francisco (TASF), Independent	8	7	88
Atlanta	Atlanta Teachers Association (ATA), NEA	27	20	74
Totals		270	185	69

attitude. Rather, three distinct, but interrelated, dimensions exist and each one contributes to an intuitive understanding of leadership orientations. To use somewhat dramatic terminology, the first might be thought of as the dimension reflecting goals; the second, strategies; and the last, tactics.[3]

Goals take into account the idea of participation. Status and dignity, the rights of teachers, the introduction of democracy in the schools, the extension of teacher control, participation rather than consultation, an equal voice in the shaping of policies which determine our professional lives—these are typical of the phrases which during the past five years have been articulated by teacher representatives throughout the nation. A central question here is: What roles do teacher leaders feel their organizations should play in determining educational policies? It is one thing to strive for increased benefits and specific changes in school conditions. It is quite another to attempt to alter the rules of the educational game.[4] Of importance in examining militancy are not demands for changes in the substance of policy but prescriptions for changes in procedures by which substantive policies are decided. Just what participatory objectives do teachers have in mind?

They may desire either a *decisive* or *consultive* role.[5] A decisive role would mean that educational policy decisions hinge upon the actual approval of teacher groups. This orientation is expressed by AFT's past-president, Charles Cogen:

> We want teachers not only to be heard, and to have some nebulous other body make the decisions taking into account what the teachers had

[3] Militancy has been conceptualized and measured in other ways. Cole, for instance, constructs a militancy index based on whether New York City teachers approved of the union's two strikes and whether they reported for work on the days the strikes were being held. Stephen Cole, "The Unionization of Teachers: Determinants of Rank-and-File Support," *Sociology of Education*, 41 (Winter, 1968), 70. See also Ronald G. Corwin, "Militant Professionalism, Initiative and Compliance in Public Education," *Sociology of Education*, 38 (Summer, 1965), 310–31.

[4] Analogous to this distinction between increased benefits and revised rules is the difference between two of the not entirely compatible goals of the war on poverty in the United States. The program seeks to end economic poverty by distributing various material perquisites. It also seeks to end the virtual exclusion of poor people from political life by distributing power. J. David Greenstone and Paul E. Peterson, "Reformers, Machines, and the War on Poverty," in James Q. Wilson, ed., *City Politics and Public Policy* (New York: John Wiley and Sons, 1968), 267–92.

[5] A similar distinction is made by Harry Eckstein, who calls attention to "negotiations" and "consultations." *Pressure Group Politics* (Stanford: Stanford University Press, 1960), 22–3.

to say, but we want teachers right in there working out the educational decisions with whoever else is concerned.[6]

A consultive role would mean that the opinions of teacher groups are taken into account but are not considered to be in any sense binding. This orientation is expressed by the director of Harvard University's Collective Negotiations Institute:

> Actually, teacher leaders simply want to establish the right of teachers to be consulted and respectfully heard on questions of educational policy. The more sophisticated teacher group spokesmen will admit it would be ludicrous to "negotiate" textbook selection, courses of study, teacher recruitment procedures, student evaluation systems, and other intricate "educational questions."[7]

In order to discover which role leaders desire, we asked a series of questions about organizational participation in several domains of educational policy-making. Leaders' goals were categorized "decisive" if they chose either of these responses to describe the proper role of teacher organizations: (1) "They should have more to say than the school board and/or administration," or (2) "They should have a voice equal to that of the school board and/or administration." Their goals were categorized "consultive" if they chose one of the following responses: (3) "They should be consulted, and the school board and/or administration should weigh heavily their advice;" (4) "They should be kept informed by the school board and/or administration, but should not necessarily be called on for advice;" or (5) "They should not be involved." Cumulating responses for the several policy domains in an index of prescribed participation, we have divided leaders into two relatively equal groups: 98 are Decisives and another 87 are Consultives.

Leadership goals appear vital. To a lesser degree, perhaps, so do leadership strategies. In the present context, strategy relates to views concerning the power of teacher organizations and also the power of other major participants in public school politics. Increasing the power of one's own group while simultaneously decreasing that of other participants would appear plausible as a strategy for achieving a decisive role in policy-making. This was the understanding of Calvin Gross, the former Superintendent of Schools of New York City. He addressed himself to the question of union strategy when he commented candidly on collective bargaining negotiations during 1963:

[6] "The President's Column," *American Teacher*, April, 1968.

[7] Joseph H. Cronin, "School Boards and Principals—Before and After Negotiations," *Phi Delta Kappan*, XLIX (November, 1967), 126.

I think what the United Federation of Teachers wants basically is more control of the school system. I mean that they would like to be able to have more say in every school and in every phase of the administration of the school system, a little more say-so in what goes on.[8]

We might expect that teacher leaders who want an equal voice in determining policies would also want their organization's power expanded and the power of boards of education, superintendents, and administrative elites diminished. Or leaders who aspired to a significant participatory role might seek an increase in their own group's power without a corresponding decrease in the power of others.

To tap strategies involving power, we asked whether teacher organizations, school boards, superintendents, and administrative chiefs at the central office or headquarters should have more, the same amount, or less power than they already possessed in several areas of educational policy-making. As anticipated, more than two-thirds of the respondents advocated greater power for their own group whatever the policy domain involved. Few leaders, however, challenged the power of members of the educational establishment. Many seemed to feel that an increase in their own influence was sufficient, since power was not limited and more for one participant did not necessarily mean less for another.

What we think of as the tactical dimension of militancy most resembles popular notions. Combativeness, tendencies to conflict, and a willingness to act forcefully, employ controversial methods, and take risks are indeed necessary ingredients of any realistic conception of teacher militancy. We can readily imagine the connection between aggressive methods on the one hand and power aspirations or ambitious participatory goals on the other. To measure dispositions toward conflict, a four-item scale has been constructed. The items, on which this combativeness scale is based, are: (1) "On most issues the leaders of teacher organizations will achieve best results by personal diplomacy—privately conferring with the board and/or administration;" (2) "Since the interests of teachers and administrators are essentially the same, teacher organizations should not campaign against administration proposals but should urge their members to support them;" (3) "Teacher organizations should not be satisfied with obtaining benefits for their members, but should strive to increase their power to share in determining policies for the school system;" and (4) "Most disputes between teachers and administrators can be resolved without the involvement of teacher organizations."[9] Those responding

8 *New York Times*, July 7, 1963.
9 The combative response to the first two items is "disagree", to the third "agree", and to the last one "not sure" or "disagree." The coefficient of reproducibility (R) is 90.4.

in combative fashion to all four items will be called Fighters (N = 60); those responding aggressively to only three, Persuaders (N = 64); and the rest, Cooperators (N = 61).

In addition to this scale, we have used another item of manifest importance. It probes the willingness of leaders to advocate forceful action by asking whether respondents go along with the statement: "If they disagree strongly with policy proposals of the school board and/or administration, teacher organizations have the obligation to call for a work stoppage, a strike, a boycott, or the refusal by teachers to sign contracts."

Analytically, goals, strategies, and tactics must be viewed as distinctive components of leadership militancy. While they may be woven from similar thread, the cloth is not identical. Participatory objectives, power prescriptions, combative dispositions, and action orientations may indeed fit neatly together, but this is not necessarily the case. One can conceive of instances in which leaders desire to participate on equal footing with school boards and administrations, and yet would not be disposed to use aggressive methods to achieve such a goal. Or conversely, it is not inconceivable that leaders, however combative, would settle for a consultive role in the arenas of educational policy-making.

If any one dimension has special significance, particularly in terms of the long-term future of teacher organizations, it is that of participation. The development of the United Federation of Teachers in New York City clearly illustrates this point.[10] It is true that from the very beginning the Federation campaigned hard for higher teacher salaries and other benefits. Yet, simultaneously, the union had as its main objective, in the words of its current president, Albert Shanker, the formation of "a movement which would give the teacher a voice—which would give him some decision-making power in his area of competence."[11] There can be little doubt that UFT's leadership, if not its membership, has looked upon participation both as a means and an end. It was naturally a means to gain improvements in salaries, personal benefits, and educational conditions. The end toward which the union was striving might well be labeled "democratic professionalism," a new system of rules and arrangements permitting prefessional educators, at whatever levels in the hierarchy, to share in formulating city-wide and school policies.

The question of whether, and to what extent, teacher groups share in determining major educational matters goes directly to the heart of educational politics and the new militancy. Therefore, goals are worth

[10] See my "New Voices in Public Education," *Teachers College Record*, LXVIII (October, 1966), 13–20.
[11] *United Teacher*, April 13, 1965.

examining in some detail. It is quite possible that leadership attitudes vary, depending upon the kinds of policies up for decision. Some leaders might feel that their organizations should be entitled to an equal voice on some matters but not on others. Whether or not orientations toward participation vary, and if so, how, appears appropriate for exploration.[12]

Consequently, in addition to asking for leadership views on educational policy generally, we have sought opinions in four more specific domains as well. What type of role do they seek on policies relating to: (1) salary—including minimum and maximum levels, range and distribution, and associated benefits; (2) personnel—including recruitment, appointment, assignment, and promotion; (3) curriculum and instruction—covering a wide variety of subjects from courses of study to instructional materials; and (4) the organization of the school system—encompassing matters like decentralization, grade levels and educational programs in various types of schools, and admissions standards.[13]

Keeping in mind the relevance of the type of policy involved, our task is to examine the linkage between participatory goals and power strategies. As can be seen in Table 15, although majorities of teacher leaders agree that their own organizations should have more power,

TABLE 15
PARTICIPATORY OBJECTIVES AND PRESCRIPTIONS FOR ORGANIZATIONAL POWER, BY POLICY DOMAIN

| | Percentages Desiring More Power for Their Own Organizations | |
Policy Domain	Decisives	Consultives
Educational policy generally	89 (84)*	64 (98)
Salaries	84 (88)	67 (91)
Personnel	93 (68)	70 (111)
Curriculum and instruction	92 (83)	59 (99)
School system organization	85 (65)	60 (117)

* Figures in parentheses are the total number of leaders favoring either a decisive or consultive role in each policy area (excluding non-responses).

[12] In inquiring into differences in orientations by policy domain, our approach parallels those of recent investigations which have shown power to be differentially exercised in a community according to the type of issue being decided. See, for example, the following: Edward C. Banfield, *Personal Influence* (Glencoe: Free Press, 1961); Robert A. Dahl, *Who Governs?* (New Haven: Yale University Press, 1961); Roscoe C. Martin and Frank J. Munger *et al., Decisions in Syracuse* (Bloomington, Ind.: Indiana University Press, 1961); and Wallace S. Sayre and Herbert Kaufman, *Governing New York City* (New York: Russell Sage, 1960).

[13] Total responses of leaders are as anticipated. Almost half (49 per cent and 46 per cent respectively) seek a decisive role for their groups on salary and curriculum policy-making, and about one-third (38 per cent and 36 per cent respectively) want a comparable say in the areas of personnel and organization.

there are differences in the proportions of Decisives and Consultives who feel this way. Approximately nine out of ten Decisives advocate increased power in the several domains. The remainder, while valuing equal rights, are probably satisfied with the share in decision-making their group is already allotted. Roughly two out of three Consultives want greater organizational influence. Although these leaders are willing to settle for a lesser share in formulating policy, they undoubtedly feel the need for more power to attain even a consultive role.

It would seem reasonable that the two categories of leaders would differ not only with regard to power prescriptions for their own groups but also in their attitudes toward the power of the educational establishment. Those with higher participatory goals should be more inclined to curtail the influence of competitor school boards, superintendents, and administrative chiefs. Those with more modest goals should be less inclined to favor diminished influence for other core participants. A majority of leaders, it should be noted, indicate that the power of board, superintendent, and bureaucracy should remain the same. But of those who challenge the status-quo distribution, significantly more Decisives than Consultives prescribe lesser influence for the educational establishment. In each of the fifteen matched comparisons presented in Table 16 differences are in the predicted direction. Not only do views of the power of one's own group differ depending on group goals, but attitudes toward that of other important participants also vary according to whether leaders demand a decisive role or will settle for a consultive one.

Is there also a relationship between goals and tactics? We would imagine, of course, that leaders advocating decisive participation would be more likely to possess combative dispositions than their less ambitious colleagues. Specifically, among leaders with high participatory goals we should discover a larger percentage of Fighters and among those with moderate objectives we should find a larger percentage of Cooperators. This proves to be so, as data in Table 17(a) indicate.[14] More than twice as many Decisives rank high (43 per cent) rather than low (18 per cent) on the combativeness scale. More than twice as many Consultives rank low (49 per cent) rather than high (21 per cent). To put it another way, nearly half of those with high participatory goals are combative as compared to only one-fifth with lesser goals. Yet some leaders do not see combat as a means to achieving an equal voice in policy-making. Some others, whose aspirations are limited, would

[14] There is no necessity to examine tactical orientations by policy domain, since our questions regarding combativeness and willingness to take forceful action did not specify types of issues. In Table 17, leadership responses for the several policy domains have been cumulated in an index of participation.

TABLE 16

PARTICIPATORY OBJECTIVES AND PRESCRIPTIONS FOR ESTABLISHMENT POWER,
BY POLICY DOMAIN

Policy Domain and Establishment Participant	Percentages Desiring Less Power for Members of the Educational Establishment	
	Decisives	Consultives
Educational Policy Generally		
Board	67 (40)*	33 (36)
Superintendent	55 (38)	33 (40)
Bureaucracy	78 (40)	32 (44)
Salaries		
Board	56 (41)	22 (37)
Superintendent	71 (42)	41 (37)
Bureaucracy	84 (38)	51 (37)
Personnel		
Board	72 (29)	50 (46)
Superintendent	73 (37)	39 (44)
Bureaucracy	88 (32)	48 (40)
Curriculum and Instruction		
Board	84 (38)	72 (39)
Superintendent	59 (39)	32 (37)
Bureaucracy	66 (41)	31 (48)
School System Organization		
Board	67 (30)	26 (43)
Superintendent	48 (31)	23 (47)
Bureaucracy	61 (31)	38 (47)

* Figures in parentheses are the total number of leaders favoring either a decisive or consultive role in each policy area (excluding non-responses and respondents who prescribed the "same amount of power").

nevertheless resort to combat. Among these deviants, the former would negotiate diplomatically to win an equal voice, the latter would fight to win benefits.

Pursuing similar logic, we would expect differences in goals to be reflected in the willingness of leaders to engage in forceful action, use novel techniques, and run recognizable risks. This turns out to be the case, as Table 17(b) shows. Two out of three Decisives are willing to strike, boycott, or impose sanctions. Only one out of three Consultives would do the same. Still, substantial numbers deviate from our expectations. However much some leaders believe in equal status, they do not consider strikes or similar measures to be suitable actions. However reluctant some are to take on a decisive role, they would strike or adopt sanctions, at least in cases of an impasse over salaries or working conditions.

TABLE 17

PARTICIPATORY OBJECTIVES AND TACTICAL ORIENTATIONS

Tactical Orientations	Decisives	Consultives
(a) *Combativeness*		
Fighters	43%	21%
Persuaders	39	30
Cooperators	18	49
	100% (98)*	100% (87)
(b) *Willingness to Strike, Boycott, or Impose Sanctions*		
Willing	63%	33%
Not Willing	37	67
	100% (97)	100% (86)

* Figures in parentheses are the total number of leaders generally favoring a decisive or consultive role (excluding non-responses).

In light of the preceding analysis there can be little dispute that goal, strategic, and tactical orientations of teacher leaders are interrelated. This should occasion little surprise. One could easily conceive the connection of the three orientations in the minds of political activists. The group leader who wants a decisive voice in policy-making should naturally prescribe greater influence for his own organization and lesser for his competitors. Especially in view of today's climate, he should be willing to take hard action in opposition to the board of education and school administration in furtherance of his goals. In contrast, the leader who is less inclined to alter the rules of the educational game should have less cause to seek a redistribution of influence or to adopt a combative posture. Nevertheless, the orientations we have been examining are not exactly the same. It is worth keeping the several dimensions distinct as we proceed to explore how group affiliation, educational conditions, and personal and situational factors relate to leadership orientations toward goals, strategies, and tactics.

The Impact of Group Affiliation

What characteristics distinguish the more from the less militantly inclined teacher leaders? One that immediately comes to mind is organizational affiliation. The effects of membership in organized groups on the attitudes and behavior of people have been demonstrated time and again by contemporary social scientists. The most obvious case is that of political party affiliation. Whether a person belongs to or identifies with the Republican or Democratic Party has major bearing on his political orientations and voting decisions, at least with regard to national affairs. On many public questions, and probably on all elections for national office, party affiliation looms as a key determinant of an individual's attitudes and behavior.[15] The analogy between political parties and teacher organizations is imperfect, of course; yet both types of groups are involved in earnest competition, trying to win adherents, votes, and the right to participate in determining governmental policies.

Previously, Chapter I noted certain doctrinal similarities and differences between NEA and AFT, as expressed in their publications and by their national representatives. On teacher participation and group power the views of association and union spokemen were not far apart. The question of combat or conflict, however, revealed sharp disagreement. Now we can test whether national doctrines are reflected in the orientations of city leaders. In other words, do those in organizations affiliated with AFT hold different opinions than those who do not belong to a union? Our contention is that the type of organization to which a leader belongs does make a difference, indeed one that is greater than a comparison of national views suggests.[16]

To explore this subject we have divided the 185 respondents into two categories. The first includes 109 Union leaders, persons on the executive boards of UFT, BTU, CTU, and SFFT, all of whom are members of the American Federation of Teachers. The second includes 76 Association leaders. In this category are grouped together 61 heads of CEA, SFCTA, and ATA, which are affiliated with the National Education Association, and 15 persons from the independent BTA and TASF.[17]

At the doctrinal level, the rights of teacher groups to participate in educational policy-making are espoused today by both NEA and AFT. Joint partnership is the ideal, whether it comes about through collective bargaining, professional negotiation, or some less formal arrangement. And both national organizations define the scope of participation broadly, covering virtually all matters of mutual concern and anything affecting the educational program. On this basis alone, one might conclude that the participatory objectives of urban Union and Association leaders are not very dissimilar. Nothing could be wider of the mark. Leaders belonging to AFT are far more disposed than their Association counterparts to prescribe for their own groups a major or equal voice in the formula-

[15] See, for example, Angus Campbell, *The American Voter* (New York: John Wiley and Sons, 1960) and V. O. Key, Jr., *Public Opinion and American Democracy* (New York: Alfred A. Knopf, 1964).

[16] What is treated here may not be the effect of organizational affiliation per se, but rather the tendency for teachers with particular dispositions to join and become active in one group instead of another. Initial attitudes predispose individuals toward certain organizations, and then the doctrinal atmosphere of the organizations reinforces prior attitudes.

[17] Combining the two types does no injustice to the militancy of NEA. If anything, independents are more militant than NEA'ers.

tion of public school policies. Seven of ten in the former category rank as Decisives on our index of participation.[18] Fewer than three of ten in the latter category rank similarly. Whatever the policy domain, differences by group affiliation persist. Union leaders are far more likely than Association leaders to prefer decisive roles. The strength of the relationships between Union affiliation and decisive goal orientations is shown summarily in Table 18(a). The higher the phi coefficient (ϕ), the stronger the relationship.[19]

TABLE 18

THE STRENGTH OF RELATIONSHIPS BETWEEN UNION AFFILIATION AND LEADERSHIP ORIENTATIONS

(a) Goal Orientations	ϕ
Decisive participation (on index)	.42*
Decisive salary participation	.40*
Decisive personnel participation	.40*
Decisive curriculum participation	.33*
Decisive school system organization participation	.42*

(b) Strategic Orientations†	ϕ
Increase in own organization's power	.39*
Decrease in school board's power	.14
Decrease in superintendent's power	.10
Decrease in administrative bureaucracy's power	.28*

(c) Tactical Orientations	ϕ
High combativeness	.51*
Willingness to take forceful action	.47*

* $p < .05$.
† Educational policy generally.

Both NEA and AFT declare that collective activity by local teacher groups is legitimate and necessary. And both are in the business of encouraging and supporting affiliates who are engaged in the pursuit of power. We would anticipate, then, that leaders in the five cities under study would pretty well agree on the strategy of increasing group power. Most of the respondents, as noted above, do prescribe increased power for their own local organizations. Still, there are differences between Union and Association representatives. For example, on educational policy generally, 89 per cent of the former but only 57 per cent of the

[18] Our index of participation is a summary measure of participatory goals in each of the several policy-making domains.

[19] In this and succeeding tables of the chapter, the phi (ϕ) coefficient has been used to measure strength of relationships. The chi-square (χ^2) test, employing the .05 level of significance, has been used to show whether a relationship is statistically significant or more likely due to chance. See Hubert M. Blalock, Jr., *Social Statistics* (New York: McGraw-Hill, 1960), 212–41.

latter category of respondents desire more influence for their groups. The relationship between Union affiliation and the desire to enhance organizational power is apparent, as is shown in Table 18(b).

Earlier it was suggested that a logical corollary of desiring more power for one's own group is proposing less power for other important participants. Moreover, national doctrines indicate that AFT tends more than its competitor to see organizational fortunes linked in a zero-sum game to the power of others. In short, the more you have, the less we have. At the local level, this also proves to be the case, as is illustrated by the coefficients for educational policy generally in Table 18(b).[20] Relationships are in the predicted direction, but only the one regarding the power of the administrative bureaucracy appears at all strong. Views toward the board of education and superintendent differ somewhat, but not to any noteworthy degree.

Tactical orientations might well be thought to distinguish most sharply between unionists, on the one hand, and NEA and independent representatives on the other, for on tactics, combat, and conflict, the two nationwide organizations are still far apart. NEA rejects the idea that conflict between teachers and school authorities is a normal state of affairs. AFT takes the view that major differences divide teachers and their employers, and many can be settled only by means of combat.

We therefore hypothesize that urban Union leaders are more combative in disposition and more willing to engage in forceful action than are urban Association leaders. On combativeness, it turns out that half of the former group, but only 12 per cent of the latter group, are Fighters. In contrast, nearly two-thirds of Association members rank as Cooperators, while only 14 per cent of Union members rank similarly. On the matter of action, differences are almost as pronounced. Two of every three Union leaders in comparison to one of every five Association leaders appear willing to strike, boycott, or impose sanctions if they disagree with the board of education or school administration. The high coefficients in Table 18(c) give distinct support to our hypothesis.

Despite the recent convergence of the two national organizations, leaders of large-city teacher organizations differ significantly in their orientations toward participation, power, and especially combat. Among our respondents from five cities, members of AFT are those most likely to adopt goals, strategies, and techniques which together comprise the major components of organizational militancy.

---

[20] Responses of leaders who said the power of the board, superintendent, and bureaucracy should remain about the same are eliminated. The reduction in the number of cases helps to account for the fact that two entries in Table 18(b) are not statistically significant.

Educational Conditions and Their Effects

Numerous studies in the field of education are devoted to the general proposition that teacher morale affects how teachers perceive and pursue their jobs. Whatever the indicators—satisfaction with teaching, contentment with working conditions, pride in a local school—these "morale" studies signify the important impact working environments may have on the perspectives of public school teachers. In Chapter II our explorations of group membership dealt with teaching situations, in terms of the numbers and kinds of pupils encountered in a school, as an indirect indicator of morale. Now we shall proceed a bit further and try to discover what effects, if any, perceptions of educational conditions have on the orientations of teacher leaders.[21] Our feeling here is that the more dissatisfied they are with the local educational environments the more likely leaders are to choose decisive goals, prescribe increased power for themselves and less for others, express combativeness, and be disposed toward dramatic action.[22]

The relationships are clear, although not as compelling as those between group affiliation and militancy. Correlation coefficients are presented in the three parts of Table 19. First, dissatisfaction with educational conditions is related to goal orientations. Among those who are satisfied, two-thirds would settle for some form of consultation. Among those who are dissatisfied, the situation is exactly reversed. Two out of three of these leaders want a decisive role. Second, dissatisfaction is associated with strategic orientations. A higher proportion of discontented than contented agree on the necessity for increased group power. Significantly more of the former than the latter would decrease the power of the school board and administrative bureaucracy. Finally, the assessments leaders make of educational conditions are linked to tactical orientations.

The harshest critics of the school environments are also the most combative. Two out of every five rank on our scale as Fighters, only one out of four ranks as a Cooperator. The distribution is just about reversed for the relatively satisfied leaders. When it comes to the willingness to act aggressively, differences are even more pronounced. Among those

---

[21] The salient educational conditions which respondents were asked to assess included salary levels, working conditions, curriculum, building facilities, administration by central headquarters, and supervision in the individual schools. An index of dissatisfaction, based on these six elements, was constructed and leaders were categorized as those scoring high, the Dissatisfied (N = 105), and those scoring low, the Satisfied (N = 80).

[22] Admittedly, the relationships might be causally reversed. Rather than dissatisfaction contributing to militant attitudes, militancy may produce dissatisfaction with educational conditions.

TABLE 19

THE STRENGTH OF RELATIONSHIPS BETWEEN DISSATISFACTION AND
LEADERSHIP ORIENTATIONS

(a) Goal Orientations	ϕ
Decisive participation (on index)	.32*
Decisive salary participation	.33*
Decisive personnel participation	.28*
Decisive curriculum participation	.26*
Decisive school system organization participation	.30*
(b) Strategic Orientations†	ϕ
Increase in own organization's power	.14*
Decrease in school board's power	.28*
Decrease in superintendent's power	.14
Decrease in administrative bureaucracy's power	.24*
(c) Tactical Orientations	ϕ
High combativeness	.24*
Willingness to take forceful action	.30*

* $p < .05$.
† Educational policy generally.

who have little complaint about salaries, working conditions, supervision, and so forth, only three in ten would engage in forceful activity. But twice that proportion of their critical colleagues expresses a willingness to strike or impose sanctions if the occasion arose.

Personal and Situational Factors and Their Effects

Analysis of aggregate data brought out the importance of sex and school division as correlates of membership in teacher organizations in New York and Boston. Less conclusively, it implied the relevance of age or length of teaching experience. We found that male, junior, and secondary school teachers were more inclined to join a union than female, senior, and elementary school teachers. In view of the comparative militancy of unions, we would imagine that personal and situational factors, such as those examined in Chapter II, would relate to the orientations of teacher leaders in five large cities.

Four hypotheses will be tested here. First, male leaders are more likely than females to have militant orientations, primarily because men generally tend to be more aggressive than women. Social expectations encourage males to be more dominant and power-oriented and females to be more receptive and submissive. Second, leaders who work in secondary schools will rank higher on the three dimensions of militancy, since they are more independent and less restricted by tight administrative controls than are their elementary school colleagues. Their frames of reference, moreover, have been shaped in an atmosphere congenial to militancy. Third, younger leaders, and fourth, those with less teaching experience also demand equal participation, prescribe power changes, and exhibit combative attitudes more than do their older and senior colleagues. Those who are younger and junior have not only had less time to accommodate to status-quo relationships in the school system, but are also most likely to have been exposed to and influenced by the new currents of militancy sweeping the nation.[23]

Correlation coefficients, reported in Table 20, generally support these

TABLE 20
THE STRENGTH OF RELATIONSHIPS BETWEEN PERSONAL AND SITUATIONAL FACTORS AND LEADERSHIP ORIENTATIONS

(a) Goal Orientations	Male ϕ	Younger ϕ	Junior ϕ	Secondary ϕ
Decisive participation (on index)	.26*	.17*	.22*	.24*
Decisive salary participation	.24*	.10	.14*	.33*
Decisive personnel participation	.20*	.22*	.20*	.20*
Decisive curriculum participation	.26*	.10	.14*	.20*
Decisive school system organization participation	.14*	.10	.10	.22*

(b) Strategic Orientations†	Male ϕ	Younger ϕ	Junior ϕ	Secondary ϕ
Increase in own organization's power	.10	.00	.00	.17*
Decrease in school board's power	−.10	.00	.22	.24
Decrease in superintendent's power	.17	.10	.10	.10
Decrease in administrative bureaucracy's power	.30*	.14	.14	.37*

(c) Tactical Orientations	Male ϕ	Younger ϕ	Junior ϕ	Secondary ϕ
High combativeness	.14*	.14*	.10	.24*
Willingness to take forceful action	.30*	.00	.14	.24*

* $p < .05$.
† Educational policy generally.

propositions. The relationships between sex, age, experience, and school division, on the one hand, and participation, on the other, are in the predicted directions for each policy domain. But only in the cases of

[23] Cole's findings on rank-and-file militancy are relevant here. In his New York City sample, 70 per cent of men and 42 per cent of women and 56 per cent of younger (below forty years) and 44 per cent of older (above forty years) teachers were militant. *Op. cit.*, 77–81. Charles Winick also found younger teachers to be more militant than older ones. "When Teachers Strike," *Teachers College Record*, 64 (April, 1963), 602.

sex and division are associations moderately strong and in every instance statistically significant. It should be noted, however, that neither sex nor division discriminates as sharply in terms of goals selected as do organizational affiliation and dissatisfaction. Concerning strategic orientations, the results are mixed, since large percentages of all teachers want their groups to have more power while relatively few seek to reduce the power of other participants. Differences between younger and older, junior and senior activists are slight in every respect. Only on the question of decreasing the authority of administrative bureaucracies are differences moderately strong, at least between men and women and elementary and secondary teachers.

On matters of tactics, once again age and teaching experience appear to have a negligible role while sex and division continue to count.[24] Men definitely are more prone to action than women. They are also rather more inclined to express combative dispositions. Junior and high school teachers, more than those in elementary schools, likewise tend to have these aggressive attitudes.

In summary, therefore, it seems that we can discard both age and teaching experience as personal factors exercising major effects on leadership orientations. They may be associated with membership in teacher groups or rank-and-file militancy, but they exert little impact on people who have achieved leadership positions. Sex and school placement, by contrast, consistently are associated with goals and tactics and at least a single aspect of power. One may argue, however, that we are assessing the same thing, since men predominate in secondary schools and women in elementary ones. Yet the relationships are not spurious. Within the ranks of both secondary and elementary teachers, male leaders tend more than their female counterparts to express decisive role orientations, combativeness, and the willingness to engage in dramatic action. And within both male and female groups, those who work in junior and senior high schools tend more than elementary teachers to express the same militant goal and tactical views.

The Determinants of Militancy

The most obvious conclusion thus far is that the orientations of Union and Association leaders differ significantly. Along each of the several dimensions of militancy, organizational differences are considerably greater than ones relating to contentment or personal and situational fac-

24 This accords with our analysis of rank-and-file behavior in the New York City teachers strike of 1962. For instance, in only 6 per cent of elementary schools but 45 per cent of junior highs and 40 per cent of academic highs did a large number of teachers go on strike.

tors. If uncertainty remains, it can be dispelled by glancing briefly at two groups of urban leaders. The first consists of those who meet several of the attitudinal criteria of militancy. They rank high on the participation index and the combativeness scale and are willing to strike or impose sanctions. The other is composed of those who meet none of these criteria. They are consultive, non-combative, and unwilling to act forcefully. Among all of the leaders affiliated with the American Federation of Teachers, about 30 per cent are in the first category. Among the non-union leaders, fewer than 4 per cent are all-out militants.[25]

Another question arises, however. Perhaps the connections between group affiliation and orientations are due to some of the other variables we have explored. Union leaders are more likely to be men, from secondary schools, and dissatisfied with educational conditions. Association leaders tend to fall into other groupings. It may be, therefore, that affiliation is linked to militancy only because members of one group differ from members of the other with respect to sex, school division, and contentment. To see whether this is so, we have controlled separately for each of these factors while examining the linkages between affiliation and the dimensions of participation and tactics.[26] The imposition of controls does not diminish the associations by a substantial degree, as the phi coefficients in Table 21 signify.

TABLE 21

ORGANIZATIONAL AFFILIATION AND LEADERSHIP MILITANCY, WITH OTHER FACTORS CONTROLLED

	Strength of Associations (ϕ)		
Union Membership	Decisive Participation	Combativeness	Willingness to Act Forcefully
Without Controls	.42*	.51*	.47*
Controlling Separately for			
Dissatisfaction	.37*	.51*	.41*
School division	.38*	.45*	.44*
Sex	.40*	.51*	.32*

* $p < .05$.

[25] Just over one-third of the leadership sample fell into these extreme categories when the two orientations were combined. All 32 who rank high on the combined dimension belong to AFT and nearly all 32 who rank low belong to NEA or independent groups.

[26] It would have been preferable to control simultaneously for all three, but the small number of cases precluded this. Eliminated from present analysis is the strategic dimension, because too few respondents advocated an alteration in the powers of the establishment and nearly all desired more power for their own groups.

Generally speaking, in each of six distinct subgroups—the dissatisfied and satisfied, secondary and elementary, and men and women—union members are far more likely than others to demand decisive roles, have combative attitudes, and be disposed toward action. Only on the matter of action do we find that the male leadership of teacher unions is at least partially responsible for the great impact attributed to group affiliation. But even here men and women differ considerably, depending upon their memberships.

If affiliation exerts such influence, do these other elements matter as well? To answer the question of whether dissatisfaction, school division, sex, and length of teaching experience make independent contributions to militant views, elaboration of our analysis controls for group affiliation. The findings in Table 22 make several things clear. First, although asso-

TABLE 22

EDUCATIONAL CONDITIONS, PERSONAL AND SITUATIONAL FACTORS, AND LEADERSHIP MILITANCY, WITH GROUP AFFILIATION CONTROLLED

Conditions, Personal and Situational Factors	Strength of Association (ϕ)		
	Decisive Participation	Combative-ness	Willingness to Act Forcefully
Dissatisfaction			
Without controls	.32*	.24*	.30*
Union	.35*	.29*	.15
Association	.04	.15	.24*
School Division			
Without controls	.24*	.24*	.24*
Union	.22*	.27*	.08
Association	.07	.08	.19
Sex			
Without controls	.26*	.14*	.30*
Union	.22*	.18	.27*
Association	.28*	.24	.24*
Teaching Experience			
Without controls	.17*	.10	.14
Union	.24*	.08	.19*
Association	.36*	.23	.06

* $p < .05$.

ciations continue after controls are applied, organization still serves as the best predictor of leadership attitudes. Second, various characteristics relate to orientations in different ways. Some are linked to attitudes of both Union and Association members, others much more to members of one group than those of another. A number strongly relate to participation, but fewer affect dispositions toward action and combativeness.

Take dissatisfaction, for instance. Within the ranks of Association members there is about as much likelihood that satisfied as well as dissatisfied leaders will desire a participatory role in educational policy-making. For union members, however, the dissatisfied overwhelmingly choose equal participation while the relatively contented divide almost equally between decisive and consultive roles. When the question concerns action, the situation changes somewhat. The degree of satisfaction with school conditions seems to have a greater effect on teachers affiliated with NEA or independent groups than on those belonging to AFT.

Whether a person's classroom is in an elementary or secondary school further helps us to distinguish union members in two respects. Secondary teachers are much more likely than their elementary colleagues to rank high on the index of participation and combativeness scale. They are only a bit more inclined to strike. School division seems to make less difference with regard to the attitudes of non-union teachers. Whatever the level, these people are not apt to have ambitious goals or aggressive attitudes. But Association teachers are somewhat more inclined to impose sanctions if they are in secondary rather than elementary schools.

No matter what their organizational affiliation, men are far more inclined than women to possess militant orientations. This holds across the board, thus signifying that it is not only the preponderance of males in unions which accounts for the relationship. True, males are more inclined to join and lead unions and this partially explains the greater militancy of their groups. Nevertheless, men and women do differ significantly in their attitudes, even after they are exposed to the doctrines of common organizations.

In several respects the time an individual has devoted to a career in teaching matters relatively little. But with regard to participatory objectives, it is quite important. Junior teachers are far more inclined than their senior colleagues to demand an equal voice in educational policies. This is especially true of Association leaders. It seems that the longer a leader of any type of group spends in the classroom, the less important alterations in the rules of the game and the more important piecemeal ameliorative improvement become to him. Younger leaders, however, have begun to respond to the pervasive strains of participatory democracy.

After examining the views of 185 teacher leaders, representing nine organizations in five major cities, we must conclude that group affiliation is the most important determinant of militant orientations. In some respects, Union and Association members generally agree. Both types of activists feel that salaries and curriculum are more legitimate areas of teacher participation than personnel and school system organization. Both at least pay lip service to the need for achieving greater group power. Otherwise, their views are widely divergent.

Association activists are not terribly dissatisfied with the ground rules determining educational policy-making. Few aspire to equal participation and even fewer believe that they should have much to say about the administrator-dominated areas of personnel and school system organization. Not many would curb the power of the educational establishment, and of these people the overwhelming majority single out the lay board of education as the target for attack. By contrast, Union activists are in a state of rebellion. They would like to participate equally with school boards and administrations, not only in certain types of matters but in all kinds. For them, hostility toward administrators is well ingrained and their main adversaries are not laymen but rather professional administrators in local schools and at central headquarters.

In light of the increasing similarity of the doctrinal positions of the National Education Association and the American Federation of Teachers, our conclusions about urban leaders may occasion some surprise. The views of local unionists are understandable. In general, they are consistent with the doctrines of participation and combat that have been enunciated for a good many years by AFT's national spokesmen. On the other hand, it seems that NEA's ideology, which has shifted markedly of late, has not yet had weighty impact on urban leaderships. There is reason to suspect that it too is catching hold, since junior teachers who head local associations are much more participatively inclined and combative than their senior colleagues. In time, much of this ideological gap may be narrowed as a result of the succession of younger people to local association leadership.

Still, a major doctrinal difference continues to separate the two national teacher organizations. NEA continues to emphasize the unity of the educational fraternity, while AFT persists in stressing the inherent conflict between teachers and administrators. It would seem that until the Association starts talking battle, instead of abstractly calling for participation, its local leaderships will be satisfied with less power than their Federation rivals. In the cities, the young are not much more predisposed to battle than the old. Opposition may prove to be the spur. Even without doctrinal direction from Washington headquarters or state capitals, local associations may be forced into combat by competitor unions or maladroit school administrations. And, once having engaged in struggle, their attitudes may undergo militant change.

But all of this omits one vital ingredient from analysis. In looking at leadership orientations, we have not taken into account the nature of specific organizations in certain cities. The views of leaders are affected strongly by group affiliation and to a lesser extent by other characteristics. They are also shaped in part by the environments in which local teacher organizations conduct their affairs. The representatives under scrutiny

here come from New York, Boston, Chicago, San Francisco, and Atlanta, and not other cities, suburbs, or towns. Their orientations, and,
even more important, the activities of their organizations, develop in particular contexts as a result of opportunities presented by the behavior
of educational chieftains and the changing rules of the educational game.
We shall now look more closely at several teacher organizations in three
cities.

IV. Patterns of Behavior

To some extent, as we have just seen, personal characteristics and satisfaction with local educational conditions play a part in determining the militancy of motivations. To a much greater degree, the militancy of teacher leaders hinges on group affiliation. Those belonging to AFT locals are likelier than others to aspire to decisive participatory roles, seek more power for themselves and less for school authorities, and express combative feelings and a willingness to act forcefully. On the basis of previous analysis, we would naturally expect leaders in each of the four union groups to be more militant in attitude than leaders in each of the five associations. The data presented in Table 23, which report the attitudes of the leaderships of the nine organizations in the five cities, support this expectation.

If one characterizes group militancy according to leadership orientations, then a number of points can readily be made. First, in the three cities where a union and one or two non-union groups coexist, the former is more militant than the latter on each of the dimensions examined. Second, the United Federation of Teachers (UFT) and the San Francisco Federation of Teachers (SFFT) appear to be the most militant organizations. Their leaders are practically unanimous in advocating decisive participation and increased organizational power. Nine-tenths of them have relatively combative attitudes and eight-tenths are willing to strike, if need be. Third, the Chicago Education Association (CEA) and the Atlanta Teachers Association (ATA) seem to be the least militant. Their leaders would settle for a consultive role in educational policy-making; they are less interested in acquiring power; and they have little disposition for combat. Only one in twenty who head ATA would take forceful action. Yet almost half of those in CEA express the willingness to strike.

Between the militant-passive extremes stand the other five groups, which vary depending upon the type of orientation considered. More than half the officials of the Boston Teachers Union (BTU) want a good deal to say about school policy, but fewer are prepared to strike in order to get what they want. On the other hand, striking does not go against

71

TABLE 23

THE MILITANCY OF TEACHER LEADERS, BY ORGANIZATION, IN FIVE CITIES

City	Organization	Affiliation	Percentages of Leaders with Militant Orientations			
			Goals	Strategy	Tactics	
			Decisive Participation*	More Power for Own Organization†	Fighter or Persuader Dispositions	Willingness to Take Forceful Action
New York	UFT	Union	85	97	92	81
Boston	BTU	Union	54	82	74	39
	BTA	Non-Union	25	88	63	25
Chicago	CTU	Union	39	65	88	72
	CEA	Non-Union	05	50	21	42
San Francisco	SFFT	Union	92	100	96	79
	SFCTA	Non-Union	45	55	46	14
	TASF	Non-Union	43	86	57	29
Atlanta	ATA	Non-Union	25	45	35	05

* Ranking "high" on index of participation.
† Educational policy in general.

the grain of the combative teachers who direct the Chicago Teachers Union (CTU). But few of them have the idea of achieving a significant role in the policy-making processes of the school system. All in all, it would appear that the San Francisco Classroom Teachers Association (SFCTA) ranks as the most militant NEA affiliate. Nearly half its leaders have decisive goals in mind. But only a handful would man the barricades to gain them. By contrast, among the leaders of the Chicago educational association, who generally have little quarrel with the current rules of the school game, a far larger number are willing to act forcefully.

Apparently, there is much more to group militancy than meets the eye of simple statistical observation. The relationship between group affiliation and militant orientations tells us something, but a great deal remains for explanation. Why are some union groups more militant than others? Similarly, why are some professional associations more militant than others?

In trying to deal with these questions, we shall have to attend to still another. This one concerns the ways in which the motivations of leaders and the actual behavior of teacher organizations are linked. Leadership orientations, we would contend, play an important part in determining the activities of teacher groups. At the same time, these orientations are in good measure the products of previous group experiences. Thus, militant views and militant behavior are reinforcing, as are acquiescent views and passive behavior. Prior activities help to shape the attitudes of present leaders. And the attitudes of present leaders are significant influences on an organization's current and future activities.

It is worthwhile, then, to devote some attention to several patterns of teacher group politics. What has happened recently in all five cities is of interest, but our focus will be on contemporary campaigns by teacher groups to change the educational rules of the game in New York, Boston, and San Francisco. In New York UFT executive board members, who responded to the leadership survey, had the experience of four years of exclusive representation, a number of strikes and strike threats, and the conclusion of several collective bargaining contracts with the board of education. Boston leaders of BTU and BTA, at the time they expressed their attitudes, were engaged in a struggle to represent teachers in negotiations with the School Committee. In San Francisco leaders responded to our survey at a time when both SFFT and SFCTA, the two major groups, were vying for power, with neither anticipating imminent victory.

CONFLICT IN NEW YORK CITY

At the risk of oversimplifying the matter, it is fair to say that competition is the hallmark of political life in New York City. To begin with, the city is one of the most culturally heterogeneous in the nation. No ethnic group, no religious group, no interest group dominates. Memberships in the multiplicity of groups and associations overlap and coalitions or alliances form, shifting from one issue to another. Common attachments and common interests are lacking. Consensus, if this word can even be used with reference to New York City, is unstable and short-lived.

"Disorganized pluralism," as one observer noted, is the term which can best be applied to New York City politics.[1] Interests constantly clash, with race pitted against race, tenants disputing landlords, unions battling City Hall, bureaucracies fighting politicians, and Democrats and Republicans in almost perpetual faction. Competition is rigorous and incessant in the numerous, separate centers of power which comprise politics and government in the city.[2] Pitched battle is the dominant phenomenon. This is not to say there are no broad grounds for agreement, possibilities for accommodation, or ways of working out arrangements to settle conflict. These features certainly exist and often come into play. But they appear subservient to the elements of competition, maneuver, and battle which give political life in New York a distinctive flavor.

Since competition and conflict are such integral features of local politics, it might be expected that school politics would include the same components. In the educational domain, as in other aspects of political life, established rules are far from sacrosanct. They are lightly rooted, and while they may lend some order and method to the continuing contest, they are also instruments wielded by contestants and wherever possible shaped to their preferences.[3] Thus, battles between the school board and superintendent, on the one hand, and the teachers union, on the other, to determine and redetermine the rules of the game and shares of influence are in accord with traditional practices of city politics. On the part of UFT, the drive for power by means of action—verbal accusations, public demonstrations, and strikes—is very much in the mainstream.

Into the "dog-eat-dog" atmosphere of New York City the United Federation of Teachers was born. It was conceived amid strife and as a result of a marriage between militant forces in the High School Teachers Association and the Teachers Guild.[4] Although the two groups had

---

[1] Bert E. Swanson, *The Struggle for Equality* (New York: Hobbs, Dorman, 1966), 57.

[2] Wallace S. Sayre and Herbert Kaufman, *Governing New York City* (New York: Russell Sage, 1960), esp. 709–16.

[3] *Ibid.*, 108.

[4] A union affiliated with AFT had existed in New York City since 1916. This local—the Teachers Union—was expelled from AFT because of intra-union fac-

sought ways to join together, they had reached an impasse because one was pledged to the restoration of a two-salary schedule, while the other favored retention of a single schedule for elementary and secondary teachers. Then a critical event occurred. Teachers in the evening high schools and the board of education came into conflict over salaries. This battle, which featured a work stoppage, led to the formation of UFT in 1960.[5] The drive for collective bargaining and power began in earnest.

"We need participation, not consultation; negotiation, not hearings," became the watchwords of the Federation in its campaign. Achieving these objectives was not an easy matter. In light of the steadfast opposition of school board and administration, the rivalries among teachers organized in innumerable ways, and the novelty of collective bargaining arrangements for public schools, the union had a tremendous fight on its hands.

Under threat of a work stoppage, scheduled for May, 1960, school authorities, who opposed collective bargaining, promised that an election would be held during the school year if 30 per cent of the staff petitioned for it. Within a month, petitions signed by over 30 per cent of the staff were submitted to the superintendent. Yet, nothing happened, as the board equivocated. In late October UFT's executive board, delegate assembly, and membership successively voted overwhelmingly in favor of a strike. Despite some last-minute concessions by the board, the real issue—who was going to speak for the teachers and with what kind of authority—could not be settled. Furthermore, the union was fabricating an image for the future, which would be useful in attracting members and keeping the organization moving. "The UFT," its newspaper declared, "is counting on its reputation as a hard-hitting, militant organization, which is not afraid to act."[6] And act it did, when it launched its first one-day strike on November 7, 1960.

The strike, which took place on the day before municipal elections, evidently worked. Mayor Robert Wagner felt the pressure and appointed a panel of labor leaders to help settle various issues in dispute. The board moved too. It appointed a five-member Advisory Commission of Inquiry to work out arrangements for an election. UFT was well satisfied with the Commission's membership and, save for a few points, with the Commission's recommendations. But the board, apparently stalling to allow other teacher groups time to mobilize, set aside the Commission's

---

tionalism and communism, and the Teachers Guild was chartered as Local 2 in 1942.

[5] For a more detailed account, see R. Joseph Monsen, Jr. and Mark W. Cannon, *The Makers of Public Policy* (New York: McGraw-Hill, 1965), 171-75.

[6] *United Teacher*, September, 1960.

definition of collective bargaining and substituted its own version. It stipulated that any agreements ". . . are terminable at will by the Board of Education" and that strikes would not be permitted.

The Federation could hardly relax. It maintained pressure on the school administration. Accusing the board of intentional delay, it threatened another strike, picketed Livingston Street headquarters of the school department, condemned the board for ignoring suggestions of the Commission, charged members with dereliction of duty in the construction and repair of school buildings, and demanded their resignations or removal by state authorities. Finally, the first step was taken. In a July referendum held by the board, an amazingly large number of teachers turned out to vote three to one in favor of collective bargaining.

A few months later an entirely new board of education took office, the previous one having been dissolved by a special act of the New York Legislature. Under the presidency of Max Rubin, the position of the new board differed from that of its predecessor. At its second meeting, the board called upon the City Labor Department to hold an election for bargaining agent as soon as possible.

There was less competition than anticipated. Entering the battle at a late date, NEA was in no position to seriously challenge the union in the forthcoming election. The Association sponsored a local alliance— the Teachers Bargaining Organization—composed of a number of groups. In order to salvage something, UFT's opponents insisted on representation by divisional levels rather than systemwide. UFT, recognizing the grab for an elementary division victory, demanded election of a single agent for the entire staff. Again the union prevailed, as the City Labor Department ruled in favor of one unit for all teachers.[7] The election was held in December, 1961, and UFT polled over 60 per cent of the vote. For all intents and purposes, the issue of which group among teacher organizations would have the potential for achieving power was unambiguously decided. The union had stood almost alone, fighting relentlessly against board, administration, and other teacher groups. Now, its popularity was on the rise. If anyone spoke for the teachers, it did. All challenges had been effectively eliminated.[8]

Having won the right to speak for 40,000 teachers, UFT's initial task was to prove itself a resolute bargainer. Its principal objective in nego-

[7] For the importance of unit determination in New York City, see Myron Lieberman and Michael H. Moskow, *Collective Negotiations for Teachers* (Chicago: Rand McNally, 1966), 141–45.

[8] Some months later, NEA set up the City Teachers Association. CTA was composed of eight groups, virtually the same ones which made up the Teachers Bargaining Organization. Born in defeat, the new group had slight chance of success.

tiating a contract in 1962 was to win substantial salary increases. High money demands, however, brought other parties into the dispute, since the school system was "financially dependent," relying on city and state for operating funds. Despite the formality of collective bargaining, there was little the board of education could do. The board's position was that until it knew how much money would be made available by city and state, it could not make a firm commitment for salary increases. UFT felt that bargaining under these conditions was absurd. It was the feeling of negotiators on both sides that they had been dealing in soap coupons rather than in dollars.

Once again, the union decided to fight. It first threatened to discourage teacher recruitment by the city unless its demands were met. Then it staged a series of demonstrations. Finally, its membership voted overwhelmingly to hold another strike. The rationale for dramatic action was simple. As David Selden wrote: "What makes the UFT different from other groups is that when we're dissatisfied, we do something about it."[9] First, there were substantive reasons for walking out. As one official of the organization put it: "Public agencies move only in response to crisis, and so we had to create one."[10] Second, there were organizational reasons. A strike was needed to assuage the feelings of indignation of rank-and-file teachers, many of whom were becoming increasingly discontented with their status and the conditions under which they worked. Members could be won by this means. In short, as UFT saw things, it had little to lose and everything to gain.

Despite last-minute efforts by Mayor Wagner and Governor Rockefeller, the strike took place. It was directed against city and state officials more than against school authorities. Spectacularly successful, the one-day walkout achieved its purposes. The mayor and governor managed to scrape together necessary funds, solving the salary dispute. But other issues remained, and, in resolving them, the union had to come to terms with the school board and administration. To preclude the possibility of a future strike while school was in session, the board insisted that a no-strike pledge be written into the contract. Although UFT proposed several alternatives, it finally agreed to a one-year pledge in order to nail down benefits which had already been agreed upon. In return, the

---

[9] *United Teacher*, April, 1961. One observer, at the time staff director of the Public Education Association, noted that the union was running a risk. "When they struck," he wrote, "I don't think they were sure that they had public support, but they felt strongly enough to do it, public or no public." *Ibid.*, April-May, 1962. In fact, they had almost no support. School administrators, the newspaper press, and civic groups all opposed the strike. Even labor was unenthusiastic.

[10] John O'Neill, quoted in Joel Kaplan, "Can a Teachers Union Be 'Professional'?" *Changing Education*, I (Summer, 1966), 41.

exclusive bargaining-agent status of the union was recognized and a strengthened grievance procedure was adopted.

The one-year contract was signed in October, 1962. In it the board emphasized that it still retained control of the school system. Indeed, it did. But UFT had pounded hard on the door of the educational establishment. One foot was already wedged inside. "We have delved into ever so many matters of so-called professional implication—guidance counselors, teacher programs, class size, and much more . . ." was the way President Charles Cogen summarized his group's achievement. Another leader, George Altomare, described gains similarly:

> Our role in policy-making is greatly enhanced . . . . We have set down, in writing, the fact that we are to be consulted on all changes; the days when we hear about changes only after they are made are gone.[11]

The following year battle once again was waged, as the board and union could not reach agreement on salaries. For UFT, direct action, which had proved itself in the past, was the only answer. However, the union was pledged by contract to forego striking until the end of the school year. If a strike could not be held while school was in session, then it could be mounted after the expiration date of the present contract. If a new one was not negotiated by the resumption of classes in September, there would be a work stoppage. A "no contract–no work" policy was voted by the membership and once again the board, city, and state were put on notice that the Federation was all too ready to wage battle.

With another strike pending, the usual efforts to achieve an eleventh-hour settlement took place. This time the mayor offered to appoint a panel of mediators and the board, despite its reluctance to allow outsiders to determine how school funds should be spent, was forced to accept. In short order, financial matters were settled, with the union winning a token amount for first-year salary increases and a more substantial amount for the second year of the contract.

Salary had been the focal objective for UFT. After all, pay was of major concern to the city's teachers, and it is doubtful that a strike could have been launched were salary not the central issue. But UFT had other objectives as well. These were of major concern to organization activists and of utmost relevance to organization power. The problem was that UFT defined its role broadly, as its proposals sprinkled liberally with the phrase "with the advice and consent of the union" made clear. For union leaders, the principal issue in contest was: "Will the Board agree

[11] *United Teacher*, October, 1962.

to give teachers a real stake in the school system by letting them share in the decisions which so vitally affect everything we do?"[12] Superintendent Gross agreed as to the nature of the issue. In a television address he accused UFT of trying to gain greater control of the school system.[13]

The outcome of negotiations constituted a major victory for the union. Aside from salaries and related benefits, it won a number of professional gains. Most significant from an organizational viewpoint, the mediation panel, by a "miracle of persuasion,"[14] broke down the board's resistance to recognizing union rights in the determination of public school policy. The preamble to the proposed agreement represented a dramatic stride forward in UFT's quest for policy-making power. It specified that ". . . the superintendent of schools or his representatives will meet and consult once a month during the school year with representatives of the United Federation of Teachers on matters of educational policy and development." The contract also satisfied another union demand of great import. It recognized the legitimacy of union chapters at the school level and provided that they could consult with school principals on contractual matters and on school policies.

By the time the contract for 1965–66 was due to be negotiated, UFT had become increasingly involved in educational policy-making at both system and school levels. Particularly in light of the provisions of 1963, collective bargaining did not have to serve as the only device for participation or the single catalyst for conflict. Still, the perennial contract remained an important means for winning benefits, improving working conditions, and strengthening the union's over-all position. And it continued to provoke conflict.

The tone was set by Albert Shanker, the union's new president, even before negotiations had begun. "We can't help wondering," he told the board of education at its annual hearing on the budget, "whether the only way to bring about progress in the school system is to have a teachers' strike pending."[15] Negotiations started in the fall. The approach was somewhat novel in that bargaining began before the board's budget was formulated. But otherwise things proceeded in customary fashion. UFT asked for more than the board thought the city could afford. The superintendent offered far less than the union had its sights on, and his offer was flatly rejected. At the end of 1964, about 1,000 teachers picketed school headquarters. During the ensuing months, teachers demon-

---

[12] *United Action*, June, 1963.
[13] *New York Times*, July 7, 1963.
[14] This phrase was used by a school board negotiator to describe the panel's impact on his side. *New York Post*, September 9, 1963.
[15] *United Teacher*, May 7, 1964.

strated at City Hall and leaders threatened another strike. No contract meant no work at the beginning of the next school year.

In accord with established precedent, a panel of mediators was appointed by the mayor. By this time, there could be little doubt, whatever the statements of various contestants, that a strike would be averted once again. The major obstacle was money, but, as Shanker pointed out: "It is very easy to resolve money issues. Somebody just has to come up with the money and that takes less than a minute."[16] It may have taken somewhat longer, but in sufficient time to head off the strike, the mayor and board agreed to the mediators' proposal. The outcome, of course, forced the board to divert funds it had set aside for educational improvements to teacher benefits. In a public statement, marked by accuracy if not grace, the board of education described what had happened:

> The crisis this year followed the same pattern as before—the spinning out of negotiations, the preparations for a strike, the appointment of mediators, and the last-minute framing of recommendations designed first and foremost to avoid a shutdown of the schools.[17]

As in the past, the authority of school board and administration had been eroded as a result of intensive pressure. And, as before, a militant union had won benefits for the city's teachers and accomplished much by way of revising the rules of the educational game.

Two years later, a similar crisis occurred as part of negotiations in a collective bargaining contract. This time, however, conflict was intensified. UFT's demands were greater than ever before, the board of education was more resistant than previously, and, to complicate matters further, community groups of Negro parents and the city-wide United Parents Association took a strong stand against union aims and tactics. Events in 1967 culminated in a bitter walkout which lasted two and one-half weeks and saw almost 80 per cent of the teachers and three-quarters of their students absent themselves from classrooms in New York City schools. One outcome of the conflict was the usual salary gain by the union, but something less than Federation leaders desired in terms of control over the educational program. Another was the imposition of penalties, including a fine of $150,000, a jail sentence given UFT's president, and the denial of check-off privileges to the union, as a result of the enforcement of a new state law regulating the conduct of public employees. A final, and perhaps most important, outcome of events was a heightening of tensions between the UFT on the one hand and board, administration, and community groups on the other.

[16] *New York Times*, September 9, 1965.
[17] *Ibid.*, September 11, 1965.

Differences over educational issues and teacher power constituted the major stumbling blocks in negotiations between the board and union. Salary, of course, was important. But negotiators on both sides were confident that money questions could be resolved, as they had been in the past. At a comparatively early stage, the school board admitted that it did not have the financial power to make an adequate salary offer to the union, and simultaneously called on the city administration to intervene so that a "fair settlement" with teachers might be reached. Mayor John Lindsay, acknowledging his responsibility for the financial plight of the board, appointed several mediators. In line with their recommendations, he finally agreed to make extra funds available to the schools. Yet a strike took place. Rather quickly, the mayor made another offer—enough to satisfy UFT leaders and members and make it evident that their tactics had again paid off. Nevertheless, the strike continued, mainly because the union insisted on greater control of matters in addition to salary.

From the outset, UFT declared its dominant concern to be improved education, not merely higher salaries. Along these lines, one of its principal objectives was to expand the city's More Effective Schools (MES) program, which it had helped institute three years before. Another was to include in the contract a new provision giving teachers the right to remove disruptive pupils from their classrooms. Still another aim—intended to benefit both teachers and pupils—involved smaller classes and increased free time for teachers to prepare their lessons.

The board's educational remedies were quite different than the union's. It resisted the expansion of MES, claiming that the program's results did not justify its huge costs. It claimed that the problem of "disruptive" children was not an appropriate matter for collective bargaining. The board went even further, mainly in order to establish a strong negotiating position. It sought to modify some provisions in the former contract, thereby taking away benefits that already had been granted employees. It called for the elimination of extra preparation periods given teachers in special service schools, because they had not been used for professional purposes. Instead these periods of relief from the classroom had interfered with the "continuity of instruction," and, by decreasing the amount of time teachers actually taught, had forced the system to hire inexperienced and substitute teachers for these schools. Another change sought by the board involved sick leave, on the grounds that present policies had led to excessive teacher absences.

Given these almost irreconcilable bargaining demands, the fact that a panel of mediators could satisfy neither side is hardly surprising. UFT was resolute in its quest for enhanced power by means of the collective bargaining contract. The board of education and school administration were just as determined to resist union demands which were designed to erode by contractual arrangements the establishment's authority to decide policies and run the schools. Eventually, conflicting demands were reconciled, but not until the most intense, prolonged, and widespread conflict had taken place. Once again, the United Federation of Teachers, although achieving no dramatic breakthroughs, had gained ground in its struggle to share power.

What had occurred in a period of a few years, from the time of UFT's organization until the escalated conflict of 1967, suggests a number of points about teacher politics in New York City. First, UFT had to impress officials outside of the educational system in order to raise teacher salaries and expand teacher benefits. This it did, with considerable success. Second, where finances were less involved and policy-making or administrative prerogatives counted more, UFT had to deal with the board and superintendent to achieve its objectives. Here, too, the union made headway, although every inch of ground was hard-fought. Third, the means to achieve each type of end was action. The strike tactic proved successful, particularly in prying additional funds loose from the city, but also in forcing educational authorities to shift priorities and cede, however grudgingly, important elements of control. For the union, conflict proved to be an advantageous pattern of school politics. As its president, Albert Shanker, commented: "Perhaps it is a bad lesson to have learned, but the city has convinced us that striking brings us gains we need and cannot get any other way."[18] On matters of both money and power the union had accepted less than it felt desirable, exhibiting a realistic willingness to reach agreement after going as far as it thought feasible under varying conditions. Compromise it did, but only when it had demonstrated its readiness to fight Livingston Street and City Hall and only when the establishment had made considerable concessions.

ACCOMMODATION IN BOSTON

One thing stands out in Boston, especially as it affects school politics. A consensus pervades the city's life. Not all groups are included, not all share the same attachments or have complementary interests. Negroes ghettoed in Roxbury and the Yankees in Back Bay dissent strongly from majority mores. Agreement is not absolute, but it is certainly striking. As far as political life goes, the Boston culture is relatively homogeneous. Irishness prodominates. With the more successful, college-educated Irish moving to the suburbs, political styles in the city have been heavily in-

[18] Quoted in A. H. Raskin, "He Leads His Teachers Up the Down Staircase," *New York Times Magazine*, September 3, 1967.

fluenced by the attitudes of the less successful ethnics, older people, and what one journalist has called the "calcified white proletariat."[19] These people have determined local habits and customs and set the tone of personalism, parochialism, and conservatism which dominates the city's politics.

No single clique or coalition rules. As in New York City, pluralism characterizes decision-making in Boston. Business is decentralized and so is politics. At one time the city was run by a political machine in the traditional sense. This is no longer true. No politician or possible combination of politicians today has enough prestige or sufficient organization to control. Instead, alliances shift among numerous political tribes. Feudal political leaders abound and political processes "revolve around personal obligations and strong political loyalties."[20] As one congressman who represents a city district described the style of politics:

> There isn't any political boss in a city like Boston. In Chicago, you call Daley and something will happen. Here you have to carefully consult the right people in each ward and section. There are established customs and territories. These cannot be breached. Also, you have to approach these people in the proper way. . . . You start by asking how their wives and kids are and this isn't just to butter them up. . . . You could say politics in this city are built on these personal relations or they are built on sand.[21]

Most recently, changes in political and ethnic style have begun to alter much of the city's public life. The traditions left behind by the Curleys and the Honey Fitzes are no longer sacrosanct. Mayor John Collins did not follow old ways, but started to shake things up. Urban redevelopment, pushed ahead by Edward Logue, also caused breaches with past customs.

Yet deep-rooted attachments to the ways in which politics are played and governments are run do not fade rapidly or without leaving a trace. Whatever the changes which are slowly developing, it seems that the schools have been left virtually untouched. According to a most perceptive investigator of the educational scene, the old order remains intact in the domain of Boston school politics. Peter Schrag, in *Village School Downtown,* convincingly presents the case that ". . . the School Com-

---

19 Nicholas von Hoffman, "Boston is an Ingrate," *Washington Post*, April 9, 1967.

20 Murray B. Levin, *The Alienated Voter* (New York: Holt, Rinehart and Winston, 1962), 7. Also Edward C. Banfield and James Q. Wilson, *City Politics* (Cambridge: Harvard University Press and M.I.T. Press, 1963), 275.

21 Quoted in Edgar Litt, *The Political Cultures of Massachusetts* (Cambridge: M.I.T. Press, 1965), 19.

mittee and the bureaucrats that administer the system still faithfully reflect the old style, the old habits, the old beliefs."[22] Reflecting a political culture, albeit one that may be eroding, the style of school politics is highly personal and parochial. A Negro candidate for the School Committee, who ran unsuccessfully as a member of a slate opposing incumbents in the 1965 election, described the consequences of this style as follows: "You can't make an impact on this town. Whenever you criticize the schools you run into the old problem—everybody has a brother or a cousin who works for the School Department, and they all think the schools are wonderful."[23]

Given the homogeneity of school personnel, where so many people are related by religion, education, experience, and habit, it would indeed be astonishing if personalism made no difference. In fact, it weighs heavily in the behavior of the Boston School Department. It would be remarkable, too, if teachers and their organizations were immune to the personal, parochial, and conservative styles that have infected the city's politics in general and schools in particular. In Schrag's opinion, the culture is highly integrated; things fit neatly together. "The School Committee, the administration, the majority of teachers, and the electorate reinforce each other."[24]

Understandably, then, the motivations of teacher leaders in Boston differ substantially from those held by leaders in New York City. Even among union members, there is little consensus on goals and tactics. Most of them are agreed on the need for organizational power, but how to achieve it and what to do with it remain unanswered questions. Few aspire to a decisive role in running the schools; for the majority, benefits seem to be the major concern. Half feel that disputes between teachers and school authorities can best be settled by personal diplomacy. Even a larger number are adverse to striking. In Boston, as in New York, the attitudes of teacher leaders and the behavior of teacher groups are congruent. But here congruence is at a lower level of militancy. Both the words and actions of Boston teacher leaders illustrate a persistent pattern of mutual accommodation, which is only occasionally interrupted by conflict.

The Boston Teachers Union and the Teachers Alliance have existed for about twenty years, three times as long as UFT. Yet organizational development here is much less advanced than in New York. UFT won collective bargaining at the very outset of its career. In fact, the Fed-

[22] (Boston: Beacon Press, 1967), 8. For a similar view, see Jonathan Kozol, *Death at an Early Age* (Boston: Houghton Mifflin, 1967).
[23] Schrag, *op. cit.,* 11–12.
[24] *Ibid.,* 73.

eration's first major effort was to work toward attainment of this end. BTU, by contrast, did not achieve comparable status until 1965, having previously engaged in many activities of which the drive for collective bargaining was not the most important one.

As much as anything else, the drive for collective bargaining illustrates the contrasting pattern of teacher-group politics in Boston. Neither BTU nor BTA was at first overly enthusiastic about gaining collective bargaining or some equivalent negotiating procedure. Certainly, neither one was inclined to launch a strenuous campaign similar to that waged by UFT. The president of the Union and the executive secretary of the Alliance were accustomed to operating informally and by means of personal negotiations when their groups' interests were at stake. Each year, when the school budget was being formulated, they followed formal channels of appeal. They testified before the Salary Adjustment Board, composed of school administrators, and before the five-member School Committee. Often they contacted the superintendent and individual members of the Committee to make their case through private persuasion.

But collective bargaining was in the air, and it could hardly be resisted by a union local. By 1963 other labor groups in the metropolitan area were pressuring the mayor and city council to grant bargaining rights to public employees. And, due to the UFT example, cues from AFT's Chicago headquarters were becoming more frequent. Furthermore, a number of newer and more militant members of the BTU executive board, allied with a professional organizer on the staff and impressed by UFT's example, had bargaining in mind as a vital objective for their group. Top union leaders simply could not ignore all this without suffering considerable embarrassment. At a meeting in June, 1963, union members voted decisively to embark on a campaign to bring collective bargaining to the Boston schools.

Leaders, who had devised their own methods of negotiating, were unenthusiastic. And few members, let alone unaffiliated teachers, seemed willing to take a hard line to accomplish a procedural rather than substantive end. Feelings against the existing rules of the educational game were neither widespread nor intense, and consequently the campaign to alter these rules was mild, not impassioned. BTU circulated petitions among teachers, propagandized through its newspaper and other literature, and appealed, as it had habitually done, to the School Committee.

Early in 1964 the union, presenting petitions signed by a majority of teachers in the system, stated its case before the Committee. BTU requested an election to ascertain whether teachers wanted bargaining and another one to determine who the bargaining agent would be. BTA did not flatly object, but its executive secretary reflected the organization's lack of enthusiasm for the idea by pointing to several questions. First, was collective bargaining by teachers even legal under state law? Second, what would happen in the eventuality of a strike? And, finally, how could the school system risk the possibility of a labor union representing educational professionals?

It was up to the School Committee to decide. The decision would be made in an environment not entirely devoid of teacher pressure, but absolutely free of coercive threats. Two committeemen, Arthur Gartland and Thomas Eisenstadt, were favorably disposed. Two others, Joseph Lee and William O'Connor, stood in opposition. The decisive vote was in the hands of Mrs. Louise Day Hicks, who was not then willing to change the status quo, and expressed doubts as to the legality of the Committee entering into a collective bargaining arrangement. Through 1964 members divided along these lines.

By the following year, things had changed. But unlike in New York, where the Federation was instrumental in promoting change, in Boston it came about not because of any action on the Union's part but as a result of other factors. The state legislature was about to pass a bill requiring boards of education, among other municipal employers, to bargain in good faith on wages, hours, and other conditions of employment. Given the likelihood of collective bargaining, there was little reason for politically ambitious members of the school committee to stand rigidly in its way.

At a meeting in October, Mrs. Hicks moved to take up the question of collective bargaining once again. "Only when the teaching staff becomes an equal partner in the educational enterprise can this school system achieve success," she maintained. Supported by Eisenstadt, she argued further the practical need for the proposed arrangement. If teachers were better organized and represented by a single agent, they would be able to work in concert with the School Committee to loosen City Hall's purse strings and obtain additional funds for public education. With Mrs. Hicks switching, the vote this time was three to two in favor of collective bargaining.[25] Due in largest measure to the energies of organized labor and action by the state legislature, BTU was on the way to getting what it half-heartedly wanted.

The election was set for November 9. Since both the question of collective bargaining and the selection of an agent were to be decided by the same ballot, the Alliance was compelled to enter the contest despite its lack of ardor for the proposed process. In any case, it hardly

[25] *Boston School Committee Minutes*, October 4, 1965.

would have been feasible to campaign against bargaining and, failing to win on that point, strive to be elected bargaining agent. Predictably, the election aroused forces of the National Education Association. For some time, NEA and the Massachusetts Teachers Association had been trying to bring BTA into the fold as an affiliated group. Now with the possibility of the American Federation of Teachers gaining power in another city and adding to its victories in New York, Cleveland, Detroit, and Philadelphia, NEA made a number of approaches to the Alliance. But affiliation, or even help, from outside was rejected. BTA thought it had a chance to win on its own, despite the union's growing margin in membership.

The outcome was a rather decisive victory for the Boston Teachers Union. Two-thirds of the teachers eligible voted. BTU received 1,602 votes, BTA 1,116; a ratio of almost three to two in favor of the union. Remarkably, only 41 teachers cast votes against collective bargaining. Given the single ballot, which undoubtedly advantaged those favoring change, teachers were disinclined to forego the chance of supporting one or another group as agent.

Negotiations between BTU representatives and school administrators got under way late in 1965. Settling the first contract was not the contentious business it had proved to be in New York. Both parties reached agreement in rather amicable fashion on salary increases, a pilot program for duty-free lunch, a reduction of class size, the limitation of teaching periods, and payments to substitute teachers. BTU's principal concern seemed to be to garner maximum material benefits and work out some machinery for processing grievances. Unlike UFT, the union here did not make any strenuous attempt to increase its power to participate in the formulation of educational policies. In fact, as one representative of management remarked, when union negotiators were confronted by their administrator counterparts with a difficult problem in search of solution their response was: "That's an administrative matter. You solve the problem." It is difficult to imagine UFT, which had vigorously fought the mayor, the board, and the school administration, taking a similar approach in dealing with the managers of public education.

MANEUVER IN SAN FRANCISCO

In some respects San Francisco resembles New York, since both cities are heterogeneous in composition. In neither does a "power elite" rule, although business interests in the former are reported to have a major and, perhaps, most influential voice. But, the resemblance does not apply much farther. The brutal competition, characteristic of New

York, is not found in San Francisco. Here one attachment is widely shared, at least by important elements of the population. The city is probably unparalleled among American metropolises in terms of its scenic beauty and wealth. Nearly all of its inhabitants are proud of their good fortune and confident of continued prosperity. Citizens, and particularly those in the middle and upper reaches of local society who appear to determine the tone of political life, agree that they live in one of the world's advantaged places and feel things cannot easily be improved. Suspicious of change, and believing that most changes are ultimately for the worse, they are not anxious to move hastily or in unchartered directions.[26]

As in Boston, political life is pervaded by parochialism and conservatism. Complacency also influences political attitudes and styles. Unlike the situation in New York, frequent and hard conflict is unnecessary. Instead, accommodation of interests is possible through moderate means. The feeling is that, above all, the climate of moderation must be preserved. In less striking fashion than in either New York or Boston, the dominant political styles of San Francisco help to shape patterns of school politics—things are fine, problems are not acute, hold the line on taxes, change must be gradual, risks need not be taken, and conflict can and should be avoided. These injunctions, embedded in the cultural terrain, establish limits within which the school board, superintendent, and administrators conduct themselves. This atmosphere also affects teachers in important ways.

In this city of moderation there is a stand-off among teacher organizations, three of whom are competing for members and support. The first and smallest is the Teachers Association of San Francisco, which was formed in 1912 and claims a membership of about 1,000. Second is the San Francisco Federation of Teachers, with approximately 1,200 members. Third is the San Francisco Classroom Teachers Association, which developed from a merger in 1965 between the Classroom Teachers Association and the local chapter of the California Teachers Association (CTA) and has a membership of about 2,500.[27] SFFT, a local of the union, and SFCTA, an affiliate of NEA and CTA, are the major contenders. But neither clearly dominates, and the contest for support and power continues unabated.

Stalemate characterizes other aspects of the scene as well. In New York and Boston the motivations of union leaders fairly well match the

[26] See Peter Schrag, *Voices in the Classroom* (Boston: Beacon Press, 1965).

[27] These estimates are not very reliable indications of group strength, since many teachers join more than one organization in order to take advantage of group benefits.

behavior of their organizations. In San Francisco, however, attitudes and behavior have diverged. While the views of leaders are extremely militant, union action has been quite restrained. Executive Board members of SFFT think like their fiery colleagues in New York but act like their moderate colleagues in Boston. Moreover, they still have some distance to travel in order to obtain collective bargaining in which they wholeheartedly believe. In this realm, too, deadlock prevails. Instead of bargaining (as AFT proposes) or professional negotiation (as NEA proposes), San Francisco teachers have only a hybrid mechanism at their disposal.

Until very recently, teachers and teacher organizations in this city had three major ways to make known their views. First, at meetings of the board of education, teacher leaders, and particularly those representing SFFT, frequently made presentations, arguing for higher salaries, other benefits, or improvements in school conditions. Although their right to address the board was recognized, there was little obligation on the parts of commissioners, as board members are titled, to take seriously what they said. "Teacher organizations make recommendations to the Board," SFFT argued. "Sometimes they are discussed; occasionally they are granted; and often they are completely disregarded."[28] According to an SFCTA official, the policy of the board was to "listen courteously and decide independently."

Another means of access for teacher groups was the Coordinating Council of Superintendent Harold Spears. One member from each employee organization, representing teacher and administrator groups, sat on the Council and met on a monthly or bi-monthly basis. Spears dominated these meetings, using the forum to hand down information, bring in his own experts, and tell representatives of the staff what he wanted them to know. The Council was a far cry from a major policy-making body, since the superintendent rarely invited consideration of significant problems. Discussion instead focused on matters such as the school calendar or discipline. As a result, teacher groups seldom raised important issues in the Council, but rather took them individually to the superintendent or school board.

A final mechanism for teacher participation was the faculty council at the local school level. The impact of faculty councils, the formation of which was encouraged by Superintendent Spears, varies from school to school. In general, however, their authority has been less than overwhelming, since principals have the power to veto council recommendations.

[28] *SFFT Reporter*, March, 1965.

Late in 1965 the situation changed. In New York, action by the state legislature in ousting the board of education had hastened the advent of collective bargaining. In Massachusetts, action by the legislature had been instrumental in the Boston School Committee's ultimate decision to hold a bargaining election. California state government also played a critical role in affecting the pattern of teacher politics in San Francisco. It passed a law authorizing teacher organizations to have a formal, if not very strong, voice in local educational policy.

Unlike other state statutes which provided for exclusive representation of teachers, the California law established a system of proportional representation. The primary purposes of the Winton Act, as the law has come to be known, were to preserve the statewide influence of the California Teachers Association and forestall collective bargaining. CTA pushed it through the state legislature, despite bitter opposition by the California Federation of Teachers, which represented union locals. The new law provides that in each community a negotiating council, representing employee organizations, be set up to "meet and confer" with the board of education or its designated representative. If more than one group claims to represent teachers and administrators, which would usually be the case, then the council has to be composed on a proportional basis, reflecting organization membership. This means that elections need not be conducted either to determine an exclusive agent or representation on the council. Instead, seats may be assigned according to the number of members enrolled by each employees organization.[29] The negotiating council, as specified in the act, is empowered to confer on "all matters relating to the definition of educational objectives, the determination of the content of courses and curricula, the selection of textbooks, and other aspects of the instructional program. . . ." in addition to "all matters relating to employment conditions and employer-employee relations."

The San Francisco school board quickly established a nine-member negotiating council and delegated the superintendent as its agent in council discussions. But the potential strength of the new body seemed limited from the outset. The attorney for the board of education rendered an opinion, showing how meager the authority of the council might be:

> . . . the Board should keep in mind [he stated] the distinction between 'confer' and 'negotiate.' The former is not a word of legal significance. . . . A meeting satisfies the 'meet' requirement; discussing the matter satisfies the 'confer' requirement. *There is no requirement to reach agreement* nor must the Board make counter-proposals.[30]

[29] Associations, with larger local memberships, did not want to give unions a chance to win majorities by attracting the votes of unaffiliated teachers. CTA persuaded the state legislature not to require elections for Council representation.

[30] Irving Breyer, quoted in *SFFT Reporter*, October, 1965. Emphasis his.

Understandably, two of the local teacher organizations were unhappy with the ground rules. SFFT refused to participate. The union had strenuously opposed the idea in Sacramento, and if seats were assigned on the basis of membership rolls it had little chance to exert major influence in the council. In addition, it regarded the whole business as a sham, which ". . . does not advance in any way the power of teachers to determine the conditions under which they work."[31] Obstacles could only be increased. On salaries, for example, a group would first have to iron out its own position, then negotiate with others represented on the council, then "meet and confer" with the superintendent, and only then take a proposal to the board. Nor did TASF agree to join the council. It also sensed that the device lacked any sanctions and might turn out to be "an administration-controlled rubber stamp." Moreover, TASF, the smallest teacher group in San Francisco, did not care to share in an arrangement where others would obviously predominate.

The only group eager to join was SFCTA, which was given seven of the nine seats on the council. Leaders of the Association are generally satisfied with the negotiating council. The former president of SFCTA thinks that all teacher groups should come together, settle things among themselves, and then speak with one voice to the superintendent and board of education. Executive Director Ralph Flynn, an NEA staff man, at one time was a strong advocate of professional negotiation. He, too, now feels that collective negotiations through the council coalition will work. In any case, the very fact that the board has been forced to come down from its "pedestal" and meet with teacher representatives on the same ground is viewed as a vast improvement. Thus, the establishment of the negotiating council was considered to be "the greatest single step" taken by the Association during the entire year.[32]

Underlying the susceptibility of NEA affiliates to this innovation in employer-employee relations is the feeling that the council would help impede the growth of union influence and deter the specter of collective bargaining. Influence and bargaining, of course, have been prime goals of SFFT. As early as 1961, the San Francisco teachers union asked the board to support a measure in the state legislature providing for collective bargaining. The board refused. Four years later SFFT requested that the board take steps leading to collective bargaining and called for a poll

---

[31] *Ibid.* Instead of resolving teacher views at the representation stage, this system of proportional representation transfers to the bargaining table the competition of views between contending teacher organizations. See Robert E. Doherty and Walter E. Oberer, *Teachers, School Boards, and Collective Bargaining* (Ithaca, N.Y.: New York State School of Industrial and Labor Relations, Cornell University, 1967), 75.

[32] San Francisco Classroom Teachers Association, *Annual Report: 1965–66*, dated May, 1966.

of all teachers to see if they wanted to be represented by one organization. With a single group bargaining on behalf of teachers, the board would be legally required to "listen, discuss, and take positive action."[33] Again, the board demurred, arguing that state law prohibited it from entering into such an agreement with a teacher organization.

Now, with a negotiating council functioning, the San Francisco union is continuing its campaign for collective bargaining. The council, according to SFFT's past president, Dan Jackson, has little meaning and "as long as teachers may be divided, allowing one organization to move in and undercut another, the teachers will suffer."[34] The present job of the union, given these conditions, is twofold. First, it must persuade teachers and the board that the negotiating council will not work to the advantage of either or both and that bargaining is essential. Second, in Jackson's words, it must project an image of "militancy, reason, and responsibility" to win widespread teacher support. Thus far emphasis seems to have been on "reason" and "responsibility" rather than "militancy." The behavior of top leaders has been restrained. They have not translated either their feelings or their words into action. Instead, until very recently they have conducted themselves in gentlemanly fashion, settled disputes quietly, eschewed the public use of inflammatory language, and acted much like union leaders in Boston.

In the view of SFFT dissidents, the union was failing in its obligations. According to their line of reasoning, a teachers union develops in three stages. In the initial one, it battles for grudging toleration of its right to exist. In the second, it tries to enlarge its rights and broaden its membership. To do this, "it may be useful tactically to play down the fundamental conflict of interest with the administration." Consequently, leadership characterized by "a more affable and diplomatic approach" comes to the fore and succeeds in making useful, peripheral gains for the local. Here is where the San Francisco Federation finds itself. It should be moving forward, into a third developmental stage, instead of lingering in its "seeming security after this is really appropriate." During maturity a union "must muster its forces for a contest of wills with the Establishment so that it can henceforth negotiate as a recognized equal." For SFFT, battle should be the order of the day and "increasingly aggressive tactics and a renewed tone of militancy" should serve as the most appropriate means in the achievement of teacher rights.[35]

---

[33] *SFFT Reporter*, March, 1965. At the same board meeting, SFCTA urged adoption of a plan to establish a negotiating council.

[34] *Ibid.*, March, 1966.

[35] This argument is eloquently made in a letter by Dick Kidd, published in *SFFT Newsletter*, February, 1966.

Top leaders, however, were not sure that the time was ripe to embark upon such a militant program. Action is necessary, according to a spokesman for the moderates, but action carries with it dangers, particularly that of losing its impact when too often called forth. An alternate source of union power is the support of a large and unified membership, which can only be attracted "by a responsible leadership that presents well thought out, sharply defined programs. . . ."[36] Action will surely be required, but the question remains as to when and under what conditions this stage of organizational development can profitably be entered.

Although the Federation has pursued a path of moderation, employing the tactics of diplomacy, it was and would doubtless continue to be more aggressive than SFCTA. On several occasions, it endeavored to turn the board against the superintendent. As long as a decade ago, it withdrew from a council of teacher organizations to make salary proposals on its own. During past years, it boycotted the negotiating council and insisted on parallel meetings with the superintendent for separate consideration of its proposals. Recently, perhaps because of the prodding of a militant faction, it resorted to direct pressure in order to persuade the board of its position on grievance machinery. Then, in early 1968 SFFT actually launched a strike, which lasted one day and was observed by only one-quarter of the city's teachers.[37] Apparently, Federation leaders had had good reason for their previous hesitance.

Differences between the association and the union are obvious, despite moderation in the past behavior of both. The former is satisfied with diplomacy and the limited role that can be played through the negotiating council. The latter recognizes the need for direct action to achieve collective bargaining and an equal voice in educational policy-making. Largely because of leadership motivations on questions of goals, strategies, and tactics, the San Francisco Federation of Teachers has the potential to follow the path blazed by its sister union in New York City. Much depends upon whether its followers are willing to be led in this direction.

[36] This argument, in rebuttal to Kidd's, is made in a letter by Stephen R. Holman, published in *SFFT Newsletter*, March, 1966.

[37] After the teachers returned, the mayor's office conducted a preference poll to determine if teachers wanted one organization to represent them in negotiation. No group received a majority. The 1968 strike and related events occurred a few years after my field research in San Francisco was completed. They seem to confirm, and not refute, my analysis of SFFT in this and succeeding chapters.

V. Opportunities for Action

The contrasting patterns of behavior by teacher organizations in New York, Boston, and San Francisco cannot be explained solely in terms of the motivations of group leaders. Militant motivation may be a prerequisite for militant action, but without *opportunities* for translating orientations into behavior it is insufficient. In the case of teacher organizations, particularly those in the three cities under present consideration, neither motivation nor opportunity alone suffices to provide an adequate explanation of behavior.[1] Both have to be taken into account.

By opportunities we mean simply the conditions and situations which facilitate or impede forceful action by teacher groups. Opportunities, in this sense, are not entirely dependent upon the perceptions of leaders. True, those with more militant orientations will interpret conditions and situations differently than their more acquiescent colleagues. Given even the slightest opportunities, their militant dispositions may propel them to take action. But the kinds of opportunities we shall explore in this chapter have lives independent of leadership orientations. In other words, even the most militantly oriented leader or teachers group may have objective cause to move cautiously rather than precipitously, diplomatically rather than combatively. By contrast, a less militant leader or group may be pushed by opportunity factors to more extreme measures.

One illustration of what we have in mind has already been considered in another context. The achievement of collective bargaining hinges not only on organizational goals but also on other considerations. In large degree, state government determines the scope or limits of opportunities in this area. In both Massachusetts and California, as has been noted, state legislation was a major factor influencing the fate of collective negotiations between teachers and their employers. Passage of legislation by state authorities enabled the Teachers Union to win representational

[1] For conceptualization along similar lines, see James D. Barber, *The Lawmakers* (New Haven: Yale University Press, 1965), 10–15. Robert L. Crain, in an examination of the militancy of civil rights groups in northern cities, makes a somewhat similar distinction. He distinguishes between the propensity of groups to act and the amount of action taken. *The Politics of School Desegregation* (Chicago: Aldine, 1968), 331–32.

authority in Boston, but only perpetuated deadlock in San Francisco. On the other hand, the Condon-Wadlin Act, and later the Taylor Act in New York, prohibited strikes and provided severe penalties. Neither had much effect, however, as UFT ignored possible penalties and violated the statutes to achieve bargaining goals.

Another class of opportunities also has been suggested in the preceding chapter. Some community political styles encourage agreement, others encourage contention. Most important are the integrative and conflictive elements, the ways in which things are held together and conflicts prevented or resolved. On the one hand, there is the political community characterized by a high degree of integration. Here, although people clash over who runs things, how public affairs are conducted, and who gets what, the pervasive features of the environment are cultural homogeneity, widely shared attachments, and complementary interests. This fits Boston, where teacher politics is marked by accommodation. It also applies to San Francisco, where conflict has been contained.

On the other hand, there is the type of political community characterized by a high degree of disintegration. Here, although there are certain fundamental agreements preventing a state of nature, the more pervasive features are cultural heterogeneity, conflicting attachments, and competing interests. These conditions describe New York City, where teacher politics are marked by conflict.

Now we shall consider other factors affecting organizational behavior. Directly relevant to the nature of group opportunities are the attitudes and practices of educational authorities, particularly school boards, superintendents, and central administrators. In New York City the general stance of educational authorities has been one of *opposition* to change in the rules of the educational game proposed by UFT. Especially in the earlier days of union development, this opposition had a great bearing on the Federation's activities. In sharp contrast, Boston groups, and most particularly the union, have struggled for power in an entirely different atmosphere. Here, board and administration have behaved in *benevolent* fashion, offering inducements for cooperation. San Francisco teachers have encountered a rather similar situation. In this city *diversion and delay,* practiced by school authorities, have had important effects on the behavioral militancy of teacher groups.

Fundamentally, of course, what count most are the attitudes of the teacher community and the kinds of opportunities they present group leaderships. The action programs launched by organizations are influenced by the views of teachers whom they are trying to recruit as members or supporters in a contest for representation. They are also influenced by the feelings of members, by group leaders competing with the incumbent leadership, and by the competition offered by rival organizations. And all of these factors are in part shaped by the attitudes and practices of educational authorities.

In general, competition, stemming either from within an organization or from a rival, has the tendency to stimulate greater militancy as far as action is concerned. On the other hand, the attitudes of rank-and-file teachers in the school system, including members and non-members alike, act as a restraining force. In New York City, despite their basic conservatism, feelings of *resentment* by teachers towards the educational establishment permitted UFT to act forcefully without fear of mass disapproval. Boston teachers, however, traditionally have exhibited *deference* and *loyalty* to authority, and thus restrained groups from taking extreme action. In San Francisco the feeling within the teacher community is best described as one of *apathy,* which made direct action programs exceedingly difficult propositions for organizations to undertake.

THE CONDUCT OF EDUCATIONAL CHIEFTAINS

In one respect the school systems of New York City, Boston, and San Francisco bear great resemblance to one another. All have resisted rather than welcomed or facilitated currents of change. Educational chieftains in each city have faithfully paid vocal homage to innovation, but have diligently avoided fundamental upheaval. School authorities in New York, mainly the board of education and secondarily the superintendent, have been more responsive to pressures for change than their counterparts elsewhere. Perhaps this is because pressures have been greater or educational leadership more enlightened. Perhaps it ties in with the competition and conflict which distinguishes political life in the nation's largest city.

Proposals for change are frequently made and seriously considered in New York City. Large numbers are adopted as policy by the school board. But whatever the proposal and whatever its source, schoolmen, at one hierarchical level or another, have banded together to protect existing programs and arrangements. Although the system is normally fragmented by criss-crossing jealousies, whenever changes are proposed factions (including administrators and teachers) unite and wage battle against any threats to their interests. As a result, even the most trivial changes that are suggested become matters of major conflict, with the defensive forces distinctly advantaged. Thus, one student of the educational scene has recently summed up: "New York City has not witnessed any meaningful change in curriculum, administrative structure, teaching recruitment, appointment and training, or general organization for at least three decades."[2] This may be an unfair assessment, but there can be little doubt that the path of innovation is tortuous indeed.

Innovation has made even less progress in Boston. True, as a result of incentives and sanctions held out by federal and state agencies, the School Department has created some new programs. It has also re-modeled its organization for school construction and entered into joint endeavors with local universities. But whatever has been done has been limited in scope and rarely of a radical nature. To a far greater degree than in New York, the board, superintendent, and administration have successfully resisted demands from federal, state, and municipal authori-ties, from educational experts, and from the city's dissenting population of Negroes. Bound together by common attachments and interests, Bos-ton's educational chieftains have been described as "a closed club of unimaginative civil servants," inbred, and lacking initiative to innovate.[3] It is difficult for an outsider to disagree with this evaluation. There has been combat, of course, but it has rarely divided the managers of public education. Unity has been preserved. Old ways have persisted and the school system has continued to function without basic disturbances.

In keeping with the basic moderation of the city, San Francisco's schools have been hesitant to embrace change. As in Boston, there exists a working consensus that the educational system is in good shape, the safety of the status quo is preferable to the risks of innovation, and ten-sion and conflict should be avoided. The board of education stands careful guard over the community purse, happily permitting the superin-tendent and professional staff to run the schools. If the system seems inert and unresponsive, this is what the school board has in mind. On their parts, the superintendent and his deputies have evidenced little desire to experiment. In fact, even if an innovation has proved itself in another setting, administrators appear ready to demonstrate how it would be of little value in San Francisco. During the past few years, like other school systems, this one has been forced to respond to problems of race and cultural deprivation. But most people, including schoolmen, believe these problems manageable and susceptible to some gradualist solution. The Negro population is small enough to make integration practicable, white attitudes are tolerant enough to preclude violent resistance, and the city's wealth is adequate to pay for compensatory services. Few be-

[2] Marilyn Gittell, *Participants and Participation* (New York: Center for Urban Education, 1967), 21.

[3] Peter Schrag, "Boston: Education's Last Hurrah," *Saturday Review* (May 21, 1966), 56.

lieve there is cause for alarm, and most would probably go along with Superintendent Harold Spears in sidestepping problems and postponing commitments as long as possible.[4]

These, then, are typical attitudes toward innovation in the three cities. Although based on somewhat different rationales and provoking slightly different schisms, the managers of public education are reluctant to adopt proposals for educational change. We might therefore anticipate that they would not welcome a change in the power status of their employees. Of particular interest here are the following questions. How do school authorities regard teacher organizations which seek a partnership in the various domains of policy-making? How do they handle the demands of teachers? Do they oppose them, accede to them, or try to evade them? The three systems have differed in their methods of dealing with teachers and teacher groups. These differences, as we shall see, help to explain typical attitudes of teachers and contrasting activities of their organizations.

Resistance and Combat

During the recent past, the school board and superintendent in New York City have had a difficult time defending the battlements of public education. In view of the size of the system, its fragmentation into semi-independent administrative sovereignties, and the plethora of outside pressures to which it has been subjected, the defensive posture is understandable. This defensiveness, in conjunction with the system's high regard for hierarchy, has affected relationships with teaching personnel as well. More so in earlier days, but even now, the board of education and successive superintendents—first, John Theobald, then Calvin Gross, and finally Bernard Donovan—have strenuously and persistently resisted encroachments on their prerogatives by the United Federation of Teachers. This resistance, often maladroit and frequently to little avail, has probably encouraged the union's militancy and the receptiveness of teachers to UFT appeals.[5]

---

[4] Peter Schrag, *Voices in the Classroom* (Boston: Beacon Press), 237, 240. The author explains that Spears' reluctance to innovate is based partly on his beliefs that no school system can be a patchwork of special programs, and no genuine change can be dictated by the central office.

[5] In a slightly different context, Ronald G. Corwin notes that the degree of militancy depends on the resistance of laymen and administrators. "In cases where laymen relinquish their control without resistance," he writes, "professionalization is not necessarily militant." "Militant Professionalism, Initiative and Compliance in Public Education," *Sociology of Education,* 38 (Summer, 1965), 315. In discussing the militancy of civil rights groups, Crain also points out that much depends upon whether the school system provokes action by refusing to acquiesce to desegregation demands. *Op. cit.,* 331.

Educational authorities began their relationship with the Federation by vigorous opposition to demands for collective bargaining. Superintendent Theobald's attitude and behavior were especially provocative. In 1959 he refused to negotiate with UFT, but instead consulted with a number of splinter organizations. Backed by the board, the superintendent evidently chose a strategy of playing off one teachers' group against another, insisting that the administration deal with all forty or so teacher organizations then in existence rather than with just one. Furthermore, according to teacher leaders, he refused to give any credit to the union for gains it had made, declaring that accomplishments resulted from his own efforts, those of the school board and supervisory staff, and the splendid cooperation of other teacher groups.

As UFT mobilized, the superintendent, in a radio talk broadcast in every public school, implied that the union was using unprofessional tactics in order to destroy its competitors. He described the threatened strike as having nothing to do with professional rights but called it "a shameful reach on the part of a few for organizational power and self-aggrandizement."[6] Adamancy by school officials, and the almost universal condemnation of union tactics proved futile. So did efforts by the administration to aid NEA in a united campaign to halt UFT.

After the advent of collective bargaining, the principal issue was the budget and teacher salaries. It soon became obvious to the Federation that its major adversary was City Hall, not the board or superintendent. During negotiations for the first contract, UFT President Cogen announced that lines of battle had changed. The board, he said, was bargaining in good faith, but

> ... at some point in the collective bargaining process it is essential that adequate funds be made available. . . . When this point was reached, the Board of Education was powerless to carry out its collective bargaining function. It was trapped. When the Board turned to Mayor Wagner, they [sic] came up against a stone wall.[7]

For some time the mayor held firm, but UFT's strike finally persuaded him to recognize union demands. Aggressive tactics paid rich dividends. No penalties were imposed, salary increases and other benefits were gained, and UFT membership grew dramatically. The rewards of militant action naturally encouraged its continuation.

Rather early in the game, however, educational chieftains began to feel the squeeze, and their sympathy with the monetary demands of teachers waned. The problem was that a pattern was emerging, jeopar-

[6] *New York Times*, October 24, 1960.
[7] *United Teacher*, April-May, 1962.

dizing their prerogatives. Under threat of a teachers' strike the mayor would make available some funds, but not enough for the board to fully accommodate UFT or even meet the terms of the agreed contract. Schoolmen still had to juggle their own budgets to find monies for the settlement. The union, through intervention by the mayor's mediators, had taken over a good part of the job of determining how school monies should be spent. The board had few illusions about the erosion of its authority. In a statement issued after the 1965 settlement, the board lamented: "If this way of budget making were to become permanent, it would end by destroying the usefulness of the board and the integrity of the educational system."[8]

What is more important, however, is that the board and superintendent appeared incapable of accepting the erosion of their power with quiet resignation. At one time or another, and in one way or another, New York City educational authorities accused the union of acting contrary to the best interests of the school system, depriving children of vital educational services, and trying to take over the school system. None of these accusations, of course, were likely to temper the militancy of the United Federation of Teachers.

Non-budgetary matters also furnished grounds for continuing conflict. Although, in the opinions of some, union demands have been moderate, school authorities have given in only most grudgingly. They have fought every inch of the way, losing gradually and retiring in orderly fashion. Their discretion over the budget, to be sure, was severely limited by the mayor's control of the municipal purse. But their prerogatives in the domains of educational policy were of little concern to City Hall. Here, at least, board and superintendent had a good chance to hold the line without fear of intervention by outsiders.

From the outset, the establishment attempted to limit the scope of collective bargaining to "terms and conditions of employment," such as salaries, pensions, sick leaves, and sabbaticals. Educational policy matters, however, were considered beyond the union's proper responsibility. In contract after contract, school authorities tried to make the distinction between "working conditions" and "educational policy." The former might be specified in a contract, but the latter, the establishment insisted, might be appended only as a policy statement. Separate treatment was more than an exercise in semantics. It was important, since alleged violations of a contract item could be appealed to an outside arbitrator, while violations of a policy statement could be appealed only to the superintendent and board.

[8] *New York Times*, September 11, 1965.

The dispute was understandable. But the issue of control, as handled by the board and superintendent, helped to nourish continued conflict. In 1963, for instance, negotiations became especially contentious. Superintendent Gross charged that UFT leaders were seeking a "form of control of the school system that goes beyond the function of a union." To make things worse, he questioned the union's legitimacy. "I have no assurance," he said, "that the group with which we sit down actually does represent the opinion of all school teachers."[9] With money issues out of the way, the issue of administrative control still could not be settled. Again Gross attacked, this time questioning the motives of the UFT leadership in trying to gain a share of administrative control. "If it should be that union officials harbor such inclinations for possible reasons of organizational prestige," he declared, ". . . these aspirations are improper and cannot be acceded to."[10] The union responded with tough words of its own.

At no time was the struggle over a contract as intense and protracted as in 1967. On this occasion, the board, led by a new president, Alfred Giardino, stood firm in the face of union demands, and, for the first time, counterattacked forcefully with demands of its own. As on so many issues previously, the board took the position that it could not delegate policy-making on More Effective Schools (MES), or any other program, to the union. The time seemed most propitious for a showdown, and school authorities were willing to risk a walkout by New York City teachers in order to resist UFT encroachments.

Although MES in the city had become a showcase for AFT's nation-wide drive to improve large-city education, the board had at its disposal an independent study questioning the program's effectiveness. And it used this to counter the union's proposal for MES expansion. Furthermore, the board had on its side the new Taylor Law, a successor statute to the unworkable Condon-Wadlin Act. As usual, the educational establishment had the backing of local civic and parent groups, the *New York Times,* and, at least implicitly, the mayor. Finally, and most important, UFT's demand to give teachers the authority to suspend unruly pupils from classrooms had alienated many people in Negro and Puerto Rican communities throughout the city, and the board counted on their support as well. In the negotiations of 1967, the positions of the contenders were firmly fixed, and only after several weeks of arduous bargaining could a compromise settlement be reached.

Conflict was not confined to formal collective bargaining. In a system regulated by a morass of administrative procedures and governed by a

9 *Ibid.,* July 18, 1963.
10 *Board of Education Press Release,* 36–63/64, September 30, 1963.

ponderous chain of command, incidents involving status-conscious administrators and rebellious teachers could be expected. Encounters were frequent at the local school level, although relatively few led to the formal processing of grievances. One aim of Livingston Street was to ensure that the authority of the school principal would not be destroyed by collective bargaining. One aim of UFT was to duplicate in each school bargaining relationships which were established for the system as a whole.

In the early days of CB, principals appealed to the superintendent because union chapters were trying to interfere with the proper conduct of their duties. Theobald sent a special directive to every school reiterating the principal's responsibility "for the instruction, direction, and control" of all members of his staff. In response, UFT argued vehemently that its representational rights applied not only at the central level but in local school affairs as well. Dictatorship could not be tolerated, maintained the union; principals should consult with their faculties and heed their views.

Today there is little doubt about the Federation's power, and consequently its rights, in local schools. UFT has gained recognition for the legitimacy of chapter organizations and has established the practice of regular monthly meetings between school leaders and principals. Friction naturally continues. Administrators and supervisors at Livingston Street and in the schools still show concern with the preservation of their prerogatives and resist union encroachment in areas they deem rightfully their own. Nor is battle merely verbal. Some local principals develop strategies, often based on the patronage at their disposal, to sap union strength in their schools. But this steady opposition has not deterred the Federation from pursuing its relentless drive for pervasive power throughout the school system.

Had the establishment the wherewithal to win, UFT might have taken a less aggressive course with the passage of years. But time and again, the establishment was forced to give way, and this further encouraged the strategies and tactics employed by the Federation from the beginning. Perhaps, as board members and superintendents constantly reaffirmed, what they wanted and what the union wanted were not very far apart. Substantive goals certainly bore some resemblance, but the two sides were at odds over the role a teacher organization should play in choosing avenues to follow toward the achievement of common ends. By 1967, tempers on both sides were short. Leaders of the educational establishment looked on teacher power with considerable dismay. Superintendent Donovan made reference to pre-union days when teachers were characterized by professionalism and dedication. Another school official summarized the establishment's feelings toward the United Federation of Teachers:

> Our experience is that the U.F.T. is more articulate than the Teamsters, the Bricklayers or other standard union types, but it uses the same basic tactic—power. . . . There is no distinctive professional approach, nor any difference based on the fact that they are in the public service or that a million children depend on their being in school. No legal, economic or educational considerations are important to the U.F.T., just naked strength.[11]

In New York City, nothing said or done by boards and administrators had solved the dispute between employers and employees or fundamentally transformed UFT's approach to power and participation. If anything, the behavior of educational chieftains fed and sustained union militancy, not diminished it.

Benevolence, Diversion, and Delay

Persistent and intense conflict, so evident in New York, has been largely absent in Boston and San Francisco. Accommodation and stalemate have been the principal patterns of school politics in these cities. Educational authorities, in part because of cultural norms and styles, have exhibited attitudes and behavior which discouraged militant activities by teacher groups and an ascendancy comparable to that of UFT in New York City.

Many people have called the Boston school system inbred and closed. "They never go outside and they never let outsiders in."[12] One outsider did enter the system, at least in a way. A professional organizer for AFT, who had served an apprenticeship in New York City, staffed the Boston Teachers Union for a few years. After she left, a local teacher took over her job, first on a part-time basis and later full-time. The superintendent, in proposing that the School Committee grant him a leave of absence to perform his duties as union business manager, made the case in typical Boston fashion: "I think it is something you should do. . . . [He is taking] the job that was formerly held by that girl who came from New York. . . . This is the Union's way of attempting to staff it with their own people."[13] The leave went through, for insiders of whatever persuasion belong to the same family and take care of one another.

---

[11] Quoted in A. H. Raskin, "He Leads His Teachers Up the Down Staircase," *New York Times Magazine*, September 3, 1967.

[12] Quoted in Schrag, "Boston: Education's Last Hurrah," *op. cit.*, 56.

[13] *Boston School Committee Minutes*, March 3, 1965. On another occasion, the board's concern was also evident. An outsider came into the system to head the office of program development, which was supported by private and federal funds.

At 15 Beacon Street, where the School Committee and department are headquartered, exist the "patterns of the small village, of the city ward, of the parish, with their strong kinship ties and their personal concerns. . . ."[14] There is pride in the system and in the people who staff it. Board members and administrators are vociferous in praising "our dedicated teachers," a phrase heard constantly. The advantages of teaching in Boston are cited time and again. As one administrator modestly confided: "And anyone who leaves our system, I think, will live to regret it."[15]

There can be no denying that the School Committee and administration sincerely have the interests of their dedicated teachers at heart. Schrag relates that Mrs. Louise Day Hicks, who has fought so doggedly to preserve the neighborhood school, took to heart the words of her dying father, "look after them—the little people, that is."[16] She has certainly tried, freely giving her protection to the neighborhoods, children, and teachers of Boston. Most of her colleagues, the superintendent, and administrators have followed suit, at least insofar as benefits for teachers are concerned.

The primary desire of educational chiefs is to raise salaries. Just about everyone connected with the system is genuinely interested in increasing salaries for the dedicated staff, even if other things have to be sacrificed. In 1965, for example, the mayor accused the School Committee of being too generous with taxpayers' money in granting salary increases to the superintendent and top administrators. Mrs. Hicks explained, however, that funds for the raises were taken from other accounts—from alterations and repairs and educational expansion programs.[17] Members of the Committee have done fairly well in providing for the system's employees. If they have not had complete success, the fault is not theirs. It lies with the mayor, who, because of his tight-fisted hold on the budget, is responsible for any defects in the school system. So goes the argument made by School Committee members, administrators, teacher leaders, and teachers alike.

Benevolence extends beyond money and material benefits. The School Committee trusts its superintendent and administrators to look after the teaching staff, but nevertheless it stands guard, ready to hear the appeal

---

One Committee member, in considering the program, noted that "eventually whoever heads this will come up through the system." The superintendent agreed. *Ibid.*, March 10, 1965.

[14] Peter Schrag, *Village School Downtown* (Boston: Beacon Press, 1967), 56.
[15] *Boston School Committee Minutes*, January 25, 1962.
[16] Schrag, *Village School Downtown, op. cit.*, 18.
[17] *Boston Globe*, April 5 and 9, 1965. Cited in Jonathan Kozol, *Death at an Early Age* (Boston: Houghton Mifflin, 1967), 142.

of employees and prepared to intervene paternalistically. It is habituated to probing into administrative matters, and does not hesitate to make decisions in individual cases when necessary. As a former chairman, William O'Connor, announced when a case came to the Committee's attention: ". . . I kind of believe that once in awhile some extenuating circumstances as here could develop, and particularly for old and faithful employees, I think we ought to spread that milk of human kindness perhaps around a little. . . ."[18]

The need to intervene in defense of employees is infrequent. In the happy family of education, the School Department listens to teacher views and entertains appeals regarding teacher needs. As long as the staff is devoted and loyal, which it has been and continues to be, it can depend upon a sympathetic hearing.

There is formal machinery too. According to Superintendent Ohrenberger, administrators and teachers consult frequently. "We have representatives in each school in attendance by subject and grade level," he proudly states. "This gives anybody in a school the opportunity to consult with his particular representative to make sure the impact of his classroom experience is made manifest to those who are in the administrative position immediately above."[19] There are monthly council meetings, attended by subject and grade-level representatives, staff meetings in each school and each elementary district, and curriculum and textbook committees which meet from time to time.

It is not difficult to appreciate that in view of the establishment's tender regard for school employees, a teacher organization might have a rough job launching an aggressive and popular campaign against the Committee or superintendent. Their doors are always open to teachers. Committee members regard the system's 7,000 employees, teachers and others alike, as their special constituency. They hear pleas and arrange for remedies. Because of the relatively small size of the system, as well as the bonds of personalism, school authorities are far more accessible to individual teachers than their counterparts at Livingston Street in New York.

If disputes develop and controversy results, another safety valve exists. Teachers always have recourse to operate through electoral politics, endorsing or opposing individuals or slates of candidates running for School Committee posts. Whereas in New York members of the board of education are appointed by the mayor from a list of candidates selected by a special panel, in Boston biennial elections determine the composition of the board. New York teachers, therefore, have little to

18 *Boston School Committee Minutes*, October 7, 1964.
19 *Boston Teacher*, February 28, 1964. For a sharp dissent, see Kozol, *op. cit.*

say in the selection of their employers; Boston teachers have the opportunity to use the machinery of electoral politics—endorsing slates, conducting campaigns, rewarding friends, and penalizing enemies. In view of their need to obtain votes, and probably because a number of them have aspirations for higher political office, members of the Boston board are likely to be more responsive to teacher demands than their counterparts in New York.

As a result, teachers also behave differently in the two cities. Direct confrontation provides the outlet for disgruntled teachers in New York; voting may serve a similar purpose in Boston. That it has not functioned this way for about a decade is attributable to the coalescence of interests between teacher organizations and most incumbent board members.

Patterns could shift, even in Boston. Teachers had chosen the more militant union over the alliance. Collective bargaining could conceivably change attitudes. BTU might possibly develop not only as a source of countervailing power and an agency to improve staff security, but also as competition in the long run to the "hierarchical togetherness nurtured by the old establishment on Beacon Street."[20] Much depends on the union's leadership as to whether it will remain in the hands of the civil servants in the Beacon Street tradition or be taken over by those who espouse reform and are willing to run risks in its behalf. Given the pervasive norms of the community, the benevolence of the educational authorities, and the nature of the teaching staff, major change is not very likely. There is little chance at present that teachers in Boston will act like their militant colleagues in New York.

In San Francisco, the educational chieftains also evidence a tendency to reward loyalty to the system, to treat teachers well, and to regard long service highly. As one illustration, the establishment is far more sympathetic to the demands of home-grown teachers than to those made by outsiders. The union's past-president, who had served for a long time, was well thought of by the superintendent and administration. In fact, his personal relationships gave him an advantage over others during the days when the superintendent's Coordinating Council functioned. Commissioners on the school board could overlook his being a union representative, since they had grown accustomed to his presentations before them throughout the years. By contrast, attitudes toward the newly arrived executive director of SFCTA were cooler, despite the fact that the association was less aggressive. He had come from Massachusetts, had never taught in the San Francisco school system, and was treated as an outsider who did not, and could not, appreciate how things were done in the city.

---

[20] This is Schrag's feeling. *Village School Downtown, op. cit.,* 68.

Once leaders become accepted as locals, however, dealing with the board and administration is not unsettling. School chieftains have worked effectively to avoid controversy by keeping teachers happy, or at least quiescent. Although union leaders desire to move forcefully in order to enhance their role in policy-making, the behavior of administrators and the school board makes it extremely difficult.

During the years he served as superintendent, Harold Spears took the same approach in dealing with teachers that he pursued with regard to other problems. His basic strategy was one of delay, in the expectation that problems would vanish. From his point of view, controversy and conflict had to be avoided at all costs, lest his superintendency and the school system be irreparably damaged. Spears agreed that teachers should participate in educational planning, but only as individual members of the educational family. He saw no need for collective activity through mobilized groups. "Teacher organizations," he stated in an interview, "should confine themselves to salary and welfare matters." Yet they seemed to him to become increasingly involved in broader areas, such as personnel and curriculum. These were matters, the superintendent felt, about which they knew little but the administration knew a great deal.

Whereas conscious strategies and specific tactics to stem teacher unrest were lacking in Boston, in San Francisco Spears was far more deliberate in his course. He exercised care to show no favor to either SFFT or SFCTA, the leading contenders for teacher affiliation. At times, he tried to play one group off against the other. If the two disagreed, he would cite their inability to reach consensus and thereby avoid the requests of each. Sometimes he advised the board of education to pay little attention to either, explaining that their proposals were calculated primarily to attract members, not to meet real school problems.

Intervention by state authorities in providing for the Negotiating Council may have complicated the superintendent's life. He preferred his Coordinating Council, which union leaders declared he used as a sounding board for his own policies and as a diversion to keep teachers from pursuing more militant paths. The new mechanism, particularly since both SFFT and TASF refused to participate, inconvenienced the superintendent who had to meet separately with them as well as with the SFCTA-dominated Negotiating Council. Yet the Council in its brief life has not curtailed the superintendent's authority to any considerable degree. And insofar as it has blocked the union's drive for collective bargaining, it may have served Spears better than he was willing to admit.

Administrators agree with their chief about teacher organizations. They see little difference between the local union and association, each of whom they feel is meddling in affairs beyond its competence. Like the superintendent, they oppose sharing administrative power with teacher groups, recalling vividly the happenings in New York City where principals have been displaced by "shop stewards." The only role for teacher organizations, according to this viewpoint, is in the area of salaries and welfare benefits.

The majority of school commissioners are inclined to let administrators worry about teacher participation. One commissioner, a union man, pays lip service to collective bargaining, but does little else to advance the cause of the SFFT. Another, who represents the dominant outlook, feels that the superintendent must run the schools and that teachers have no business attempting a take-over. Still another commissioner believes that teacher groups have a right to take positions and offer proposals, not just on salaries and related matters but on a wide variety of educational questions. In his opinion, collective bargaining will and, indeed, should come sometime in the future.

All in all, the board has steered clear of controversy and conflict. Members see little difference between SFFT and SFCTA, except that the former talks louder and more often. They are not sanguine about the machinery established by the Winton Act, but do not intend to act rashly. With the retirement of Spears in mid-1967, the lay leaders of public education were content to stand fast until his successor in the superintendency either devised a new strategy or adopted the old one for coping with teacher organizations.

The system has waited teachers out. Periodic salary increases, voted by the board, helped Spears deter teacher agitation. The superintendent acted with acumen, benevolently, yet authoritatively. He encouraged the formation of faculty councils in the schools to drain off teacher energies into harmless activities and away from collective action through teacher organizations. He also managed to delay acting on various proposals advanced by SFFT and SFCTA, referring them to his subordinates. They, in turn, adroitly handled teacher representatives. One assistant superintendent worked well with the organizations, another could resist most of their demands.

Unity of purpose, momentum, and action do not come easy to San Francisco's teachers. At the local school level, the thrust of teacher groups is blunted. In the high schools, faculty councils capture the attention of the staffs. Principals in the junior highs, backed by an influential assistant superintendent at headquarters, manage to distribute a disproportionate share of small inducements to their faculties. In the elementary schools, principals rule in dictatorial fashion, and few teachers are willing to take issue or agitate for the union or association. For a number of reasons, the blend of benevolence and authoritarianism, skillfully practiced by central and local educational leaders, has restrained militant behavior by teacher organizations. Only a few in San Francisco were ready to take the risks of forceful action, but their numbers have definitely been growing.

TEACHER COMMUNITIES AND PROBLEMS OF REPRESENTATION

In explaining variations in organizational behavior, the conduct of the school board and superintendent must be taken into account. A blend of benevolence and authoritarianism by educational authorities in Boston and San Francisco has provided little opportunity for teacher rebellion, while resistance by the establishment in New York has evidently furnished ample opportunity. Perhaps, what counts even more than establishment performance is the way the teacher community as a whole perceives group action and group programs. Community norms and styles undoubtedly shape the expectations of local teachers. So do the practices of educational leaders. In turn, the attitudes of teachers toward school affairs and their willingness to engage in combat exert a major influence on what organizational leaders do. On the one hand, it appears that rank-and-file views exercise limits on the militancy of group policy or group action. On the other, it seems that competition to the leadership from activists within an organization creates pressures which propel incumbent leaders to increased militancy.

Rank-and-File Constraints

Unlike teachers in many other places, those in New York City have never seriously restrained the militancy of the organization espousing their interests. From the days when UFT was first formed, the city's teachers rallied to its support, voting for collective bargaining, electing the Federation as agent, striking in substantial numbers on two occasions, becoming members, and expressing the willingness to wage battle before each contract came due. Then in 1967 about three-quarters of New York City's teachers staged a walkout lasting two and one-half weeks, which paralyzed the school system and helped the union advance some steps further toward its goal of equal participation in educational policy-making.

The morale of teachers had been at such low ebb that UFT's job of mobilization, in retrospect at least, appeared relatively easy. In the 1950's and in the first years of the next decade, teacher resentment toward the Livingston Street hierarchy grew with the scandals involving the board and superintendent, the state department's harsh criticism of the city's schools, and the efforts of administrators to halt the union's rise to power. Yet, things were not then as predictable as they now seem to have been. Would teachers actually resort to action? Union leaders were doubtful, because they believed teachers to be conservative, submissive, and wary of a group and activities that might be considered anti-professional. But, as Cole demonstrates, the composition of the New York City teaching force had been changing. By 1960, there existed a large number of teachers, who, however conservative, were predisposed to favor the union's program and were ready for action.[21]

Since the early days, conflict between employers and employees has continued to heighten feelings of union solidarity on the parts of teachers. Even with morale improving as teachers developed a sense of potency, many remained discontented with the administration of the school system. According to one survey of teachers, for instance, nearly all felt that the job they were doing was not appreciated and the prestige they merited was not forthcoming. Almost half thought that the new board of education was no better than the old one which had been ousted. It, too, did not really care about their welfare.[22] UFT leaders diligently encouraged this kind of discontent. In statement after statement and in campaign after campaign they made repeated reference, as is illustrated in the union's literature, to the autocratic and anti-professional structure of the school system.

Despite the passage of time and the opportunity for collaborative arrangements to develop, both UFT and teachers in general maintain a good portion of their early hostility toward the establishment. One indication of this was the Federation's refusal to permit the creation of a separate AFT local to represent the supervisory staff in New York. Another was evidenced in Superintendent Bernard Donovan's public criticism of UFT for what he thought its unreasonable antagonism. Donovan condemned the "cold war" between classroom teachers and their supervisors. He maintained that the "class struggle" pervading life in the system had been cynically nurtured by the union; that it did not reflect realities, but instead was "a straw man set up to emotionalize membership campaigns;" that its only results were to engender bitterness and divert attention from important educational problems.[23] The existence of widespread attitudes of resentment is also suggested by rank-and-file responses to a UFT survey conducted in 1965.[24] While 78 per cent of the respondents reported that they had received supervision from

[21] Stephen Cole, "The Unionization of Teachers: Determinants of Rank-and-File Support," *Sociology of Education*, 41 (Winter, 1968), 67–8, 84–7.

[22] The opinions were sampled by Cole, but are not yet published. He has kindly made his findings available to me.

[23] *Board of Education Press Release*, 315–64/65, May 11, 1965.

[24] About 7,500 teachers, or one-fifth of the staff, responded to the union questionnaire. Sampling procedures were not employed. Results were made available to the author by UFT.

a superior during the year, only 27 per cent expressed the belief that they needed such supervision to help them in their classroom work. Union leaders were of the same view. In the leadership survey, two-thirds of executive board members said that school supervision was poor; three-quarters felt similarly about administration by headquarters.

The education editor of the *New York Times* summed up teacher attitudes well. According to him, the crucial issue underlying the militancy of New York teachers is their hostility toward the local chieftains of public education. In part, this is a reflection of a general city-syndrome of distrust of the "power structure." In part, it results from the belief that "in the vastness of the political and educational system nothing ever changes—least of all for the better."[25] Discontent, distrust, and resentment exist, but they have not led to paralysis. They have been effectively exploited by UFT leaders in the organization's continuing drive for power.

Although teachers have generally applauded UFT's behavior, it would be incorrect to infer that rank-and-file attitudes have had no influence at all. UFT leaders, in anticipation of union elections, have given weight to the wishes of their constituents. In their minds, the wishes of teachers meant that the Federation had to concentrate on the improvement of salaries and related benefits. Although the union pursued other matters as well, it was the salary issue which perennially led to an impasse, a strike threat, or an actual strike.

In late 1962, for example, leaders accepted a no-strike clause in their contract, despite their abhorrence of such a provision. They could do little else, since no issues relating to material benefits were unresolved. And only on these issues would teachers, they felt, give active support. Yet, five years later, UFT could go much further. Salaries again were a major issue, and one of the principal reasons a strike was called when schools opened in September. After several days, the mayor made additional funds available and the salary issue was effectively settled. This time, however, UFT leaders insisted that a written contract satisfy union demands on a number of points before they would recommend that teachers return to school. In effect, then, the 1967 walkout lasted as long as it did not because of a deadlock on salaries but because of contention over questions of educational policy, and by whom such questions should be resolved.

One reason for the emphasis on salaries is the belief by union leaders that money matters are the most important to their constituents. Interestingly, however, their views of what teachers want from collective

[25] Fred Hechinger, *New York Times*, September 6, 1965.

bargaining negotiations, what they themselves desire, and what teachers actually want, are not entirely consonant. This is in part because rank-and-file define bargaining objectives more narrowly than do union leaders. The former think in terms of conditions of employment, the latter conceive of bargaining possibilities more expansively.

In the 1965 union survey, which we have already cited, one question asked teachers to list in order of priority the three most important objectives the UFT should strive to win in collective bargaining negotiations. In our survey of members of the executive board, ten items were listed. Nine of the possible negotiating objectives were ones that had been coded in the union survey and the tenth, not specified in union findings because too few respondents mentioned it, was "greater influence for UFT and UFT chapters." We asked leaders to indicate which they personally considered and which they believed teachers considered the three top priority goals for the union to achieve through collective bargaining. The results of both surveys are shown in Table 24.

TABLE 24

TEACHER AND LEADER VIEWS OF UFT COLLECTIVE BARGAINING PRIORITIES, 1965

	Percentages Choosing Item as One of Three Top-Priority Objectives		
Collective Bargaining Item	Teacher Preferences* (N = 7572)	Leaders' Perceptions of Teacher Preferences† (N = 39)	Leaders' Preferences† (N = 39)
Better pension programs	60	03	03
Smaller class size	48	59	62
Increased health and welfare benefits	19	21	03
More preparation periods, fewer teaching hours	16	23	18
Higher salaries	13	74	62
Solution of disciplinary problems	08	56	36
Better staff rotation procedures	07	00	03
Less clerical work	05	46	26
More and better educational supplies	04	05	21
Greater influence for UFT and UFT chapters	—	10	67

* UFT Classroom Teachers' Questionnaire.

† Leadership survey.

Somewhat surprisingly, since pension provisions are determined by state statute, 60 per cent of the teachers mentioned better pension programs as a top priority item. Almost half felt the same way about smaller class size. Only 13 per cent mentioned salaries. The preferences and perceptions of union leaders are congruent with those of rank-and-file in a number of respects. Corresponding percentages agree on the need for smaller classes and perceive this item as important to teachers. Perceptions are generally in accord also on health and welfare benefits, preparation periods and teaching hours, staff rotation procedures, and educational supplies. In a number of instances, however, views diverge markedly.[26] Leadership attitudes and perceptions, on the one hand, and teacher preferences, on the other, disagree on pension programs, solutions to disciplinary problems, and salaries as major objectives. Furthermore, few teachers apparently care very much about organizational gains, as compared to other gains that might be achieved by bargaining. The lack of saliency here is correctly perceived by leaders, even though two-thirds of them naturally feel that greater influence for UFT is a prime goal.

Despite incongruence between rank-and-file and leadership opinions, the administrative committee and executive board of UFT have been able to exercise discretion in establishing priorities without jeopardizing constituent support. Still, with all the support incumbent leaders have received, they feel some constraints and there are some directions they cannot freely pursue. As Gittell pointed out in her study of educational participation in New York City, UFT leaders see a conflict between educational and professional goals, which they regard highly, and the narrow interests of rank-and-file members. "In some instances," she wrote, "the Union leaders expressed concern that their own positions of power might be threatened if they violated the narrower interests of their membership."[27]

But ways existed to serve the interests of all, as UFT proposals in 1967 demonstrated. Teacher preferences, at least as perceived by Federation leaders, were reflected in bargaining for higher salaries, smaller class size, and the authority for teachers to suspend disruptive children. Leadership preferences, and perhaps those of many members as well, were reflected in bargaining for the expansion of More Effective Schools and the insistence that UFT play a greater part in formulating and

[26] Rank order correlations, based on percentages mentioning each item, show no association between these views. Using Kendall's tau, the coefficients are: teacher preferences and leadership perceptions of teacher preferences, $+.02$; teacher preferences and leadership preferences, $-.20$.

[27] *Op. cit.*, 15.

reviewing educational programs. Given the huge variety of items which might be pursued in collective bargaining, union functionaries had considerable scope for making choices and establishing priorities. Yet this freedom was not unrestrained. It had to be exercised with care and sensitivity.

In contrast to New York, public school pedagogues in Boston and San Francisco have been relatively quiescent. In neither city do they feel particularly aggrieved. Boston teachers respond to the personalism of the system and the benevolence of their superiors with deference and loyalty. They are in no mood for major rebellion. San Francisco teachers share in the general complacency of the community and seem satisfied with inducements given them by the board and administration. With the exception of a few activists, they are overwhelmingly apathetic.

The great majority of teachers in Boston have been serving in the system for a long time. Many began their careers during the Depression. Partly as a consequence of having been given jobs when so many others were unemployed, a large nucleus has developed feelings of deep loyalty toward the system and its managers. These feelings have been reinforced by a solicitous School Committee and paternalistic administration. Therefore, the belief is widespread that teachers' interests will be given proper attention. For preferment, they need only to make themselves known downtown, to be patient, and to keep from rocking the boat. As individuals, they deal on an individual basis, and not by means of collective action, for people, not classes or categories or groups, are what count at Beacon Street.

Although teachers join employee groups and have recently declared in favor of collective bargaining, their concept of the role of organization is extremely narrow. They have engaged in collective action throughout the years, but generally their main concerns have been salaries and related material benefits.[28] They feel that the main obstacle is not the School Committee or administration, but the mayor. His control over the school budget, rather than any lack of empathy for their plight by educational authorities, stands in the way of necessary improvements. Leaders of BTU and BTA reflect their constituents' dissatisfaction with levels of teacher welfare. They are more dissatisfied with salaries than any other educational condition. The next greatest irritant is the inadequacy of building facilities. Both of these items are perceived by teachers and leaders alike to be the prime responsibility of the mayor.

---

[28] Attitudes within the teacher community resemble those of organized labor. Despite its large membership and monetary resources, labor does not play an important part in city politics. This is because Boston's labor movement is "pragmatic and conservative rather than ideological and radical." Edward C. Banfield, *Big City Politics* (New York: Random House, 1965), 48.

In view of the kindnesses they receive from their superiors and the image they have of the penurious mayor, Boston teachers have little cause to make war on educational authorities. Feelings of class strife, if they exist at all, are limited to a small minority in the union. There is no reason, then, to take militant action. Even on seemingly important matters teachers are disinclined to act rashly or take risks. Some are willing to demonstrate, but few are ready to strike or impose similar sanctions. In fact, after BTU picketed the School Department during its successful campaign for sick-leave benefits, one official reported a membership drop of several hundreds. Union members, and other teachers as well, might be willing to demonstrate before City Hall, but they are not inclined to embarrass their employers and friends at 15 Beacon Street.

Group leaders in San Francisco, particularly those in the union, are a different breed than those in Boston. But they are, to a major degree, immobilized by the indifference and apathy which pervades the teaching community. This atmosphere results in large measure from general satisfaction with salaries and benefits. Salaries are higher than those of teachers in most cities of comparable size and they compete favorably with those offered in many affluent communities of the Bay area. Not only salaries, but also teaching conditions and freedom for the individual in the classroom are considered by most teachers to be satisfactory.

The Teachers Association of San Francisco, in reviewing the state of local education in 1963–64, undoubtedly echoed the satisfaction of an overwhelming majority. In its newsletter it commented that the board and superintendent "have not been unkind" and noted that they had provided in a single year a salary increase of almost 5 per cent, the granting of full pay for teachers taking a six-month sabbatical, extra pay for extra-curricular services, and the use of non-professional employees for routine supervision in the elementary schools.[29] Later on, TASF expressed its contentment with the status quo in another vein, commenting on the so-called rebellion of teachers in urban areas:

> It is quite amazing to hear these Easterners express themselves in this manner. . . . What we take for granted in San Francisco today is comparatively unknown to teachers in other sections of the United States. They are just catching up.[30]

Naturally, teachers talk about improvements when the question of reform is raised. SFCTA asked teachers in a survey it ran to rate items that should be given top priority by the new Negotiating Council. Almost

[29] *TASF Bulletin*, October, 1964.
[30] *Ibid.*, December-January, 1965.

1,000 individuals responded. Most mentioned class size. Elementary and junior high teachers were also concerned about discipline, annual promotions, and salaries, in that order. Senior high teachers ranked clerical help, discipline, and salary to be next in importance to class size.[31] But they are not about to resort to collective action to achieve change.

SFCTA members, according to one association officer, are extremely apathetic. A large majority are interested mainly in the types of services, such as insurance coverage, provided by the organization. But leaders feel they have to take members as they come if they are to build their group's strength and overcome the union challenge. The predominant view among Association followers is "let the leadership do it." Among leaders, the feeling prevails that they cannot move too fast and cannot move at all without carefully taking the pulse of the membership.

Association activists think that SFFT, in contrast, is able to take a stand on any issue without the risk of membership disavowal. In part, this is true. Federation followers, like their leaders, are liberal with words. They may be more attached to their group than mere "insurance members," but on the whole they also are rather apathetic. Many live outside of the city and are consequently less involved in the general problems of urban education and less able to attend union meetings. They look to their leaders, and not to themselves, to accomplish whatever has to be done to further their interests. "This is a paternalistic system from top to bottom," one dissident member of SFFT explained. "We've grown up in it, we've accommodated to it." If the board and superintendent need prodding, then let the union president and his associates do it—they have talked effectively in the past; let them continue in the same manner now.

The passivity of teachers to whom the union must appeal has influenced the behavior of leaders, if not their objectives and preferred tactics. SFFT presidents have felt severely restricted by rank-and-file indifference. Fearful of pressing, they move cautiously ahead. Recently, when they did act, rank-and-file support was limited. SFFT picketed the school department on the matter of grievance procedures, but afterwards a number of teachers informed their leaders that they refused to walk a picket line again merely to obtain grievance machinery. The union also launched a strike in 1968, but only one-quarter of the system's teachers responded.

Competitive Pressures

Frequently, competition between rival groups engenders increased militancy in both. Such, of course, has been one outcome of the national

---

[31] *SFCTA Update*, February, 1966.

competition between NEA and AFT. It applies also to individual locales where each contestant for membership and representational power attempts to offer more than the other. Among the organizations in the cities under present consideration, competition between rivals has primarily had the effect of impelling non-union groups toward greater militancy than might have been the case otherwise. What concerns us presently, however, is a different kind of competition—the challenge by organizational activists who demand more militant behavior than established leaders propose or rank-and-file would seem to condone.

Top leadership of the United Federation of Teachers has never been entirely secure in its incumbency. Internal opposition and internal pressure from a more radical faction have confronted the Cogen-Shanker majority from the outset of UFT's life. Although challengers have never swept an election for officers of the union, the impact of a semi-organized opposition has been important.[32] By provision of the UFT constitution, elections are held annually. At-large officers, such as the president, secretary and some executive board members, run in even-numbered years. Those who are elected by unionists in their respective divisions, such as the vice presidents for elementary, junior high, academic high, vocational high schools, and executive board members, run in odd-numbered years.

In 1962 the internal opposition was led by Roger Parente. One of the original organizers of UFT and a vice-president for vocational high schools, Parente's group spurred the union to increased militancy and contested the election of officers. Twenty-five candidates, headed by President Cogen, banded together as a Unity slate and won handily. Cogen polled more than two-thirds of the vote and Shanker, running for secretary, polled almost three-fifths. By the following year, opposition to the incumbents was better organized. Calling itself SPUR, it managed to capture the vice-presidency for junior high schools in the divisional elections. This put intense pressure on the Unity leadership to strive hard for gains in collective bargaining that year.

With Cogen about to contest for the presidency of the American Federation of Teachers, Shanker headed the Unity committee in 1964. Ben Mazen, a former vice president, led the opposition SPUR slate of 21 candidates. Again Unity swept the election, taking all of the positions. Shanker received almost two-thirds of the 11,390 ballots cast for president while five other members of his ticket received from two-thirds to three-quarters of the vote. The following year, Sol Jaffe and Ben Mazen led a group called STAFF and challenged Shanker's party. Again the

[32] UFT is one of the few labor unions in which "outs" periodically challenge "ins." Another is the International Typographical Union. See Seymour Martin Lipset *et al.*, *Union Democracy* (New York: Doubleday Anchor, 1962).

outcome was one-sided. With 36 positions to be filled, Unity elected 34 of its candidates. One independent won. So did Mazen, who was elected to the executive board and became a lonely in-house critic. The leadership had consolidated its power by 1965; much, but not all, of the pressure from an organized opposition had diminished.[33]

Annual elections are not the only means by which the leadership is held accountable. Another device permits the more militant wing of UFT to impress its views on the administrative committee and executive board during periods between elections. A delegate assembly, composed of one representative for each ten members of a school chapter, meets monthly and has authority to overrule leadership recommendations. During the life of UFT, the delegate assembly has proved to be more aggressively inclined than the top leadership. Its very existence has undoubtedly impelled Cogen and Shanker to greater militancy than the rank-and-file might have desired.

In one outstanding instance the assembly, later backed by a membership vote, turned down a recommendation of the leadership. Last-minute talks were held in 1962 between union representatives and Mayor Wagner to halt the strike scheduled in April. When the mayor promised to appoint a fact-finding commission to devise a solution to the impasse, the executive board recommended that the strike be postponed a week until the commission made its report. The delegate assembly rebuffed Cogen and his allies, postponed the strike only one day, and called for a referendum by the membership. At a mass meeting of members Cogen argued against an immediate walk-out, but Parente and Deputy President Samuel Hochberg favored action the next morning. By a vote of 2,544 to 2,231, the opposition's resolution to strike on April 11 carried and events then took their course. When, in return for certain assurances, leaders called the strike off after one day, criticism from members of the delegate assembly was intense.

With rare exception, however, UFT's leadership has received strong support for its policies and actions from delegates and the mass of its membership alike. Everyone favored combat as a means of resolving contractual disputes. In 1962, 1963, 1965, and 1967, rank-and-file

---

[33] In the most recent leadership election, Shanker won an unprecedented victory, gaining about 78 per cent of the 24,628 votes cast. Two challengers—one heading the STAFF slate and the other leading the New Coalition—split the remainder rather evenly. The major issue of the campaign was the union's position on decentralization or community control of the city's schools. Shanker's group favored moderate and gradual decentralization. The New Coalition rejected UFT's previous position and supported thorough community control. The outcome surely indicates that the incumbent leadership has faithfully represented the views of union members.

members were as agreed as their delegates and leaders on the need to strike. In referenda during these years, 85 to 98 per cent of those voting cast ballots in favor of proposed strikes. On the adoption of the "no contract–no work" policy, 85 per cent of those voting supported the proposal.

Membership support was also overwhelming on the acceptance of executive board recommendations to approve negotiated contracts. But on these decisions—to reach agreement rather than to take action—the delegate assembly was less united. Larger proportions of its members than of the leadership or rank and file expressed dissatisfaction with negotiated outcomes and wanted to hold out for more than was obtained. In 1962, on the first contract, only six of 38 members of the executive board opposed the final recommendations of UFT's negotiating committee. Only 10 per cent of the union's membership voted against acceptance. However, 35 per cent of representatives in the assembly opposed the contract. On the second contract, negotiated the following year, the executive board split the same way. Only 3 per cent of the union's voting membership cast ballots in opposition. But again 35 per cent of the assembly wanted to hold out for something better. In 1965, voting on the contract was along similar lines: about 10 per cent of the executive board, 15 per cent of the membership, and 30 per cent of the delegate assembly dissented from majority agreement. In the 1967 vote on the contract, the executive board was more deeply divided, with 13 members opposed. But once again the greatest opposition came from the delegate assembly, where one-third of the representatives voted against accepting the contract.[34]

Union leaders, as elections and referenda indicate, have been able to satisfy passive and active members alike. Despite a split over the 1967 contract, it is fair to say that a generally united leadership has withstood continuing factional opposition from a small minority within. It has at the same time been able to win rather solid support for its policies and campaigns from the mass membership. Radicals in the delegate assembly, however, pose a constant threat. They have the potential to overrule the leadership, and thereby keep UFT from abandoning its militancy or becoming too friendly in its dealings with the educational establishment.

Factionalism in the Boston Teachers Union has produced corresponding results. BTU's top leadership, far more conservative than UFT's,

[34] One method of comparing dissent is by computing indices of cohesion for the executive board, the membership, and the delegate assembly. On the basis of the voting on contracts, reported above, the average cohesion of each group respectively is 67, 78, and 34. The measurement used is the Rice Index of Cohesion. See Lee F. Anderson *et al.*, *Legislative Roll-Call Analysis* (Evanston: Ill.: Northwestern University Press, 1966), 32–5.

has for the past five years or so been under pressure from a more militant wing within. Until 1962, a small group rotated top leadership positions in the union. In that year, a change occurred, due largely to events in New York City and the arrival in Boston of a professional organizer sent by AFT. Militancy began to increase among high school teachers and the faculty of the city's most prestigious school, Boston Latin, began forming the nucleus of a liberal faction within BTU. For a while, the influence of the professional organizer and the militants, who worked together, was predominant. A vigorous campaign to win sick-leave benefits was launched. It included demonstrations and picketing, rare phenomena among teachers in Boston. After the campaign proved successful, the organizer and militant wing thought seriously of escalation in order to achieve benefits and collective bargaining procedures. They were not averse to striking if necessary.

Conservatives in the leadership recaptured control, however. The AFT organizer moved to another job and any escalation was effectively blocked. Nevertheless, the impact of this upsurge could not be denied. Since 1964, the Boston Teachers Union has demonstrated greater militancy than it had shown in the years prior to 1962. A liberal faction, although a distinct minority, continued to agitate from within. It might not hope to gain control, but its presence would be felt as BTU embarked upon its new career as bargaining agent for the city's teachers.

Internal competition also affects the life of the teacher union in San Francisco. Here, the motivations of incumbent leaders and their opponents are not very dissimilar. But there are differences over the kinds of action to be launched and matters of timing. A radical opposition, called the Activists, is in favor of striking. Top leaders, however sympathetic to the abstract idea of a strike to achieve SFFT ends, are dubious about its practicality in San Francisco. According to them, the Activists are irresponsible—hot-headed and too anxious to act without giving enough thought to the probable consequences of precipitate action.

The Federation's leaders fear teacher reactions to increased militancy by their group. Neither collective bargaining nor improved grievance machinery appear to them to mean much to San Francisco teachers. Therefore, they prefer to wait. Their strategy is not to behave rashly but rather to stand apart from the Negotiating Council, buy time, and press a program that might attract about 400 additional members as well as sufficient support to win a bargaining election.

Activists are impatient with merely suggesting programs. They argue that relations between SFFT and the school board have deteriorated alarmingly, and that the Winton Act created an intolerable obstacle to union representation of teachers. As a result, the Federation's ability to influence educational affairs is not only static but is actually less than at any time in the last fifteen years. Furthermore, they maintain, the membership favors direct action to secure group demands, as was evidenced by its willingness to participate in public demonstrations. In view of this situation, Activists have insisted on an all-out drive for collective bargaining and preparation for a strike, which might be necessary to force the board to agree to an election.

SFFT radicals could not persuade the majority leadership of the correctness of their perceptions or the practicality of their proposals, but they kept the issue of action very much alive. In 1966, for the first time in SFFT's history, two parties contested an election. An Activist slate ran against a Committee to Elect Effective Leadership. Although activists did not feel sufficiently strong to contest the office of president with an extremely popular moderate leader, they did run candidates for fourteen other positions. Only one was elected, and this one because moderates put forward only six candidates for seven positions as delegates to the City Labor Council. Of about 450 votes cast in five two-man races, candidates running on the Effective Leadership slate polled on the average of 80 per cent. Only about 90 union members voted consistently for the opposition. This was hardly enough of a showing to gain control, but the number was sufficient to indicate to SFFT leaders the potential power of the minority within.

Two years later the union did strike, and after the mayor's quick intervention a preference poll was conducted to determine whether teachers wanted a single organization to represent them in negotiations. No group received a majority of the approximately 4,500 teachers who were employed in the system. SFCTA, the local association, came closest with 2,061 votes. SFFT, however, won only 1,834 votes.[35] The city's teachers were still not ready to choose.

CONTRASTS IN GROUP BEHAVIOR

In Chapter IV we described three contrasting patterns of teacher politics: coinflict in New York City; accommodation in Boston; and maneuver in San Francisco. In the present chapter we attempted an explanation of why patterns differ from one city to another. An important reason, cited earlier, involves differences among leadership orientations toward goals, strategies, and tactics. But an explanation of organizational behavior requires moving beyond organizational motivation. Opportunities for action, in addition to leadership militancy, must exist. Whether they do or not, as seen from the vantage of group leaders, de-

[35] *American Teacher*, April, 1968.

pends upon a number of factors operative in the local environment—the styles of the political community, the conduct of educational chieftains, and the dispositions of teachers and teacher activists in the school system. No single one is decisive.

Militant behavior is encouraged by a congruence of factors in New York City. The competitiveness of political life and the almost perpetual conflict which keep things unsettled furnish a natural setting for a combative teacher organization. A rigid, hierarchical school system in which educational authorities strenuously resist UFT encroachments upon their prerogatives provides further steam for union militancy. Teachers become resentful, union radicals become impassioned, and leaders learn that forceful tactics are the best means of achieving group goals and maintaining personal power.

In Boston, by contrast, congruent factors serve to deter aggressive behavior by teacher groups. Community styles stress personalism. Large majorities, particularly those concerned with school affairs, agree that whatever disputes exist can best be settled amicably. Elections of School Committee members provide a safety valve and also foster responsiveness to teacher claims. The system of public education is led by people whose benevolence induces deference and loyalty on the part of the teaching staff. Except for a few activists in BTU, who are influenced by the goals, methods, and accomplishments of the New York Federation, the overwhelming number of teachers are willing to go along with the system and gratefully accept agreements reached by their leaders in the union and at Beacon Street.

San Francisco presents a somewhat different picture. Union leaders are not content with educational arrangements, but complacency pervades the community and renders many teachers apathetic to group efforts to mobilize them. A combination of paternalism and authoritarianism which infuses relationships in the system makes it even more difficult for organizations to spur teachers to action. Content with life and its rewards, members of the teaching community are willing to let their representatives maneuver for advantage but are reluctant to commit themselves to one specific group or to battle with the local chieftains of public education.

Militant attitudes and behavior are likely to persist in New York City. Just as likely, moderation should continue to prevail in Boston. In San Francisco, however, change is very possible. The environment here is less structured, the superintendency may be undergoing transformation, and SFFT's leadership—incumbents and opponents alike—are pledged to militant goals and militant tactics.

VI. The Government of Education

In view of the increased assertiveness and organization of teachers today, we might expect power to have shifted somewhat in their favor. Certainly, school authorities have been forced to revise the rules of the educational game in order to provide expanded opportunities for participation by teacher organizations. But just how much recent changes have meant in terms of educational policy-making remains to be seen.

To properly treat the organizational influence of teachers, it is necessary first to examine how educational power is generally distributed in large city school systems. In other words, before assessing the contemporary role of teacher organizations, we shall try to respond to the question that Neal Gross posed some years ago—"Who runs our schools?"[1] Thorough analysis of educational power in five cities is not our objective. Yet, attention must be paid to the subject. For the policy-making power of teacher organizations can best be understood by comparative analysis—not only comparisons among cities but also among major participants in the government of public education.

PERCEPTIONS OF POWER

How is educational power distributed in New York City, Boston, Chicago, San Francisco, and Atlanta? Which participants have the greatest say in determining public school policy in these large cities? What about teacher groups; how do they compare in influence to other major participants? Do differences in the distribution of power depend upon the types of policy being decided? Few would deny that these questions are important ones.

In an effort to suggest answers to them in this and the following chapter, we have relied on several different kinds of information: first, the perceptions of the leaders of nine teacher organizations in the five cities as revealed in our leadership survey;[2] second, the expert opinions of school system investigators in the cities under consideration;[3] third,

1 *Who Runs Our Schools?* (New York: John Wiley and Sons, 1958).
2 See Chapter III, above, for a description of the survey.
3 Research associates, participating in the Large City Education Systems Study

123

the author's own field study and interviewing in New York, Boston, and San Francisco; and fourth, other analyses, particularly of New York and Chicago.

The basic data for systematic comparisons are the perceptions of teacher leaders. The operating assumption is that members of the executive boards of various teacher groups are in a good position to evaluate the influence of major participants in public education. Several items in the leadership questionnaire asked for assessments of whether several listed individuals and groups had "much," "some," or "little" power in deciding various kinds of educational policy. Responses, particularly when supplemented by other evidence, offer a useful map of the distribution of power, among participants and by city and policy domain.

We are well aware of the conceptual and measurement difficulties which challenge students of "power."[4] Scientific discretion would suggest that the concept be avoided. But this hardly seems possible if one is dealing with the potency of teacher groups today. Teacher leaders are accustomed to thinking about power in the school system. It is striking that when they comment casually on the subject they speak essentially the same language. Terms like "power," "influence," and "voice" all have wide currency and meaningful elements in common. For present purposes, they are presumed to be equivalent and to relate to degrees of control over policy choices or decisions.

Another problem should be mentioned. Our procedures resemble those used in many "community power" studies, all of which involve some variation of asking individuals to assess the relative power of other individuals or groups. In basing comparisons upon the views of teacher leaders, we are dealing with the "reputations" certain individuals and groups have and not necessarily with the actual power they exercise.[5]

---

conducted by Syracuse University, have been very helpful in confirming the accuracy of teacher perceptions. Each associate spent about two years working in the central office of the school department and studying various aspects of a particular city system.

[4] For a summary analysis of conceptual approaches and measurement procedures, see James G. March, "The Power of Power," in David Easton, ed., *Varieties of Political Theory* (Englewood Cliffs: Prentice-Hall, 1966), 39–70. For a superbly reasoned statement of conceptual and empirical difficulties, see Robert A. Dahl, "The Concept of Power," in Nelson W. Polsby *et al.*, eds., *Politics and Social Life* (Boston: Houghton Mifflin, 1963), 106–19.

[5] Whether or not reputational power and actual power are the same is a subject that has been debated extensively. See, for example, the following: William V. D'Antonio and Eugene C. Erickson, "The Reputational Technique as a Measure of Community Power," *American Sociological Review*, XXVII (June, 1962), 362–76; Nelson W. Polsby, *Community Power and Political Theory* (New Haven: Yale University Press, 1963); Robert Presthus, *Men at the Top* (New York: Oxford University Press, 1964); Arnold M. Rose, *The Power Structure* (New York: Oxford University Press, 1966), 255–97; and Raymond E. Wolfinger,

Furthermore, unlike other reputational analyses, this one bases its findings about power on the views of people occupying one position only, that of nominal leadership in a teachers group. Power distributions as perceived by organization leaders may, of course, differ from those seen by people in other positions—board members, principals, newspaper reporters, citizens—in the same city. Either or several sets of perceptions conceivably could be out of line with reality.

Although their accuracy cannot be proved, we believe that leadership perceptions provide valuable information about influence in educational affairs. In view of other evidence, they loom not merely as images but as fairly good indications of who has power over school policy. With few exceptions, leadership perceptions, the opinions of investigators in the cities, the evaluations of other observers, and the author's field research are mutually supportive.[6] Nor is there any reason to think that some teacher leaders perceive power differently than others, merely as a result of different experiences and attitudes. We have shown in Chapter III that leaders differ in their goal and tactical orientations according to several factors, most prominently organizational affiliation. But within each city there are no such patterns in perceptions of power. Group membership, satisfaction, age and experience, and teaching position make no difference.[7]

Our analysis concentrates on core participants in education. These we arbitrarily define as the mayor, board of education, superintendent, administrative bureaucracy at headquarters, school principals, and teacher organizations. Except for the mayor, whose role is of special interest,

---

"Reputation and Reality in the Study of 'Community Power'," *American Sociological Review*, XXV (October, 1960), 636–44. In general, our procedure is similar to the "issue-specific reputational method," advocated by Terry N. Clark, in "The Concept of Power," Terry N. Clark, ed., *Community Structure and Decision-Making: Comparative Analyses* (San Francisco: Chandler, 1968), 77–8.

[6] It should be noted that, in one way or another, nearly every study of power depends on someone's perceptions for its conclusions. Even those which employ the decision-making process or issue-analysis approach, and not reputations, rely on the reports of participants, newspaper accounts, or on the investigator's own observations. In either case, the perceptions of individuals concerning participants who had initiated proposals that were adopted, vetoed proposals initiated by others, or offered proposals that were turned down are extremely important. One of the best examples of an excellent power study, which nevertheless fails to come to grips with the perceptional problem, is Robert A. Dahl, *Who Governs?* (New Haven: Yale University Press, 1961). See especially the author's methodological appendix explaining how he determines "as far as possible, who *really* influences decisions," 332–36.

[7] In San Francisco, for instance, similar proportions of SFFT and SFCTA leaders assign "much" power to the same individuals and groups. In New York, elementary teachers are just as likely as secondary ones to recognize the major role of the mayor in salary determinations.

all the others are either legally or professionally involved in various aspects of education. Few would deny the likely significance of these core participants. But some may question whether they exhaust power holders in a school system. What about other individuals and groups whose influence may be as great or greater: business and labor organizations; civic and parents associations; civil rights, ethnic, and neighborhood groups; the local "power elite;" and the mass public? The possible influence of any one or a number of them cannot be discounted.

Some investigators, especially those studying smaller school systems, have uncovered illustrations of influence by informal members of power elites.[8] Others have demonstrated that ethnic groups, various categoric groups, and community electorates exercise influence over school decisions.[9] Still others have shown how and to what extent civil rights groups and "neighborhood school" coalitions have played a part in the formulation of certain educational policies.[10] In New York City, particularly, neighborhood groups have recently been accorded substantial authority. They play an increasingly important role. Nevertheless, there is reason to believe that in large cities, although perhaps not in small towns or suburbs, continuing power resides with those who are at the core of the system—those whose concerns are direct, whose motivations persist, and whose positions allow frequent opportunity to influence policy decisions.[11]

[8] Ralph B. Kimbrough, *Political Power and Educational Decision-Making* (Chicago: Rand McNally, 1964), and Arthur J. Vidich and Joseph Bensman, *Small Town in Mass Society* (New York: Doubleday Anchor, 1960), 174–201. An excellent analysis of indirect influence is Robert L. Crain and James J. Vanecko, "Elite Influence in School Desegregation," in James Q. Wilson, ed., *City Politics and Public Policy* (New York: John Wiley and Sons, 1968), 127–48.

[9] Robert E. Agger, "The Politics of Local Education: A Comparative Study of Community Decision-Making," in Donald E. Tope, ed., *A Forward Look—The Preparation of School Administrators 1970* (Eugene, Oregon: Bureau of Educational Research, University of Oregon, 1960), 131–72; Herbert J. Gans, *The Levittowners* (New York: Pantheon, 1967), 86–103; Louis H. Masotti, "Patterns of White and Nonwhite School Referenda Participation and Support: Cleveland, 1960–64," in Marilyn Gittell, ed., *Educating an Urban Population* (Beverly Hills, Calif.: Sage Publications, 1967), 240–55; and Alan Rosenthal, "The Special Case of Public Education," in Richard T. Frost, ed., *Cases in State and Local Government* (Englewood Cliffs: Prentice-Hall, 1961), 62–75.

[10] Robert L. Crain, *School Desegregation in the North* (Chicago: National Opinion Research Center, University of Chicago, 1966); Robert L. Crain and David Street, "School Desegregation and School Decision-Making," *Urban Affairs Quarterly*, II (September, 1966), 64–82; David Rogers, "Obstacles to School Desegregation in New York City," in Gittell, *op. cit.*, 155–84; and Bert E. Swanson, *The Struggle for Equality* (New York: Hobbs, Dorman, 1966).

[11] Cf., Edward C. Banfield, *Political Influence* (New York: Free Press, 1961); Dahl, *Who Governs?, op. cit.;* and Wallace S. Sayre and Herbert Kaufman, *Governing New York City* (New York: Russell Sage, 1960). On education, specifically,

Our major objective, in any case, is not to consider every possible influential or to describe as fully as possible patterns of educational influence. It is mainly to see how the power of teacher organizations compares to that of some other recognized participants, each of whom has a potential voice in one or several areas of policy-making.

Since power often tends to develop along subject matter or functional lines and since each area of governmental activity tends to develop its own distinct power structure, we shall again examine general domains of policy. As was the procedure in Chapter III, our method here is to examine how influence is distributed in the areas of salaries, personnel, curriculum and instruction, and the organization of the school system. Presumably, distributions will differ from one domain to the next, with one participant having more to say about one kind of policy but less to say about another. Here, too, we are not exhaustive.

Perceptions of teacher leaders on matters such as school construction, working conditions, and integration have not been solicited. Power may vary in these areas as well. Take school integration, for example. There is reason to believe that school boards today play a greater role in developing integration policies than they do in establishing other kinds of policies.[12] Admittedly, then, we cannot confidently generalize from salary, personnel, curriculum, and system organization to the entire school system. But these do constitute more than a trivial range of issues. So we ask indulgence for occasional generalization—usually buttressed by other information—which extends beyond leadership perceptions of power in these four domains.

Distributions of Power

The four sections of Table 25 report teacher-leader perceptions of *who* has power with regard to *what*. Each section pertains to one policy area and presents percentages of teacher leaders in each city attributing "much" power to each participant. According to these perceptions, educational policy-making is dominated by those legally entrusted with the

---

see: Marilyn Gittell and T. Edward Hollander, *Six Urban School Districts* (New York: Praeger, 1968); Robert L. Crain, *The Politics of School Desegregation* (Chicago: Aldine, 1968); and Alan Rosenthal, ed., *Governing Education: A Reader on Politics, Power, and Public School Policy* (New York: Doubleday Anchor, forthcoming).

12 According to Crain, the school board sets the tone of the integration decision, while the superintendent plays a less important role. *The Politics of School Desegregation, op. cit.,* 358. Also Peter Schrag, *Village School Downtown* (Boston: Beacon Press, 1967), and Marilyn Gittell, *Participants and Participation* (New York: Center for Urban Education, 1967). Especially with respect to integration, there is often a huge gap between policy-making and policy-execution; between the adoption of policy and its implementation.

TABLE 25

THE DISTRIBUTION OF EDUCATIONAL POWER

Core Participants	Percentages of Teacher Leaders Attributing "Much" Power to Core Participants in Five Cities*				
	New York (N = 39)	Boston (N = 36)	Chicago (N = 37)	San Francisco (N = 53)	Atlanta (N = 20)
Salary Policy					
Mayor	82	94	29	26	10
Board	51	60	62	100	85
Superintendent	44	20	87	48	90
Bureaucracy	05	23	09	02	25
Principals	00	03	00	00	00
Teacher Organizations†					
AFT Affiliated	63	25	03	12	—
NEA Affiliated	—	—	03	04	15
Independent	—	00	—	00	—
Personnel Policy					
Mayor	03	06	14	12	00
Board	55	80	33	61	65
Superintendent	100	86	92	87	90
Bureaucracy	56	66	40	56	35
Principals	10	06	03	25	05
Teacher Organizations†					
AFT Affiliated	08	11	06	04	—
NEA Affiliated	—	—	00	02	10
Independent	—	00	—	00	—
Curriculum Policy					
Mayor	03	00	00	00	00
Board	32	51	22	46	45
Superintendent	84	97	92	94	85
Bureaucracy	82	85	69	56	60
Principals	26	26	14	28	25
Teacher Organizations†					
AFT Affiliated	00	09	00	00	—
NEA Affiliated	—	—	00	04	05
Independent	—	00	—	02	—
School Organization Policy					
Mayor	16	12	18	08	05
Board	81	89	53	82	70
Superintendent	87	86	89	89	95
Bureaucracy	47	63	35	34	45
Principals	05	11	08	14	05
Teacher Organizations†					
AFT Affiliated	00	11	00	00	—
NEA Affiliated	—	—	00	02	05
Independent	—	00	—	02	—

* Numbers of respondents vary slightly due to non-responses on some items.

† Assessments are based on the views of all teacher leaders in the city, not only those who head the particular organization classified. Leaders of each group, in short, rate the power of their rival as well as their own power.

responsibility. The board of education, theoretically entitled to set policy, and the superintendent, as the board's executive officer, share predominant power. Mayors, too, have some say, but only on particular matters and only in some cities. Headquarters bureaucracies, as one might expect, play a substantial role in personnel and curriculum, but principals and teacher organizations have little say in most matters of educational policy.

Salaries: In New York and Boston there is consensus on the influential role of the mayor. There is less agreement on the power of the board of education. Elsewhere, the mayor appears to have little control over teacher salaries. In Atlanta, nearly all leaders agree that the board and superintendent jointly determine salary policy. In Chicago, strength resides mainly with the superintendency, secondarily with the board. By contrast, in San Francisco every leader respondent asserts the primacy of the board of education. As far as teacher organizations are concerned, only UFT has an influential part in setting salaries. Few leaders in cities other than New York think that local teacher groups have much to say even about an issue as close to their interests as this one.

Personnel: Extremely few of our respondents attribute much power to mayor, principals, or teacher groups. Nearly all agree on the strength of the superintendent. Only in Boston is his position contested by an aggressive school board. In three cities—New York, Boston, and San Francisco—more than half the leaders also attribute significant power to headquarters bureaucracies when policy involves personnel.

Curriculum: Similar perceptions hold for the distribution of power in the domain of curriculum and instruction. Hardly a leader ascribes influence to either mayors or teacher organizations. Here, too, superintendents seem to dominate, with school boards playing lesser roles—particularly in New York and Chicago. Administrative chieftains at the central office are thought to wield substantial influence, and in New York and Boston they share power with the superintendent.

Organization of the School System: A few, but certainly not many respondents, perceive mayoral involvement in the various issues affecting the organization of the district school system. Fewer attribute much power to principals and hardly any believe teacher groups potent in this domain. Once again the superintendent emerges as the key figure, although laymen on boards of education also are thought powerful. In New York, San Francisco, and Atlanta policy-making on organizational matters seems to be shared exclusively by superintendent and board. In Boston the bureaucracy also is believed to have a considerable voice. In Chicago, on these issues as on others, the superintendent stands alone in terms of power.

Relative Power

Examining perceptional data in the above manner, while useful as an introduction, is not sufficient. Scrutiny of percentages of responses does not tell enough about differences in the power of core participants.

Recognition of relative power is necessary. Especially in assessing the contemporary influence of teacher organizations, we must inquire not only whether they are believed to have power, but also how much more or less they have than other contestants. Differences count.

If we are to make comparisons among cities and among policy areas, some method of estimating differences would be helpful. For instance, the fact that 100 per cent of the respondents in New York and 92 per cent in Chicago feel that the superintendent has much to say about personnel policy does not tell us enough. To appreciate the superintendent's authoritative position, we must at the same time take cognizance of the power of his nearest competitors. In New York, roughly half of the teacher leaders believe the board and bureaucracy powerful in this domain, whereas in Chicago only a third feel similarly. This suggests that the superintendent's position in these two cities is not quite the same.

In order to standardize power attributions and facilitate comparison, we have constructed an index of relative power. The index is based on the perceptions of teacher leaders. In each policy domain, each of the six participants has been assigned a score of two for every attribution of "much" power and one for every attribution of "some" power. Scores have been added, giving a total power attribution figure for each city. Let us assume for the sake of analysis that if power were equally parcelled among the six participants each would score one-sixth of the total. Some, of course, score higher and others lower. The ratio of a participant's perceived power to his expected power constitutes his index of relative power within a city's educational system.

Power attribution scores and indices of relative power are reported in Table 26 for core participants in each policy domain of the five large cities. An example of index calculations may be helpful at this point. Take the power of the San Francisco school board on salary. The total attribution in this domain is 289. This means that if power were equally divided among the six participants each would score 48. The board has a score of 104, based on 52 responses attributing to it "much" power. The ratio of 104 to 48, or 2.17, is the relative power index of the board in this policy area.

In succeeding tables in this and the following chapter we go one step further, reporting not indices of relative power but rather differences between the indices of specified participants. Thus, for example, the difference between the index of relative salary power of the San Francisco board and superintendent is 0.65, in favor of the former. Despite these calculations, we do not want to give the impression of precision in measuring power. Our object is to make comparison by city and by domain somewhat easier and clearer.

TABLE 26

AN INDEX OF RELATIVE EDUCATIONAL POWER

Core Participant and Policy Domain	New York		Boston		Chicago		San Francisco		Atlanta	
	PAS*	IRP†	PAS	IRP	PAS	IRP	PAS	IRP	PAS	IRP
Mayor										
Salary	67	1.63	68	1.79	35	1.06	48	1.00	9	0.41
Personnel	13	0.30	15	0.38	19	0.54	25	0.42	3	0.15
Curriculum	6	0.16	4	0.11	8	0.23	9	0.16	2	0.10
Organization	28	0.67	18	0.46	24	0.67	28	0.52	5	0.24
Board										
Salary	56	1.37	56	1.47	59	1.79	104	2.17	37	1.68
Personnel	57	1.33	63	1.62	42	1.20	77	1.31	30	1.50
Curriculum	41	1.08	47	1.24	35	1.00	68	1.24	26	1.24
Organization	67	1.60	66	1.69	54	1.50	91	1.69	34	1.62
Superintendent										
Salary	48	1.17	35	0.92	69	2.09	73	1.52	38	1.73
Personnel	76	1.77	65	1.67	71	2.03	97	1.64	38	1.90
Curriculum	69	1.82	69	1.82	71	2.03	102	1.85	37	1.76
Organization	69	1.64	64	1.64	70	1.94	98	1.81	39	1.86
Bureaucracy										
Salary	12	0.29	31	0.82	17	0.52	15	0.31	19	0.86
Personnel	58	1.35	56	1.44	46	1.31	78	1.32	24	1.20
Curriculum	68	1.79	63	1.66	60	1.71	78	1.42	31	1.48
Organization	51	1.21	54	1.38	44	1.22	63	1.17	26	1.24
Principals										
Salary	3	0.07	5	0.13	3	0.09	8	0.17	10	0.45
Personnel	27	0.63	20	0.51	16	0.46	55	0.93	14	0.70
Curriculum	41	1.08	32	0.84	29	0.83	53	0.96	20	0.95
Organization	18	0.43	19	0.49	18	0.50	37	0.69	14	0.67
Teacher Organization										
Salary	59	1.44	30	0.79	16	0.48	41	0.85	21	0.95
Personnel	28	0.65	17	0.44	19	0.54	20	0.34	10	0.50
Curriculum	4	0.11	14	0.37	7	0.20	19	0.35	9	0.43
Organization	18	0.43	12	0.31	7	0.19	8	0.15	7	0.33
Totals										
Salary	245	(41)‡	225	(38)	199	(33)	289	(48)	134	(22)
Personnel	259	(43)	236	(39)	213	(35)	352	(59)	119	(20)
Curriculum	229	(38)	229	(38)	210	(35)	329	(55)	125	(21)
Organization	251	(42)	233	(39)	217	(36)	325	(54)	125	(21)

* Power attribution score.
† Index of relative power.
‡ Expected power attribution.

INDEPENDENCE FROM MAYORAL CONTROL

American educators are in the vanguard of those public-spirited citizens who inveigh loudly and campaign vigorously against "political interference" in the management of local public education. The separation of politics and education has become an article of faith among schoolmen and publics alike. Nevertheless, there is evidence that the separation is bridged in practice, if not in theory. To stress the obvious, it is bridged differently in different places and with regard to different issues.

It may be assumed that mayors of large cities, as top political leaders wishing to maximize their power, would intervene frequently in educational affairs. This is not the case. Even when school systems and municipal governments are formally intertwined, the facts of political life buttress separation. Mayoral detachments from school politics may seem surprising, but as two investigators point out, ". . . the mayor who tries to run the schools would be taking a great risk for a very small reward."[13]

Whatever the formal arrangements, the school systems of New York, Boston, Chicago, San Francisco, and Atlanta share in common a large measure of independence. In Table 27 we present a comparative descrip-

TABLE 27
RELATIVE INDEPENDENCE FROM MAYORAL CONTROL*

Policy Domain	New York	Boston	Chicago	San Francisco	Atlanta
Salary	−0.26	−0.32	+1.03	+1.17	+1.32
Personnel	+1.47	+1.29	+1.49	+1.22	+1.75
Curriculum	+1.66	+1.71	+1.80	+1.69	+1.66
School System Organization	+0.97	+1.23	+1.27	+1.29	+1.62

* A plus indicates that the difference between the relative power indices of the mayor and the superintendent or board runs in the direction of the superintendent or board; a minus indicates the opposite.

tion of mayoral control, based on the evaluations of teacher leaders and our index of relative power. The entries report the difference between the relative power of the mayor and the relative power of the board or superintendent for each city and each policy domain.[14]

It is plain that in only one of the four areas we have specifically examined does the mayor have substantial influence. On teacher salaries he is relatively more powerful than boards or superintendents in New York and Boston, but less so in Chicago, San Francisco, and Atlanta. On other matters, his influence is comparatively insignificant in each place. Although minor disparities exist, in general the independence of school systems is greatest in the area of curriculum, next in personnel, then in the organization of the school system, and least in teacher salaries. Our comparisons of teacher leader evaluations suggest that mayors and mu-

[13] Crain and Street, *op. cit.,* 75.

[14] In choosing between the score of the board and superintendent, we selected in each instance the higher of the two and then compared it to the score of the mayor. If the mayor's is higher, the entry is negative; if the superintendent's or board's is higher, the entry is positive. For example, take the entry describing mayoral control of curriculum in Chicago. The mayor's power index is 0.23 and the superintendent's is 2.03 (Table 26). The difference between the two is 1.80, which is considered positive since it runs in the direction of school independence.

nicipal officials have little say in operational matters—somewhat more in New York and Boston, somewhat less in Chicago and San Francisco, and the least in Atlanta. Generally speaking, these assessments appear accurate. Other data tend to confirm teacher leader perceptions as we have used them in the index of relative power. They also suggest three contrasting patterns of mayoral involvement.

Separation of Powers

In theory, it would seem that a mayor's potential influence in school affairs is based fundamentally on two factors. First, it hinges on how school board members are selected and to what extent they owe their positions to the mayor. Does he control appointments or are board members chosen independently of his desires? In this regard, Chicago, San Francisco, and Atlanta differ from one another. Atlanta's board is elected. In San Francisco, the mayor nominates members, who are voted into office by popular election. In Chicago, the mayor appoints from a list of candidates proposed by a screening panel which he in turn controls. It is doubful, however, that the relative separation of municipal and school powers in these cities depends on the process by which the board is selected.

More important is the mayor's official role in the budgetary process. The question is whether the school system determines its operating budget or is restricted by the mayor to an amount determined by community resources. In other words, is the system fiscally independent or fiscally dependent?[15] More accurately, since all school systems are dependent upon the public for support, the question should be phrased in terms of the degree of formal dependence. Budgets, of course, affect every aspect of school affairs. In view of the proportion of funds spent on teaching personnel, however, the relationship between budgetary power and salary power is particularly intimate. In neither Chicago, San Francisco, nor Atlanta does the mayor possess formal authority over the school budget comparable to that possessed by mayors in New York City and Boston. In none of the three cities does he play a major role in the determination of salary policies.

Atlanta's elected board determines its own budget and sets necessary tax rates without obtaining the approval of the mayor or other municipal officials. Chicago's mayor similarly has little formal authority.

[15] Despite the popularity of debating the merits of fiscal independence, it is difficult to realistically portray school-municipal relationships as either one or the other. See H. Thomas James *et al.*, *Determinants of Educational Expenditures in Large Cities of the United States* (Stanford: School of Education, Stanford University, 1966).

The school board formulates a budget, forwards it to the City Council, and the latter sets a property tax rate sufficient to yield the needed school revenues. But since the tax rate cannot exceed the maximum established by the state, the mayor has an indirect voice due to his influence in the Illinois legislature.[16] In San Francisco, too, mayoral authority is lacking, for the school budget cannot be reduced by city officials. The Board of Supervisors is required to levy a tax sufficient to raise revenues specified by the board of education.

In part because they are not delegated formal responsibility for educational expenditures, mayors in these three cities feel compelled to permit school authorities considerable latitude in determining budgets and other policies. With the exception of fitful and cautious involvement on matters of school desegregation and other scattered issues, mayors such as Ivan Allen of Atlanta, and George Christopher and John Shelley of San Francisco have stood apart from the problems and decisions of public education.

Even a most skillful and powerful mayor, like Richard Daley of Chicago, recognizes the separation of schools from municipal government. The schools are by no means subject to his control, for he prefers to remain aloof from educational affairs, leaving problems to the superintendent and the board. During recent years, for instance, Daley took no responsibility for the heated controversies surrounding the administration of General Superintendent Benjamin Willis. Yet he did give the superintendent tacit backing.[17] In other ways as well, the mayor rendered noteworthy assistance to the educational establishment, working behind the scenes to stifle criticism of the schools and intervening to get federal aid which had been held up by the U.S. Department of Health, Education and Welfare because of segregation.

Lately, however, even in cities where powers are essentially separate, mayors have seen fit to involve their offices in the settlement of disputes

[16] The Chicago schools have used the maximum permissible tax rate for a number of years. Therefore, as a matter of fact, the state legislature largely determines the district's budget. Mayor Daley certainly has a say in the matter. *Ibid.*, 82.

[17] It is probable that without this support Willis would have been forced from his position before 1966. See Hal Higdon, "A Minority Objects, But Daley is Chicago," *New York Times Magazine,* September 11, 1966. Also Kevin P. Buckley and Richard Cotton, "Chicago: The Marchers and the Machine," *The Reporter* (November 4, 1965), 30–1. Since the departure of Willis, however, Mayor Daley has taken a more prominent role in public education. In 1968, the Chicago screening panel refused to recommend the reappointment of two school board members, both of whom opposed integration. The mayor renominated both men, and the school board, by a six-to-five vote, reinstated the two. Mary Ellman, "Chicago! Behind The 'I Will' Spirit, It Is Nervous And Erratic," *New York Times Magazine,* July 14, 1968.

between the school board and teachers. In Chicago, Mayor Daley intervened in 1967 and 1968 when the Teachers Union threatened to strike after its negotiating demands were turned down by the board of education. In San Francisco, the new mayor, Joseph Alioto, tried unsuccessfully to prevent a union strike, but then played a major role in settling it quickly. It would seem that militant teacher tactics help prod mayors into the domains of public education and require them to exercise important influence on salary and budgetary policies.

Sharing of Powers

Although mayors and city officials in Chicago, San Francisco, and Atlanta do not play major roles in educational policy-making, their influence is indirectly felt. In some areas, particularly as a result of civil rights pressures, they are forced to take a position or come to the defense of the school system. But they gladly allow other officials the job of making decisions. With regard to the school budget also, they make no authoritative choices, but their views, like those of many eminent citizens in the community, are heeded by board members, superintendents, and top administrators, all of whom calculate the political and economic realities of municipal life in arriving at budget estimates.

In two cities, however, mayors are formally obliged to play a greater part in educational affairs. John Collins in Boston and Robert Wagner in New York could avoid involvement on many issues, but they were required to participate publicly in the budgetary processes of education, even though their decisions were greatly limited by the amount of resources available for public purposes and the competing demands upon them. Still, it seems fair to say that these mayors had direct influence in the determination of teacher salaries and indirect influence elsewhere.

Enough has been said in Chapter IV about the part of the New York mayor in the determination of teacher salaries. He is one of the most important decision-makers, "for it is he, more than any other single person who shapes educational expenditures" in the city.[18] He must respond, of course, to the demands of the teachers union, but just where the salary line is drawn is largely his decision to make. Thus, collective bargaining between the board and superintendent, on the one hand, and the UFT, on the other, is something of a fiction. It serves a purpose in bringing contenders closer together on matters of salaries, but it mainly sets the stage for eventual intervention by the mayor and his mediators.

In Boston, too, the mayor has a stranglehold on school finance. He possesses the authority to decide how much in the way of new or addi-

[18] James, *op. cit.*, 160. Appendix B of this work provides a valuable account of the budget process in New York.

tional monies will be spent on public education. In other words, he controls the amount of funds which exceeds the previous year's school budget. This naturally includes any salary increases. Customarily, the School Committee, on the recommendation of the Board of Superintendents, formulates a budget and presents it to the mayor. He calls for a cut, and the Committee resubmits a pared budget for his consideration. After negotiations, a compromise is reached in which the mayor bends a little but the School Committee usually bends more.[19]

The budgetary powers of New York and Boston mayors affect not only salaries but other educational policies as well. Insofar as changes in the organization of the school system necessitate funds for new buildings, additional personnel, or extra materials, mayors and other municipal officials exercise influence. Their role is indirect, however, and hence they are not perceived by teacher leaders and others as major participants in various policy areas.

Mayors have not intervened in matters of curriculum, matters such as use of I.Q. tests, or decisions as to whether a system with comprehensive high schools is preferable to one with both academic and vocational ones. Problems of school system personnel, including the appointment or election of board members and the selection of superintendents, have been beyond their chosen purview. Robert Wagner, for instance, was gratified with the change made in the procedure for selecting school board members in 1961. Instead of direct appointment, nominations by a non-partisan screening panel served to protect him from immediate pressures and future recriminations.

Like their colleagues in Chicago, San Francisco, and Atlanta, the mayors of New York and Boston remained aloof from most school affairs, although they were obligated to regularly decide on budgets, and this they did. Occasionally, they were forced by pressures and unavoidable crises to speak out, as happened when boycotts and demonstrations occurred during battles over school integration. When this was necessary, it was done as generally and ambiguously as possible. They did not choose to take the initiative. Mayors John Collins and Robert Wagner no doubt felt they had troubles enough without seeking others in the maelstrom of public education.

---

[19] In 1965 the Committee asked for $6 million over its prior budget, but Mayor Collins would allow only $2 million. Finally, he made an additional $200,000 available. At a meeting between the mayor and the School Committee, the following exchange took place: *School Committee Chairman*: We are very grateful for the $200,000. We would like more. *Mayor Collins*: You should sit here every day and talk to every department head. . . . He wants more money. *School Committee Chairman*: Of course you know our department is the most important. *Mayor Collins*: Everybody says the same thing. *Boston School Committee Minutes*, May 25, 1965.

Integration of Powers

Before the administration of John Lindsay had time to establish itself in office, Marilyn Gittell portrayed "the isolation of school administration from the city government" as the most significant trend during the past two decades of education in New York.[20] At this writing, however, the trend appears to be reversed. Under Lindsay, the role of the mayor has changed. Unlike other executives whom we have considered, he is voluntarily involving himself and his office in the affairs of the school system and trying to become an important influence on policy-making in public education.[21] His position is that educational policy cannot be so insulated from City Hall that it conflicts with the over-all strategy of elected city officials. As a result of the recent enlargement of the school board and the resignation of several old members, the mayor now commands majority support, at least on the issue of school decentralization. John Lindsay's exceptional behavior may not affect mayoral strategies elsewhere, but it merits specific attention.

From the very beginning, Lindsay promised a departure in the mayor's role. In his campaign for office, he proclaimed an affirmative duty to lead, taking the view that, despite the board's independent status, the people still held him, as mayor, responsible for public education. Leadership meant, in one major respect, active participation in the school system's budgetary processes. Lindsay acknowledged his problem here, for quite early he stated:

> If the Mayor becomes involved in controversial issues he is accused of political interference. And yet if the educational budget grows without visible improvement, the Mayor is accused of fiscal mismanagement. Unavoidably—as the city's highest elected official and as the man who signs the vast educational budgets—the Mayor is responsible for how well the educational system is performing its functions.[22]

The new mayor went further. He publicly criticized the budgetary procedures of the school system and privately induced the board to make changes. Then, in early 1967, Mayor Lindsay expanded his budgetary authority, despite objections from all sides.

Under a practice instituted by Wagner in 1962, the board received a lump-sum appropriation from the city and was permitted to allocate it as it pleased. In the belief that the board of education should be treated the same as any other city departments, Lindsay moved to replace the

[20] *Participants and Participation, op. cit.,* 47. The reader should recall that UFT leaders were surveyed before Lindsay succeeded Wagner as mayor.

[21] Lindsay, it would seem, is attempting to emulate the leadership of Richard Lee in New Haven. See Dahl, *Who Governs?, op. cit.,* esp. 203–14.

[22] *New York Times,* April 30, 1966.

"lump-sum" budget with a "line-by-line" one. Reaction was immediate, with board and superintendent, the Public Education Association, and the *New York Times* objecting intensely to the mayor's action. But the administration maintained its position, explaining that the board would retain authority to transfer certain budgeted funds (those *within*—not between—broadly stated programs), but not all.

Like Wagner before him, Mayor Lindsay could not avoid involvement when the board of education and UFT reached an impasse in bargaining on salaries. Under pressure from the board, Lindsay named a mediator six weeks in advance of the 1967 school opening. By contrast, Wagner had waited until the last possible moment before appointing mediators. When mediation showed no immediate results, Lindsay appointed a three-man panel, without consulting the union as had been the habit of his predecessor. When the panel presented its recommendations, no effort was made to obtain the approval of UFT's leadership, as had been the practice previously.

In 1963 and 1965 Mayor Wagner managed to avert teacher strikes; in 1967 a long work stoppage took place, even though Lindsay agreed to allocate more funds than those proposed by his mediation panel. Throughout the stoppage, Lindsay took charge on the behalf of management. The board of education, according to UFT's president, did not function during these weeks except when the mayor called members together to override the position of the board president.[23] Finally, in contrast to the precedent set by Wagner of dispensing with punitive measures once a settlement had been reached, neither the new mayor nor the board agreed to overlook the penalties of the Taylor Act when the teachers returned to work. As a result of Lindsay's independent line and his refusal to attend to the political niceties of bargaining, relationships between the union and the mayor became cooler. But the same type of pattern was evolving in the relationship between the mayor and the educational establishment.

An interventionist mayor, determined to integrate municipal powers, might be expected to increase his authority over the school budget and take a harder line on salary negotiations, but Lindsay's words and actions extended well beyond the fiscal realm. In the early days of his administration, the mayor took the occasion of addressing a joint meeting of the Elementary and Junior High School Principals Associations to back grade reorganization and decentralization policies of the board, which his audience faced with less than enthusiasm.

Later on, he made similar use of another speaking engagement. Ad-

[23] "A Talk with Albert Shanker," *Phi Delta Kappan*, XLIX (January, 1968), 256.

dressing PEA, the board's bastion of elite support, he asserted that New York was not receiving its money's worth in education. Shortly thereafter, Lindsay verbally intervened once again, this time for more immediate cause since the context was a heated dispute over Intermediate School 201 in East Harlem. Under pressure from neighborhood groups, Superintendent Donovan and the board had agreed to a plan which would have given community representatives virtual veto power over school appointments. In defense of the board's own prerogatives, the mayor announced that parents should not control the appointments of school principals and teachers. And, as if to fan the flames, he accused the board of handling the affair in clumsy fashion and isolating the school system from the community.

These verbal sallies illustrated a new outlook from City Hall. However threatening, taken alone they might have been insignificant. But Lindsay took other steps as well. He established the Human Resources Administration to oversee, among other programs, a good part of the federally financed pre-kindergarten programs operated in poverty areas of the city. Then, in mid-1967, the mayor appointed a chief policy advisor on educational matters and Director of the Office of Education Liaison in HRA, further threatening the autonomy of the school board.

Whether by design or not, Lindsay was afforded still another opportunity for intervention. In order to obtain additional financial aid for the city's schools, the Lindsay administration submitted to the state legislature a plan which divided New York City into five separate counties. Under this arrangement, the low values of property in Queens, Richmond, and the Bronx would produce $100 million more in aid than if real estate in the city were taken as a whole. The legislature appropriated the extra monies, but required in return that the mayor submit a proposal to decentralize the city's school system.

Lindsay took on the responsibility, agreed to cooperate with the school system, and appointed a panel, headed by McGeorge Bundy and including the board president, to advise him. Like the Bundy committee, the mayor recommended that the school system be broken down into largely autonomous, locally governed community districts and submitted his decentralization program to the state legislature for approval. One of the features of his proposed plan was mayoral authority to decide how funds would be allocated among the new districts. Thus Lindsay sought to gain greater control over the school budget and, in effect, a more significant role in the determination of educational policies.

Lindsay has tried to allay the fears of the government of public education, not by changing his overall design but only by belated doses of tact. After criticizing the schools and being criticized harshly in return, he reappraised them as the finest in the country but in need of improvement. After revising education's budgetary processes in the face of strong opposition, his office referred to the change as a matter of "budgetary tidiness rather than policy control." Having taken on the job of school decentralization, in the face of fears expressed by educational leaders in city and state alike, he assigned the work to a prestigious committee of his appointees on which the representative of the school board had only a minority voice. Despite his continued interventions, he has assured the educational establishment that he does not want to take part in relationships between individual schools and their communities, have influence over administrators or teachers, dictate the curriculum, or run the school system.[24]

It cannot be denied, however, that Lindsay has purposefully sought to alter the mayor's role. In large part he has succeeded. In the words of UFT President Albert Shanker: ". . . at the present time there is no real function for the Board of Education. . . . The city administration is calling the shots on all important matters, not only budgetary but in such areas as community involvement."[25] The wall between City Hall and education still stands, but it has surely been breached.

BOARD, SUPERINTENDENT, AND BUREAUCRACY

Generally, the mayor's role in school affairs is indirect or limit-setting rather than direct or initiative-taking. More directly involved, and more intimately concerned with a broad range of educational issues, are boards of education, superintendents, and administrative bureaucracies. People in these positions are delegated, either by the state or by one another, primary responsibility for deciding public school policies. Many studies have dealt normatively with the functions of lay members of school boards and professional administrators. Some have explored the role orientations of superintendents and board members. But few have investigated the comparative prominence in decision-making and school system influence of boards, superintendents, and bureaucracies.

It might be expected that in the five large cities under consideration the superintendent is the leader rather than the servant of the school board. As Roscoe Martin wrote, in describing the contemporary power of the superintendent, ". . . he is at least as much a policy maker as he is a manager in the narrow sense; for he enjoys an expertise, a professional reputation, and a community position which combine to give him an

[24] In an address to PEA, *New York Times,* April 28, 1967.
[25] "A Talk with Albert Shanker," *op. cit.,* 256.

almost irresistible voice in school affairs."[26] Surely, the superintendent has considerable resources at his disposal, but whether and in what instances he chooses to exploit them is another matter. The superintendency role affords the incumbent potential power, but his actual power ". . . is dependent on both the man and the situation."[27]

In this section we shall examine the question of professional control of public school systems. Our interest centers on two aspects of the problem: first, how the superintendent's power compares with that of the board of education, and second, how it compares with the power of his own administrative bureaucracy. In other words, what is the distribution of influence among top laymen and top professionals in various policy domains of education in the cities under investigation?

Following the same mode of analysis used in the discussion of mayoral control, Table 28 offers a comparative description of the power

TABLE 28
RELATIVE POWER OF THE SUPERINTENDENCY, COMPARED
TO THE BOARD OF EDUCATION*

Policy Domain	New York	Boston	Chicago	San Francisco	Atlanta
Salary	−0.20	−0.55	+0.30	−0.65	+0.05
Personnel	+0.44	+0.05	+0.83	+0.33	+0.40
Curriculum	+0.74	+0.58	+1.03	+0.61	+0.52
School System Organization	+0.04	−0.05	+0.44	+0.12	+0.24

* A plus indicates that the difference between the relative power indices of the board of education and the superintendent runs in the direction of the superintendent; a minus indicates the opposite.

of the superintendency versus that of the school board. On the basis of the evaluations of teacher leaders and our index of relative power, several points deserve mention. First, although the superintendent is generally reputed to be more influential than the board, the distribution of power varies by policy domain. In each of the five cities, the superintendent's relative power is greatest in the area of curriculum, next personnel, then school system organization, and least salaries. Second, the superintendent's power varies significantly by city also. In Chicago his influence is greatest, in Boston least, whatever the issue being decided.

A superintendent's influence, however, cannot simply be determined by his relationship with the board of education. His control over educa-

[26] *Government and the Suburban School* (Syracuse: Syracuse University Press, 1963), 61.
[27] Roald F. Campbell *et al.*, *The Organization and Control of American Schools* (Columbus, Ohio: Charles E. Merrill, 1965), 217.

tional policy also depends on how he shares influence with those below him in the hierarchy. A chief executive may well dominate his board of directors, but in turn be dominated by his administrative staff. Table 29

TABLE 29
RELATIVE POWER OF THE SUPERINTENDENCY, COMPARED
TO THE ADMINISTRATIVE BUREAUCRACY*

Policy Domain	New York	Boston	Chicago	San Francisco	Atlanta
Salary	+0.88	+0.10	+1.57	+1.21	+0.87
Personnel	+0.42	+0.23	+0.72	+0.32	+0.70
Curriculum	+0.03	+0.16	+0.32	+0.43	+0.28
School System Organization	+0.43	+0.26	+0.72	+0.64	+0.62

* A plus indicates that the difference between the relative power indices of the superintendent and the administrative bureaucracy runs in the direction of the superintendent.

does not suggest that this is the case in any of the five cities. Generally, superintendents exercise greater influence than administrative bureaucracies, but there are interesting variations by policy and city. Save for Boston, chief administrators have much more to say about teacher salaries than do their staffs. Only in the area of curriculum and instruction do administrative subordinates have a voice comparable to their own. The Boston bureaucracy shares power with its chief executive, while in New York, the bureaucracy plays a somewhat subordinate role and in San Francisco and Atlanta an even lesser one. In Chicago, bureaucratic leaders are totally subservient to the superintendent.

Closer scrutiny of policy-making processes in four cities tends to confirm the comparative description presented above.[28] It also suggests several patterns in the distribution of influence among establishment participants. Two school systems demonstrate a balance of powers. In New York, balance is based on the abilities of board, superintendent, and bureaucracy to check one another by blocking, retarding, or watering down any proposal disagreeable to any one of them. In San Francisco, balance results from consensus among participants who hold similar views on policy change. Two systems demonstrate a relative imbalance of powers. In Boston, the five-member board is significantly and ex-

[28] An important exception is New York's school bureaucracy. It seems to play a greater role, notably in defending against proposed innovations, than the one teacher leaders ascribe. According to David Rogers: ". . . even Superintendent Donovan, an able administrator and astute politician who has been able to use the limited powers of his office more effectively than most of his predecessors, can be subverted quite readily by his staff." In "New York City Schools: A Sick Bureaucracy," *Saturday Review* (July 20, 1968), 59–60. See his *110 Livingston Street* (New York: Random House, 1968).

tensively involved in school policy, and the independence of both superintendent and bureaucracy is notably curtailed. In Chicago, by contrast, the imbalance runs the other way, for here the chief adminis-trator (at least during the regime of Benjamin Willis) ruled almost absolutely.

Checks and Balances

In New York, as elsewhere, the superintendent is the central decision-maker of the school system. Yet he is a relatively limited chief executive, restricted on the one side by a school board which attempts to establish policy and on the other by a bureaucracy which resists unsettling change. Some years ago, Wallace Sayre and Herbert Kaufman described his role: "In sum, the superintendent of schools presides over but cannot lead the school system."[29] Today, the situation is essentially unchanged. The superintendent's opportunities for initiative are limited, for he is torn between board and bureaucracy. If he subscribes to the policy views of the former, he risks the wrath of the latter. If he moves at a pace satisfactory to the latter, he is almost sure to be criticized by the former. In a system where conflict is frequent and intense and where the mayor, citizens, and teachers have begun to play a participatory role, the superintendent must walk a tightrope, exerting some leadership but avoiding debilitating battle.

At least since 1961, the board of education has made serious efforts to assert its power as a policy-making body. Conscious of the tasks it faced in exerting control over a huge school system, the board has tried to strengthen itself and at the same time effectively oversee the managerial job being done by its superintendent and his staff. Continuing efforts to develop membership specialization and add professional staff indicate the board's intention to actively involve itself in policy and implementa-tion. Additional evidence was provided by the board's role in hiring and dismissing a superintendent. Without doubt, one of the most significant personnel decisions in a school system is the selection of a superintendent. Even more significant, though rather infrequent, is his dismissal. In each of these aspects of personnel policy, the New York City board has played a decisive role.

Before the appointment of Calvin Gross, the tradition in New York was to promote someone within the system to the superintendency rather than to take a serious look outside when a vacancy occurred. When the new board took office and John Theobald left the superintendency, pressures for a successor to the chief executive position were strong. The

[29] *Op. cit.*, 282.

Public Education Association, as it had in the past, favored an outsider. But administrators, through their associations, insisted upon an insider.

Feelings were intense, as Max Rubin, board president at the time, recalled. His worst moment as president, he mentioned, came when he told a group at school headquarters of a nationwide search to find a man for the job and was booed as a result.[30] Nevertheless, the board chose to hire from outside, and with the help of an advisory committee, finally appointed Calvin Gross, then superintendent of the Pittsburgh school system. As a sop to the educational bureaucracy, it promoted three of the system's own candidates to positions as deputy superintendents, and thereby helped undermine the new superintendent before his career even began. Gross came to New York virtually alone, and, as it turned out, unequipped to deal with the obstacles he encountered within the system—the professional staff associations and the headquarters departments, which viewed him as a threat to the sanctity of their own influence.

Gross's tenure was shorter than the six-year term of his appointment. A variety of factors precipitated his downfall. He was attacked from outside and undermined from within, but the principal agency in his removal was the board of education, and particularly its president. Almost from the outset, superintendent and members of the board came into conflict. Members privately charged that Gross failed to exercise capable leadership, and thereupon the board started to build its own staff despite his opposition. Differences arose also over the superintendent's handling of school integration and school decentralization and his negotiations with the teachers union. At one point, the board refused to go along with his nominations of several new associate superintendents and at another it began to take over his administrative job. Finally, the decision to replace him was made, not when civil rights groups or others sought his removal, but when the board apparently decided it could no longer tolerate what it considered vacillating and weak leadership. Despite the difficulties imposed by state law, the board ousted Superintendent Gross. No one in the system came to his defense and many were delighted to see him go. His successor was Bernard Donovan, a child of the system and first in line among insiders for the top job.

These manifestations of board power do not lend themselves to facile generalization. For while the board has asserted itself from time to time, the superintendent and administrative bureaucracy have had continuing responsibility for the development of system-wide policies. Although they are responsive to the board's over-all preferences, the

[30] Martin Mayer, "Close to Midnight for the New York Schools," *New York Times Magazine,* May 2, 1965.

professionals dominate budget-making. Save for occasional interventions by the board, as in the choice of a superintendent, the professionals also dominate the domain of personnel policy. High administrative positions are filled on the nomination of the superintendent. He, in turn, is restricted by the tradition of promotion from within the ranks, the strength of headquarters divisions, and the lobbying of administrative and supervisory associations. On curriculum, too, participation by the board is spasmodic. It leans heavily on the initiatives of the headquarters staff—a deputy superintendent, the assistant superintendent in charge of the Bureau of Curriculum Research, and heads of divisions. As a board president admitted concerning curriculum and related matters: "I think the most important factor here is that, in the areas which are so-called policy-making, the Board must look to, and *heavily rely upon,* the advice of the superintendent and his staff." An outside observer was even stronger: "Actually, the professionals make policy and carry it out, and it is difficult to say just what the board does."[31]

In recent years, the board of education has devoted a good part of its energies to mediating disputes. Civil rights pressures and demands for control of local schools by Negro parents have forced it to spend considerable time on problems of site selection, relationships between individual schools and neighborhood groups, and attempts to stem local crises and extinguish brush fires. These same stimuli, however, have impelled the board to assert itself and play a major role in the formulation of educational policy.

Continuing controversy has caused the adoption, maintenance, and implementation of new policy to proceed at only the most gradual pace. The gap between policy statements and their implementation has been especially great. Nevertheless, the board and superintendent by working together have been able to embark upon major change. A reorganization of grade levels in the schools slowly moved ahead, despite opposition by the educational bureaucracy and associations of secondary school principals. The conversion from separate vocational schools to comprehensive high schools was also decided, despite outcries from high school principals and supervisory groups, but progress here has been extremely slow. A pilot program of meaningful decentralization was finally undertaken, despite prolonged resistance by central headquarters administrators and school principals.[32]

[31] *Board of Education Press Release* 347–61/62, March 21, 1962 (emphasis added), and Rogers, "New York City Schools: A Sick Bureaucracy," *op. cit.,* 47.

[32] In this case, however, initiative was taken from the educational establishment by the mayor and his special panel, probably on the assumption that change would not come in time if the school system were left to its own devices. But establish-

With regard to each of these programs, demands for further integration or increased local control provided the impetus and the board responded affirmatively, but influential elements within the school system resisted change. While the board spoke primarily for members of the New York community, the superintendent had to represent the views of the staff upon whom he depended for support. In some instances, such as the establishment of comprehensive high schools, the superintendent, besieged by principals and faculties, retreated from his original position in support of the board's policy. His was the discomforting task of trying to reconcile the demands of citizens and the desires of laymen with the interests of the school system's professionals. In this environment of intense pressure and firm resistance, the superintendent and board have worked together and evolved educational policy. In the process, the superintendent followed the guidelines and preferences established by the board, but tailored his proposals and specific directives to the tastes of members of the system he administered. In turn, the board accepted the superintendent's judgment on the schedule and details of implementation, but insisted on maintaining over-all control. The board of education, and most recently the mayor, determined the general direction. How far, how fast, and in what specific manner the giant school system would move were matters largely determined by the professional staff.

Superintendent-Board Collaboration

Compared to the superintendent in New York, Harold Spears did not have a difficult time with either the board or the small bureaucracy at Van Ness Street in San Francisco. Although the board is not a rubber stamp for administrative proposals, there is a presumption that the superintendent, as an educational expert acting in good faith, is usually correct in his policy recommendations. Therefore, individual commissioners pause before taking issue with him, feeling that in any dispute they and not the superintendent are likely to be wrong. On his part, Spears restricts his suggestions to those he thinks the board will accept, tactically avoiding clear-cut positions and tailoring his proposals to ensure legitimation by the board. Once he has formulated a position, it generally is adopted. A proposal which does not have his assent, by contrast, has little chance of passage.

Collaboration between the superintendent and board of education comes easily, since both parties share, with almost everyone else, the belief that educational changes should be gradual and taxes should not

---

ment forces, including the board, supervisory associations, and the teachers union banded together to prevent a program for radical decentralization from being enacted by the 1968 session of the state legislature.

rise too steeply. The school budget is prepared by Spears, who keeps a sharp eye on the tax ceiling. He presents the budget, exclusive of salary increases, and suggests to the board just how much it can afford for teachers if there is to be no increase in tax rates. Members of the board then decide on salaries, taking factors other than taxes into consideration. First, they try to match salaries paid in other large cities and in the Bay area. Second, they assess the raises given by the mayor and Board of Supervisors to public employees of the city and give their classified personnel the same. This ordinarily sets the floor for teacher salary increases. Third, they take demands made by teacher organizations into account.

If the board dominates policy-making on salaries, the superintendent has a relatively free hand in other areas. There has been no serious controversy over curriculum since about 1960. At that time, following the Soviet Union's launching of the first Sputnik, there was a flurry of proposals and wide involvement in this domain. A majority of commissioners felt strongly and contracted with a group of university professors to recommend improvements in the school system's curriculum. The "Professors Report" won support from the board, but the superintendent argued that recommended changes would be administratively difficult to accomplish. He could not ignore the report, however, so he put a number of the proposals into practice, keeping substantial change to a bare minimum.[33] Since then, the superintendent has faced no comparable challenge to his authority. As one observer of the system commented: "Nothing gets done unless he wants it done, and he usually doesn't want it done."

The board has been forced to exercise some judgment independent of the superintendent on issues related to school integration. It has taken action by appointing an *ad hoc* committee, which proposed a compensatory educational program. On several occasions it has virtually instructed the superintendent to resolve issues and formulate policies. But even on racial imbalance, where the tendency in other cities is for school boards rather than superintendents to make decisions, the board delegated major power to Spears and looked to him for leadership.[34]

[33] See Robert D. Lee, Jr., "Educational Ideology and Decision-Making in the San Francisco Public Schools, 1956–1966" (Syracuse University, unpublished Ph.D. dissertation, 1967).

[34] In his studies of integration in eight cities, Robert L. Crain found that in all except San Francisco the superintendent played a minor role in comparison with the school board. He explains that since there was a lack of clear leadership on the board, as a result of conflict between political and non-political appointees, the superintendent took over many of the board's functions. *The Politics of School Desegregation, op. cit.,* 187. See also Lee, *op. cit.,* 162–74.

Quite unlike superintendents in New York, Spears has had no problem controlling his administrative staff. Top-level administrators in the system serve as faithful lieutenants to the superintendent. In conformity with the city's conservative tradition and in step with the board and chief executive, assistant superintendents at headquarters are little inclined to advocate substantial change. Had Spears or the school board chosen to push innovative policies, the small central office bureaucracy might have offered resistance, but active resistance was quite unnecessary in a relatively inert system. The administrative staff contented itself with the application of moderate policies, leaving critical decisions to the tender mercies of board and superintendent.

Dominance of Laymen

Boston's superintendent of schools confronts a more aggressive board than do his administrator colleagues in New York and San Francisco. Although the School Committee and professionals see eye to eye on broad policies, the superintendent's discretion is restricted on nearly all types of issues. For one reason or another, the five elected members of the board have insisted on deciding not only integration and budgetary policies but many trivial matters as well.

The previous superintendent, an interim appointee who served until October, 1963, was extremely loath to accept responsibility for major decisions. In 1962, for example, after the mayor cut its budget, the School Committee decided to adhere to the salary raises it had voted and delete the "most expendable" of items for the improvement of educational programs. When a board member asked what could be eliminated, Superintendent Frederick J. Gillis replied: "What you are going to do to reduce the budget now, a quarter of a million dollars, I haven't the slightest idea. It is up to the School Committee to select what they [sic] are going to cut out of the budget."[35] The present superintendent, William H. Ohrenberger, is more willing than his predecessor to take on responsibility in formulating the budget and revising it after the mayor's perennial cuts. He has been reluctant to fight the School Committee, but he has pushed as far as his bosses have allowed.[36]

Usually this has not been very far. On matters concerning school integration, for instance, the School Committee has undeniably determined policy. With few exceptions, Ohrenberger has conformed to dominant views on the Committee. In response to a state report critical

[35] *Boston School Committee Minutes*, June 25, 1962.
[36] Peter Schrag points out that Ohrenberger was responsible for beginning compensatory and experimental programs and initiating cooperative programs with Harvard. *Op. cit.*, 56–7.

of racial imbalance in the Boston school system, he questioned whether there was sufficient evidence to show that such a condition was educationally harmful and went on to shift responsibility for change from the schools to the neighborhoods. The Committee majority agreed to his report, although some aspects were not welcomed by all members. In conformance with majority opinion, Ohrenberger recommended that the Committee refuse to cooperate with the U.S. Office of Education in distributing a questionnaire on racial attitudes to pupils and teachers. On one occasion, however, the superintendent went too far. He suggested that the city bus several hundred children from overcrowded schools in Negro sections to under-utilized white schools. This the Committee refused to do, although at a later date it relented somewhat in order to qualify for state aid that had been held up because of its failure to comply with state law on racial imbalance.

Decisive intervention by laymen extends beyond the highly-charged area of school integration, into matters that would appear primarily administrative in nature. In protecting the interests of its staff and the public, the Committee exercises close supervision of personnel and school organization and some degree of oversight in the domain of curriculum and instruction as well.

The board has shown no desire for major policy overhaul or expert study of personnel practices. But, to a greater extent than other boards we have considered, the one in Boston has maintained constant involvement in questions of who should be appointed or promoted to administrative and teaching positions in the system, often acquiescing in the superintendent's nominations, but occasionally turning them down. This persistent intervention provoked one dissenting member to lament that the Committee did not have the time to involve itself in administrative detail. "Whether we are basically trusting souls or not," he said, "we have to repose a certain degree of trust in the administrators. . . ."[37]

If the interests of school or neighborhood groups contradict the opinions of professionals, the Committee has little difficulty making a choice. It inevitably decides in the people's favor, largely because the people have an opportunity to vote in school elections. Whenever the administration recommended closing a school or combining one with another, the Committee's decision hinged on the number of parents who objected. Consolidations were put off when parents complained; they were undertaken when they had little impact in the neighborhoods. Sometimes, curriculum too was decided on this basis. On one occasion, for example, the administration, reacting to a budgetary squeeze, pro-

[37] *Boston School Committee Minutes,* October 17, 1962.

posed that sewing instruction in the fifth grade be abolished. The School Committee complied, but shortly thereafter, when parents objected strenuously, it reinstated sewing instruction.

Perhaps the most graphic example of the weakness of the headquarters administration is the conduct of Boston Latin, the city's prestigious high school. "Because of its reputation," Schrag writes, "the Latin School operates like a quasi-independent barony within a feudal structure. . . ."[38] On questions concerning its organization and curriculum, the Committee responds to a powerful, organized constituency. The superintendent and his deputies have little power when confronted by a Latin School coalition, including the headmaster, department heads, parents representatives, students, and alumni. In one instance, the central administration recommended the elimination of instruction in military science and the curtailment of the Latin language requirement. Opposition from the school was intense, and the Committee vetoed the recommendations. At another point, a proposal to liberalize admissions to the school was voted down when the headmaster raised objection.

On many issues, of course, the School Committee delegates authority and no problem arises. Unless people protest, curriculum is left to the superintendent and headquarters chiefs, who, together with school principals, formulate courses of study and make minor alterations. For example, when several revised curricula were before the Committee for decision, an assistant superintendent testified: ". . . we feel that you people on the Committee have enough policy matters to take care of so we don't want to burden you with reading courses of study. . . ." Approval was quickly given.[39] Nor can the superintendent himself be apprised of every matter. He leaves many things to the judgment of his subordinates. As one board member commented, ". . . we have seen many occasions when policy has been established without the full knowledge of the Committee and to some extent without the knowledge of the superintendent."[40]

Nevertheless, it is fair to say that the School Committee has exercised a remarkable degree of control over the entire range of educational affairs in Boston. Even a highly politicized, energetic board such as this one cannot decide every conceivable question. But, on those it overlooks, it can be reasonably sure that the superintendent and top administrators at Beacon Street perform in general accord with School Committee desires.

[38] *Op. cit.*, 79.
[39] *Boston School Committee Minutes*, April 26, 1965.
[40] *Ibid.*, September 10, 1962.

Dominance of the Superintendent

During his thirteen-year reign as General Superintendent of the Chicago school system, Benjamin Willis exhibited the type of personal, political, and professional domination seldom found on the American educational scene. Few will deny that he was the central educational policy-maker in the city. Called by one participant "a giant of inertia, inequity, injustice, intransigence, and trained incapacity" and by others a tyrant ruling by fear, Willis dictated policy for the schools until he was replaced as superintendent in 1966.[41]

Whether the board of education, legally entrusted with control by state statute, abdicated power or had it usurped by the superintendent is difficult to say.[42] Willis certainly had built-in advantages. He set the agenda for board meetings, initiated proposals, and directed the staff to study whatever problems he considered important. The board depended on the superintendent for its information, and Willis deluged members with materials, many of which concerned trivia. At times, as one observer has noted, the superintendent lectured his employers, treating them like "a group of slow-witted schoolboys" and reading reports which were rarely distributed to members before meetings.[43]

For a variety of reasons, including its lay character, its lack of information, and the fact that a majority of members either supported Willis or was sufficiently confused and frightened not to interfere, the board deferred completely to the superintendent. Satisfied to mull over building projects and permit their energies to be diffused, most members floundered in a morass of operating details, unable to focus on basic issues, standards, and goals. There can be little doubt that, with the exception of a few abortive rebellions, the board abjectly tolerated its chief administrator's autocracy and refused to do anything that "might even inadvertently or by implication" undermine his authority. In each and every domain, policies were for the superintendent to determine.

With regard to the school budget, and consequently teacher salaries, Willis provided leadership. According to a former board member:

> Despite the fact that the budget process is in many respects the keystone of the Board's role . . . , the general superintendent appeared to regard board concern with budgetary practices as an intrusion. The Board did

---

[41] Charles and Bonnie Remsberg, "Chicago: Legacy of an Ice Age," *Saturday Review* (May 20, 1967), 73, 74, 91.

[42] Unless otherwise noted, this section is based largely on the account of a former board member, Joseph Pois, *The School Board Crisis: A Chicago Case Study* (Chicago: Educational Methods, 1964).

[43] Peter Schrag, *Voices in the Classroom* (Boston: Beacon Press, 1965), 59.

not resent this attitude. In fact, discussions of the subject engendered uneasiness and apprehensions that admissions of inability to cope with intricacies of the budget would reflect on the intellectual capacities of the board members.[44]

Personnel, too, fell within the superintendent's jurisdiction. He controlled procedures for the examination and certification of teachers, made appointments to the positions of assistant principal, district superintendent, associate superintendent, and many other positions, and rejected any but the most *pro forma* discussion of his decisions by the board. Laymen played no role, unwilling as they were to review and evaluate personnel policy, and confident that the improvement of salary schedules would compensate for any personnel shortcomings.

In theory, the general outlines and policies of the educational program and curriculum in Chicago are determined jointly by board and administration. In fact, of course, the board had little to say. Dependent as they were on professionals for curriculum-related information, members possessed no understanding of alternatives to program recommendations of administrative personnel. Furthermore, they showed even more diffidence than usual on matters of substantive education and even less inclination than customary to oppose the overwhelming pressures exerted by the superintendent and his staff in advocacy of a program.

On school integration, where pressures have been great and board involvement unavoidable, Superintendent Willis pretty well had his way. In most cases when confronted by civil rights demands, large-city superintendents have responded defensively, but school boards have had little difficulty in taking control.[45] In Chicago, until the end of his regime, Willis managed to maintain control of decisions relating to school integration. He successfully delayed a survey of the public schools, although the board earnestly desired one. He refused to carry out a policy mandated by the board. In one of the few instances when a weak effort was made to overrule him, he threatened to resign, forcing the board to back down completely. In mid-1963 the board appointed a panel, headed by Philip Hauser, to suggest measures for school integration. But long after the committee's report had been completed and adopted, the superintendent had still not implemented its recommendations. Hauser explained the dilemma: "Willis has shown that he will not follow any recommendation of this report unless it is shoved down his throat by the board—and they [sic] have not shown the spirit or inclination to do this consistently."[46]

[44] Pois, *op. cit.,* 178–79.
[45] Crain and Street, *op. cit.,* 69–70.
[46] Buckley and Cotton, *op. cit.,* 31. Since the new superintendent, James Red-

In no city under study has the board been weaker or the superintendent more powerful.[47] In none have superintendents had their own way so completely with both their lay superiors and their professional subordinates.[48] Like decision-makers elsewhere, the Chicago superintendent's dominance depended to some extent on community acquiescence. As long as his general policies had the tacit support of the city's political machine, the business community, and the press, Benjamin Willis could run the school system as autocratically as his desires and skills would allow.

mond, assumed office, some change has taken place. Unlike his predecessor, Redmond moved vigorously to respond to demands for integrated and quality education even if it meant much higher school costs. His proposals, however, met strong resistance within the Chicago community, and very little of the ambitious "Redmond Plan" was actually implemented. Ellman, *op. cit.*, 58.

[47] Gittell and Hollander, on the basis of their study of six cities, claim that the Chicago board is stronger than that of New York, primarily because the former meets more often in executive session. *Op. cit.*, 87. We doubt seriously that this factor compensated for the almost total domination of the system by Willis.

[48] Gittell and Hollander note that Superintendent Willis "undertook almost everything himself despite objection from his staff." *Ibid.*, 190.

VII. Organizational Influence

A decade ago, one would have had to search diligently to discover an opinion characterizing teachers as effectual in the grand affairs of educational decision-making. The prevailing view was appropriately expressed by Daniel Griffiths. "Teachers as a group," he wrote, "have little or no say in the formulation of school policy."[1] Today, educational influence is apparently shifting. Across the country teachers have increased the size of their pay envelopes and won a host of fringe benefits. In some places they have put limits on class size and the number of teaching periods each week. In others they have gained a voice in curriculum matters and in determining which textbooks pupils will use. Recently, Wesley Wildman maintained that, given the high professional autonomy and the low visibility of classroom activities, individual teachers acting alone are far from powerless. In concert with their colleagues their power is increased. Moreover, a formal framework of collective bargaining or professional negotiation further enhances their power.[2]

Yet, according to contemporary teacher leaders in five large cities, the influence of their own groups is still meager, especially in comparison to that of the educational establishment. By and large, they play a negligible part in determining school policies, as is shown in Table 30 by the large differences in indices of relative power between teacher groups and other powerfully perceived participants. It may be that leaders tend to underestimate their own influence, for self-assessments are less objectively reliable than evaluations of others.[3] Nevertheless, admissions of group impotence cannot wholly be dismissed.

[1] *Human Relations in School Administration* (New York: Appleton-Century-Crofts, 1956), 106.

[2] "Implications of Teacher Bargaining for School Administration," *Phi Delta Kappan*, XLVI (December, 1964), 155.

[3] Or they may have a vested interest in avoiding widespread acceptance of the view that teacher organizations are weak. See Myron Lieberman, "Power and Policy in Education," in Stanley M. Elam *et al.*, eds., *Readings on Collective Negotiations in Public Education* (Chicago: Rand McNally, 1967), 39.

TABLE 30
RELATIVE POWERLESSNESS OF TEACHER ORGANIZATIONS*

Policy Domain	New York	Boston	Chicago	San Francisco	Atlanta
Salary	−0.19	−1.00	−1.61	−1.32	−0.78
Personnel	−1.12	−1.23	−1.49	−1.30	−1.40
Curriculum	−1.71	−1.45	−1.83	−1.50	−1.33
School System Organization	−1.21	−1.38	−1.75	−1.66	−1.53

* A minus indicates that the difference between the relative power indices of teacher organizations and the most powerfully perceived participant (whether mayor, board, or superintendent) runs in the direction of the latter.

Nor can comparative evaluations, based on leadership perceptions be discounted.

These data on relative power show that, except in New York, where members of UFT's executive board attribute substantial influence to their own organization on salaries, teacher groups are much weaker than mayors, boards, superintendents, or whoever happens to dominate in a particular policy domain. Predictably, they have somewhat more to say about salaries, and perhaps personnel, and much less to say about curriculum and the organization of the school system. It is noteworthy also that in New York, where pluralism prevails and bargaining has become institutionalized, teachers emerge more powerful than elsewhere. In Chicago, where the superintendent reigns supreme, they seem weakest. And in Boston, with the beginnings of collective bargaining, leaders feel stronger than in San Francisco, where group relations appear deadlocked. Further examination of teacher organizations in New York, Boston, and San Francisco will serve to flesh out these comparisons.

EFFORTS AND EFFECTS

Like modern corporations, which today are as concerned with their own perpetuation and power as with profits, contemporary teacher groups are as interested in their own strength as in securing advantages for teachers. In the economic sphere, corporate survival depends on making profits; in education, the health of a local association or union depends on winning benefits. As we suggested earlier, organizational strength and substantive gains are inextricably linked. One significant effect of group efforts in domains of policy is to increase rank-and-file support, membership, and the chance of representational recognition. For instance, UFT's demands in 1960 were specifically calculated to appeal to various groups of teachers. Collective bargaining might be attractive to all. Progress toward a duty-free lunch period for elementary teachers was designed to gain support at the union's weakest point. Five days of annual sick leave for full-time substitutes was to consolidate support in the junior high schools where half the staff was made up of permanent substitutes. Equalization of salary steps and promotional increments was to attract newer, younger teachers.[4]

In addition to organizational strengthening, group efforts help to determine the distribution of influence on a range of educational policies. Here we shall deal with educational policy in a somewhat different fashion than before. Of concern, first, are the efforts and the impact of teacher organizations on matters where they seek personal and material rewards for their constituents. These we shall call *position* issues. With regard to a few, involving economic welfare, such as salaries and fringe benefits, potential gains are most concrete. With regard to others, involving working conditions and covering a range from in-service courses to class size, potential gains are somewhat less personal and more abstract. Of concern also are organizational efforts and impact on what we shall term *style* issues, where rewards tend to be more impersonal and less immediate. They include questions of educational leadership, curriculum policy, and the structure of the school system.[5]

Position Issues—Economic Welfare

There can be little doubt that teacher organizations have concentrated their energies on achieving higher salary schedules and winning related benefits. In New York City, salary concessions have been a critical goal of UFT bargaining in 1962, 1963, 1965, and 1967; in Boston, the teachers union did not even submit proposals beyond salaries and fringe benefits until 1964; and in San Francisco, SFFT leaders readily admit that "pork-chop" issues, primarily salaries, have been the union's principal focus throughout the years.

Enough has already been said about bargaining in New York to indicate UFT's substantial accomplishments. Perhaps the union could have won even higher salaries, as some people allege. Time after time, however, it upset the normal processes of educational budgeting, ignored the board's authority, and threatened to embarrass the mayor if additional funds were not allocated for increased salaries. Prior to 1965, the board

---

[4] Joel Kaplan, "Can a Teachers Union be 'Professional'?" *Changing Education,* I (Summer, 1966), 39–40.

[5] This conceptualization follows lines similar to Bernard Berelson *et al., Voting* (Chicago: University of Chicago Press, 1954), 184, and Lewis A. Froman, Jr., *People and Politics* (Englewood Cliffs: Prentice-Hall, 1962), 24–7. In the field of education, distinction is frequently made between "conditions of employment" and "educational policy." See Myron Lieberman and Michael H. Moskow, *Collective Negotiations For Teachers* (Chicago: Rand McNally, 1966), 226–28.

submitted its budget to the mayor before collective bargaining began in earnest. As a result, UFT publicly bypassed the board and exerted pressure on the mayor, who was forced to intervene. In 1965, the board attempted a different approach, hoping to maintain its authority. On the recommendation of the superintendent, it included $20 million in the school budget to cover union demands. But this was only a minimum. The Federation insisted on much more, and finally emerged from mediation with about $65 million, very close to the amount it actually expected.[6] The superintendent and board had to revise their educational programming in order to provide a good portion of the funds for the settlement. As before, the board lamented that it was being forced "to adopt a different scale of budgetary priorities than those which it has deemed to be in the best interests of the school system."[7]

On other issues as well, the teachers union has had an impact on policies affecting economic welfare. It not only won attractive fringe benefits, such as health insurance paid in full and substantially higher compensation for extra-duty activities performed after school hours, but it also intervened in matters of salary administration, remedying particular inequities through union grievance machinery. Finally, the union has been able to veto schemes which it found harmful. For instance, proposals by the administration to award salary differentials to teachers in special service schools were repeatedly opposed by UFT and consequently were never put into effect.[8]

In Boston, where the School Committee's budget must be accepted by the mayor, teachers have fared less well. Before collective bargaining, teacher groups presented their salary requests annually before the Salary Adjustment Board, a group of assistant superintendents at Beacon Street. The latter formulated a salary schedule with an eye toward keeping expenditures within limits that the mayor would deem reasonable. The School Committee then adopted a schedule, insulating itself as much as possible from the organized demands of teacher groups.

Given the mayor's perennial cuts in its budget, Boston educational authorities have had to make adjustments by reallocating funds among different educational purposes. They have tried always to put salaries

---

[6] H. Thomas James *et al., Determinants of Educational Expenditures in Large Cities of the United States* (Stanford: School of Education, Stanford University, 1966), 171.

[7] *New York Times,* September 11, 1965.

[8] One salary matter on which the union has been notably unsuccessful is the supervisors' index. Enacted into state law in 1963, the index gears the pay increases of supervisors to those of teachers. Despite continued attempts to have the law repealed, UFT and the Empire State Federation of Teachers have been unable to persuade the state legislature.

first, both because of the personalism which pervades the system and the competition for teachers by wealthy suburban school districts in the vicinity. Their attitude is summed up by one administrative official, who said with regard to salaries: "Even without any requests, teachers would have received what they did." Yet school authorities could not completely satisfy teachers, since they confronted an almost insurmountable obstacle. "I want to assure you," one Committee member explained to teacher representatives, "that if you folks can tell us where we will get the money, we will give it to you. . . . Our problem now is convincing the Mayor to give us an adequate amount."[9]

As far as salaries were concerned, teacher organizations in Boston did not go beyond putting forward demands, making a case to the School Committee, and pleading that it stand up to the mayor and put the burden for cuts on his shoulders. On a related matter, however, teachers resorted to a vigorous campaign, the likes of which had rarely been seen in Boston. The issue was a sick-leave policy, which had been raised by teacher groups year after year. Due largely to BTU's professional organizer, the union in the fall of 1962 began pressing for a policy of fifteen days sick leave with full pay and a cumulative sick-leave bank. Over 1,000 individuals signed petitions, as BTU sought to mobilize teachers for organizational advantage.[10]

Union leaders lobbied persuasively behind the scenes, and at the December meetings of the School Committee hundreds of teachers crowded in to display their strength and ensure adoption of BTU's plan. Members of the Committee went along with the proposal, but like most policy processes, this one did not end with their general acquiescence. BTU offered to meet and work out rules governing the use of sick leave provisions. Without consulting the union, the Committee responded to a proposal of the school administration and instituted stringent safeguards to prevent abuse of the new sick-leave system. Teachers persuaded the Committee to rescind some of these safeguards. They apparently managed to overcome others, since the mayor later asked the superintendent and school administration to crack down on the most flagrant abuses.

On matters of economic welfare, teacher groups in San Francisco have been more successful than their counterparts in Boston. Because of the school board's willingness and power to raise salaries and provide other benefits, SFFT and SFCTA have not had to use pressure tactics to guarantee regular improvements. During the past decade, salary increases have averaged about 4 per cent a year, and just once—in

[9] *Boston School Committee Minutes,* February 14, 1963.
[10] The recruitment effects of the campaign are mentioned in Chapter II, above.

1959—did the board outrage teachers by granting only a meager raise. It also agreed to a proposed sick-leave policy and, without even involving the superintendent, consented to a liberalized sabbatical program. The board of education has truly sympathized with teacher welfare interests. Nonetheless, organizations, and particularly SFFT, deserve some credit for influence, since they serve as a constant and vocal reminder that teachers merit greater rewards.

Position Issues—Working Conditions

The number of issues falling within the scope of conditions of employment is impressive and group demands for improvement are extensive. Teacher organizations spend a good portion of their energies seeking changes which would lighten their work load—duty-free lunch periods, special personnel and teacher aides, increased time for preparation and a reduction in the number of instructional periods, relief from noninstructional and clerical duties, limitations on class size, and so forth. Accomplishments in this area, however, do not match demands; and on this basis particularly the comparative influence of teacher groups in New York, Boston, and San Francisco can be assessed.

By any standards of judgment, UFT has far outpaced other groups in terms of the type and number of gains made during the past several years. The 1962 contract provided benefits too numerous to mention in their entirety here. Included were the relief of teachers from noninstructional chores, duty-free lunch periods for elementary teachers, more time for lesson preparation, consultation on teachers' programs, and the rotation of assignments. Subsequent contracts expanded and improved these benefits. The union, moreover, has not been satisfied to rely entirely on provisions of the collective bargaining agreement. It has worked outside of the formal contract as well. For example, in 1964 the union mobilized almost 10,000 elementary teachers in a campaign to persuade the school administration to revise the reading record card, which it claimed imposed a senseless clerical burden on teachers. A year later, UFT objected to teachers having to score batteries of Iowa tests given to their classes on the grounds that this was a non-professional chore. In both instances the administration responded positively.

Then, in 1967, the union took another stride forward in its efforts to improve working conditions. In negotiating with the board, it demanded that teachers be given the authority to suspend disruptive children from their classrooms. The board, under great pressure from local groups to resist, would not agree to such a provision. But the contract finally did specify the creation of local review boards on which teachers, local representatives, and outside experts would serve together. Here, too, UFT had addressed itself to a problem which disturbed many of its members. Here, too, the union had been able to achieve a mechanism which offered new possibilities for teacher control of their working environments.

By contrast to UFT, teacher organizations in Boston have achieved little. Where money has not been at issue they have had some success, for the School Committee has been disposed to please the teachers even at the displeasure of the administration. In 1963, for instance, the administration organized a series of after-school lectures on education and race and required teachers in sixteen districts to attend. BTU objected, first, because it had not been consulted in planning the series and, second, because of the compulsory nature of the in-service lectures. As a result, attendance became voluntary. But on issues involving money, and especially before collective bargaining, teachers have encountered obstacles. In 1962 BTU and BTA complained that secondary school teachers should not be required to check cafeteria receipts. No remedy was obtained until two years later, since neither the Board of Superintendents nor the School Committee could devise an inexpensive solution. On another occasion, the School Committee was called on to give elementary teachers two free periods per week. Due to the high cost and the mayor's curtailment of funds, the proposal was voted down.

The campaign by BTU for a duty-free lunch period illustrates how difficult it is in Boston to achieve change, even when a teacher organization makes a concerted effort. The union began its drive to relieve elementary teachers of lunchroom chores in late 1962. Not until June of the following year did the School Committee take up the matter, and then it referred BTU's proposal to the superintendent. During the summer, the union and BTA met with a subcommittee of administrators to work out a plan. Because of disagreement between the two groups, the School Committee decided to poll teachers on alternative possibilities and to solicit by ballot the views of parents. From September until the end of the year, polls were taken, additional conferences were held, and the two teacher organizations continued to squabble over the merits of each one's plan. In January, 1964, teachers voted once again and parents were sent a questionnaire. Although teachers favored the duty-free lunch proposal, parents divided almost equally, and the school administration began to voice serious objections. As a compromise, the School Committee voted to include $17,000 in its preliminary budget request for an experimental program in four schools to begin in September. Once again, however, a budgetary ceiling imposed by the mayor forced the Committee to cut back and the pilot program was abandoned. Not until September, 1966, four years after BTU's campaign started, did the union achieve duty-free lunch periods, and then only as a pilot program in twelve schools.

In San Francisco, funds have not proved to be quite the problem that they have in Boston. Several years ago, teacher groups, supported by the administration, easily persuaded the board to grant duty-free lunch periods. More recently, SFFT urged the school system to develop data processing and thereby lighten the clerical burden of teachers. The board agreed, if funds could be obtained. Teachers have been able to effect minor improvements on other issues also, primarily because the superintendent offered no resistance. But when the school administration believed its authority endangered, change did not come easily at all. Such was the case when both SFFT and SFCTA pressed for the adoption of grievance procedures in the school system.

For some time the union had advocated a formal process of settling grievances, but both the board and the superintendent evaded the issue. The establishment of the Negotiating Council, however, set the stage for a direct confrontation. SFCTA introduced its own proposal at the Council. This was unsatisfactory to the administration, mainly because it threatened the authority of school principals. Superintendent Spears thereupon broke off negotiations with the Council, and issued a plan of his own.

Now the teacher groups objected, because the superintendent's plan provided neither for representation at the local school level nor for the right to appeal to the board of education. SFCTA took steps to obtain a court injunction to prevent the board from considering Spears' proposal, arguing that he had ignored the machinery of the legally established Negotiating Council. SFFT, in an extraordinary step for a San Francisco group, mobilized its forces and took action. It distributed petitions, picketed school headquarters, and staged a walkout at a meeting of the board of education. Under pressures such as these, the superintendent withdrew his proposal from the board agenda, and the issue was deadlocked. The union, in particular, had pressed hard, but it still failed to achieve the grievance procedures it deemed so necessary and had advocated over the years.

An excellent illustration of the comparative influence of teacher groups is the issue of class size. The average number of pupils in each class differs from one school system to another. This is one reason why the problem is likely to be given different priorities in the three cities. Nevertheless, the reduction of class size has been an objective of teacher organizations in each place.

The Boston Teachers Union had little difficulty negotiating the issue during its first contract. The administration did not offer objections, since average class size in the system was even lower than the union requested.[11] "We didn't give them a thing," one administrator commented, unmindful that a troublesome precedent might have been established for future negotiations. The point is that, unlike the situation in New York, school authorities in Boston did not consider union negotiators their adversaries, and so were less mindful of precedent. SFFT, on the other hand, made little headway here, except perhaps to keep pupil loads of teachers from rising. During the period from 1957 to 1965, for instance, the union made four presentations before the board of education. Yet the board never proposed a reduction, ordered a study, or even indicated whether it thought classes of forty too large. Nor did any of the group's proposals receive serious response from the superintendent, save for his questioning of the reliability of SFFT statistics. Only after the union conducted a one-day strike in 1968, which the mayor helped settle, did the school administration, now led by a new superintendent, make concessions. It agreed to institute limits on class size, provide school aides, and allow teachers preparation periods free from administrative assignments.[12]

In New York City, by contrast, union influence has been notable. Not until 1963 did UFT earnestly press to have class size limitations written into its contract. At that time, a reduction in class size ranked as one of the union's main objectives. But the board declared the issue non-negotiable, since the number of pupils assigned to a teacher was a matter of educational policy, not working conditions. It was ready to limit class size, but was unwilling to write restrictions into the contract. It was absolutely essential for the union that limits be in the contract and not merely stated as policy, which could be changed at will by the board with no recourse by UFT.

Fortuitous circumstances helped the Federation achieve an advantageous compromise. When the mayor's mediators intervened at the last moment, board negotiators asked that the disagreement on salaries be settled first. The mediators suggested it be resolved last, after other items had been cleared away. This put the board under pressure to give way on non-wage issues in order to soften UFT resistance when salaries came up for discussion. As a result, the board relented, and the final contract included limitations, allowed certain exceptions, and permitted teachers to file a grievance if their pupil loads became too heavy. Thus, class size was established as "a proper subject for negotiation and regu-

[11] There are other explanations. Some suggest that the administration gave in because a ceiling would make it easier to deny transfers to Negro children who sought to attend schools outside their neighborhoods.

[12] *American Teacher,* April, 1968.

lation through a collective bargaining contract clause."[13] In subsequent contracts the union managed, slowly but surely, to reduce the size of classes in the city's schools.

Teacher organizations not only direct their efforts toward improving working conditions, but also try to prevent the board and administration from moving in directions they believe contrary to the interests of their constituents. Take the matter of the length of the school day or the school year. In Boston, citizens groups and at least one Committee member advocated lengthening the school day. Because of teacher opposition and the administration's lack of concern, the idea received little serious attention. In San Francisco, however, the administration recommended that the board extend the school day for elementary teachers. The board asked no questions, ignored teacher groups, offered no explanation, but just extended the day.

In sharp contrast, UFT has exercised an almost absolute veto over proposals it found unsatisfactory. The board in 1965 considered holding classes on George Washington's birthday. But when the idea aroused the union, it was abandoned. The following year, the board, supported by parent and community groups, actually voted to extend the school year by two days. UFT's president thereupon threatened that teachers would not report two days earlier and, if their pay were docked, they would strike. The board finally backed down and rescinded its policy.

There is probably no better example of the union's veto power than its action on the issue of the assignment and retention of teachers in the city's difficult schools. In a number of respects, the union agreed with educational authorities, helping to reduce transfers from these schools. But one alternative, emanating from a joint report issued by the Board of Superintendents and Board of Examiners in 1962, called for a salary differential to teachers and supervisors in slum schools. UFT objected, and no plan was adopted. Two years later the idea of "combat pay" was again advanced, only to be vetoed by the Federation. Then, in mid-1965, the board announced a policy of involuntary assignments to assure the equitable distribution of experienced teachers throughout the system.

UFT responded by condemning the board for ignoring the real problems of slum schools and threatened to close the schools rather than permit teachers to be forcibly transferred or rotated. The board again gave in, appointing a School-Community Committee for Educational Excellence, to handle the problem. In early 1966, the committee, one of whose members was the UFT president, rejected both extra pay and forced rotation, because these procedures would lower the morale of

[13] David Selden, "Class Size and the New York Contract," *Phi Delta Kappan,* XLV (March, 1964), 283–87.

teachers. Instead it recommended a new training program and other measures designed to improve the quality of the city's teaching force. Clearly, the union had again emerged victorious.

But victory in the domain of personnel policy may have been short-lived. By 1967, the Federation was facing the most imposing challenge it had yet encountered. The power it had gradually accumulated and the arrangements it had devised by dint of hard work were threatened by the trend toward decentralization. While recognizing the need for greater community involvement in educational affairs, UFT leaders were understandably anxious about the possibility of conflict between parent power and teacher power in the local schools. The union had worked to convince teachers to cooperate in three experimental school decentralization projects launched by the board of education with the backing of the Ford Foundation. UFT was willing to be pragmatic and flexible, but worried about the effects of community control on local teachers.[14] Then, during the walkout of 1967, a number of community groups were extremely critical of the union and insisted on screening striking teachers before they returned to their classrooms. This caused UFT to reassess its position.

The union finally objected to any plan that would allow community groups to exercise control over the hiring of teachers.[15] It opposed the decentralization programs advocated by the Bundy panel, by Mayor Lindsay, and by the State Board of Regents. Together with the New York City board of education, UFT fought hard to substitute a relatively mild plan for one that was substantially stronger. Primarily because of the union's pressure, the bill which was enacted in 1968 made some changes but effectively postponed decision until the following year.[16]

Granting the need for some dispersal of school authority, UFT leaders reflect the fears of their constituents that hiring, promotion, and tenure policies would be adversely affected by militant groups who might gain control. Recent events have shown these fears to be well grounded.

[14] *The Center Forum*, 2 (January 26, 1968), 1. The union, in fact, had helped to draw up the original proposal for the Ocean Hill-Brownsville demonstration district. But when the time came to elect permanent teacher representatives, the union refused to participate. Martin Mayer, "Frustration is the Word for Ocean Hill," *New York Times Magazine*, May 19, 1968.

[15] UFT supported a suit brought by the Council of Supervisory Associations to prohibit the school board from appointing district administrators and principals approved by local groups in the three demonstration districts. The State Supreme Court ruled that the board's method of appointing principals, but not administrators, was outside normal channels and therefore illegal.

[16] *New York Times*, May 26, May 28, and June 2, 1968. It was reported that Shanker threatened to use union funds to defeat legislators who cast votes against his group's position. *Ibid.*, May 25, 1968.

The most dramatic controversy occurred in the Ocean Hill-Brownsville demonstration school district. Here the community governing board tried to dismiss nineteen teachers and supervisors without preferring formal charges. UFT came immediately to their defense, called a walkout, and prompted two-thirds of the district's teachers to boycott the schools for more than a month during the 1967–68 academic year.

The UFT is in a difficult position as a result of intense demands for decentralization and community control. Newly acquired organizational influence is in serious jeopardy. A radical decrease in central educational authority not only would force local chapters to wage battle for themselves, but it would also curtail the union's ability to make citywide demands, achieve comprehensive gains, and share in the shaping of overall educational policy. As one observer noted: "There is always the simple, organizational reality that a big union must have a big enemy to face."[17]

Style Issues

A favorable resolution of matters involving working conditions or economic welfare promises direct, immediate, and personal benefits to teachers. Obviously, any change in a school system has implications for conditions of employment, since every policy affects the working lives of teachers in one way or another. But some changes are of a different order than others. Some do not confer direct advantage. Improvements in the quality of the teaching force, the education of the underprivileged, curricula offerings, or the way in which schools are organized and managed are mainly designed to serve the entire system and only indirectly promise to help individual teachers.

On matters like these, most commentators would agree, teacher organizations devote minimal energy and play an insignificant role. In view of organizational imperatives, stemming largely from the interests of their constituents, their inability in these affairs of educational policy is understandable. Still, teacher organizations have participated in deciding "style" issues, sometimes lending support to a coalition, but only infrequently taking the initiative or exercising leadership. If organizational influence is based in part on effort and accomplishment here, once again teachers in New York emerge as relatively potent, while those in Boston and San Francisco appear weak.

Each of the teacher groups in these cities has participated in one

[17] Joseph Featherstone, "Community Control of Our Schools," *The New Republic* (January 13, 1968), 17. The issues of school decentralization and community control confront other large city unions as well, as the heated debate at AFT's 1968 convention demonstrated.

coalition or another for purposes of achieving a mutually desirable and generally long-range goal. As a rule, however, teachers have been supporting actors in casts dominated by others.

Take the issue of school integration. The United Federation of Teachers has actively supported civil rights campaigns, working in close collaboration with the Public Education Association and the United Parents Association. In the civil rights boycott of 1964, the union was strong in coming to the defense of over 3,000 teachers who stayed away from school, refusing on grounds of conscience to cross boycott picket lines. It has also endorsed board proposals, such as educational parks, and has been far more receptive than most staff groups to other changes designed to promote school integration.

San Francisco teacher groups have also become involved in the school integration controversy. As early as 1962, SFFT declared itself in favor of school desegregation and recommended that the board of education appoint a citizens' committee to formulate a program to alleviate the problem. During the last few years, both the union and SFCTA have been represented on the Coordinating Council for Integrated Schools, although neither organization has raised integration to priority status or been willing to become closely aligned with the civil rights movement. Nonetheless, they have been vocal enough to disturb the superintendent, who felt that teachers should have supported the administration and board instead of taking sides with citizens groups and criticizing the school system.

Only in Boston have teachers avoided a position on this issue. The Teachers Alliance would not declare itself, primarily because of a sharp split in members' attitudes. A small faction in BTU endeavored to fashion a pro-civil rights policy. But the union as a whole ignored racial imbalance, arguing that the real problem was economic, not racial, and the real need was money from the mayor, not integration.

Other issues have also prompted concern by teacher organizations. In Boston, they have endorsed and campaigned for candidates in School Committee elections, although their electoral impact since 1957 has probably been slight.[18] Officially, they have not been involved in the selection of a superintendent, but leaders of both BTU and BTA worked informally and jointly with administrators to ensure the appointment of an insider. Finally, they have taken a stand on what School Committee members, administrators, and teachers all believe to be the critical issue

[18] The election of 1957, one remembered by group leaders and School Committee members alike, illustrates that teachers could make their electoral weight felt. BTA campaigned against three incumbents and was instrumental in electing its own slate to the Committee.

in Boston—the mayor's control over the educational budget. In San Francisco and New York as well, teacher groups have staked out positions and occasionally spent some time, working alone or in conjunction with other participants, on questions concerning personnel, the organization of the system, or increased state and local funding for public education.[19]

Teacher leadership, however, is extremely rare. Organizations do offer, as planks in their total platforms, recommendations and demands pertaining to what we have labeled "style" issues. That is usually as far as they go. With the initiation of collective bargaining, the Boston Teachers Union listed a large number of items in its agenda for negotiations, including the appointment of a committee to study programming for language laboratories, immediate construction of a new high school, a remedial reading program, and the establishment of more special classes. Yet few of these were earnestly put forward for bargaining. By contrast, teacher organizations in San Francisco, despite their weaker status, have frequently initiated proposals concerning school curriculum and related matters. SFFT, for instance, has presented the board with programs on departmentalization in elementary schools, ungraded classes at the primary levels, the education of gifted children, and reading elevation. SFCTA, although giving less attention to these matters, has endorsed expansion of pre-school education and increased library, counseling, and guidance services.

The participation of teachers is limited, however, and their impact is negligible. Group leaders have been content to make proposals in the hope that central office administrators would be prompted to incorporate their ideas in administration programs. SFFT and SFCTA leaders acknowledged scant influence, and Superintendent Spears, referring to the role of teacher organizations, simply commented: "I can't think of anything they accomplished."

Both the efforts and accomplishments of UFT have been far greater, despite declarations of weakness by members of the executive board. No doubt, the power of the New York union does not match that of the board, superintendent, or administrative bureaucracy on issues peripheral to the material interests of the teaching staff. Although UFT wants a decisive role on questions of curriculum, textbook selection, and research projects, progress has been slow.

[19] UFT, for instance, is one of 42 city-wide and local organizations belonging to the Citizens Coalition for an Adequate Education Budget, which was formed in 1968. When Mayor Lindsay cut $150 million from the 1968–69 school budget, the public relations director of the union stated: "This is an absolute disgrace, and Lindsay ought to be called in on it. He supports school decentralization and then he cuts down the funds." *New York Times,* April 2, 1968.

Unlike many other educational groups, however, the union has engaged itself and made some headway. One problem in which it has been involved is teacher recruitment. Because a shortage of teachers imperils objectives for smaller classes and more preparation time, UFT has constantly tried to improve recruitment procedures. It has prodded the administration to make reforms and has even conducted recruitment activities on its own. Another related problem where the union has attempted to play a role is teacher retention. It proposed an experimental nursery school to care for the children of former teachers and thereby permit them to return to teaching careers they had given up.

On another significant issue, UFT developed a program, initiated action, recruited support, and persuaded school authorities to go along— not very far, but at least to some extent. The "More Effective Schools" (MES) program undeniably illustrates initiative and influence, seldom exercised by a local teachers organization. The plan for more effective schools was conceived by a union committee in 1962 and approved by the executive board and delegate assembly in early 1963. UFT recognized that piecemeal, diluted reforms, such as minor reductions in class size, were not sufficient to improve slum schools. Instead, it called for a program of much smaller classes, greatly increased services, union participation in the selection of personnel, and staff involvement in instructional decisions to begin as a pilot program in about twenty schools. Although it was unsuccessful in efforts to negotiate MES in its 1963 contract, the board agreed that the subject could be considered by the superintendent in his periodic consultation with Federation representatives.

UFT did not merely propose; it acted. A Citizens Committee for Effective Schools was formed, almost 200,000 brochures were distributed, and union chapters were mobilized to stimulate grass-roots support. The program was launched at a propitious time, since the superintendent had just been instructed by the board to come up with recommendations to improve education in disadvantaged areas of the city. MES constituted an appropriate and acceptable approach to the board's policy of "quality, integrated education." Consequently, agreement was reached rather quickly. A joint planning committee, composed of representatives of the superintendent, UFT, and Council of Supervisory Associations was appointed. The committee proposed a program, which, although scaled down, was adopted and instituted in ten schools in the fall of 1964. A year later eleven additional schools were added, so that 21 schools were part of MES by late 1967.

Union participation continued, although implementation was primarily in the hands of the administration. There were difficulties, of course. From the UFT's point of view, leadership was confused, personnel and supplies insufficient, and bureaucratic interference troublesome. From the board's point of view, there had been some reluctance by teachers to assume responsibility and by supervisors to listen to and accept staff suggestions in cooperative planning endeavors. Nevertheless, these problems had been worked on by active UFT chapters, and generally teacher-supervisor relations proved satisfactory.

The major problem was the program's high cost. Expenditures per pupil were substantially greater than in other elementary schools. This was a principal reason why two board members, including the president, voted against an expansion of MES in 1965. Then, in 1967, during collective bargaining negotiations, the question of cost assumed major proportions. With UFT calling for an expansion of the program to all ghetto schools, the board president called for its curtailment. He argued that there were too many specialists in the 21 schools and that a good number should be reassigned to improve education in all 267 schools of the disadvantaged areas. Once again, the union waged battle, encouraging the formation of a Citywide More Effective Schools Parents Association, launching demonstrations, and appealing to city officials to help defend and extend MES.

On its part, the union was firmly committed to MES for a variety of reasons. First, the program lent credence to the group's claim of caring not only for the welfare of its members but also for that of the children in slum schools. Second, it had been adopted by the American Federation of Teachers, and New York City served as a showcase for the promotion of this union innovation in large-city school districts across the country. Third, sponsorship furnished UFT with a mechanism for continuing involvement and additional gains in power in the domains of educational policy-making. Thus, when its contract was up for renegotiation in 1967, UFT began by proposing an expansion of MES to all ghetto schools, at the rate of 90 a year for three years. As bargaining ensued, it reduced its demand for expansion to a total of 60 schools, then to about 40, and ultimately had to settle for something else entirely.

The board proved resolute. It favored the curtailment of an expensive program, whose results, it argued, did not justify the costs. In this holding operation the board was supported by a study conducted by the Center for Urban Education, a federally financed research and education agency. The Center's study found that, although the program had aroused enthusiasm, interest, and hope among administrators and teachers in the participating schools, it made no significant difference in the performance of the children involved.[20] The board was naturally reluctant to spend millions of additional dollars on MES, particularly since it was already committed to other enrichment experiments in elementary education which it considered to be of at least equal merit. Moreover, a contract provision infringing on the board's own policy-making powers was quite objectionable. Policy decisions, the board had always insisted, could not be delegated to the union or be negotiated by processes of collective bargaining.

The dispute was ultimately settled, but not until it had caused the Federation to extend its walkout at the beginning of the school year past the time when an agreement on salaries had been reached. As previously, each side was forced to give ground, although UFT undoubtedly yielded more than its adversary. The board refused to commit itself to an expansion of MES or to any other specific project. It did agree, however, to devote $10 million to the development of new elementary programs, with not less than half given over to "intensive programs for the reorganization and improvement of additional schools." To achieve a final settlement, it also agreed to establish a work group, composed equally of board, union, and community representatives, which would make recommendations regarding the use of the special fund.

As a result of the 1967 contest, UFT's innovation in educational programming was blocked, at least temporarily. The board had held firm, refusing to negotiate MES and then insisting that it would have the last word on policy. In return, the union's demand for a greater voice in educational direction was formally recognized once again.[21] But this time UFT had to settle for coequal status on an advisory group, while superintendent and board retained the power of final decision. The New York City union, unlike other teacher organizations, had truly exercised an unprecedented degree of influence in promoting a major educational program of its own. But when school authorities held fast, permitting the strike to run its course, the UFT was forced to yield. Militant action

[20] David J. Fox, *Expansion of the More Effective Schools Program* (Center for Urban Education, September, 1967). A month later, the union issued a study of its own, criticizing the Center's conclusions and producing findings which demonstrated substantial achievement by MES pupils. In early 1968, the office of educational research of the school administration issued an evaluation, based on a methodology somewhat different than the Center's, which showed greater improvement by MES pupils. For a discussion of the controversy over these evaluations of MES, see the special supplement in *The Urban Review*, 2 (May, 1968), 15–34.

[21] Still, when the mayor cut from the 1968–69 school budget more than $50 million in funds required to continue present programs at their current levels, he did not touch the $10 million set aside for intensive improvement by the UFT-board agreement. *Board of Education Press Release*, 310–67/68, April 2, 1968.

alone proved insufficient to bring the union the type of power over educational policy which it had resolutely sought.

THE NATURE OF GROUP INFLUENCE

In each of these three cities, leaders of teacher organizations feel that their groups have had only the merest impact on public school policies. Differences among their subjective evaluations exist, but they are not overwhelming. From a more objective perspective, however, differences appear larger. Issue analysis suggests that there is greater variation in group influence than reputational data alone would indicate. Indeed, contrasts are sharp among teacher organizations in the scope and intensity of their efforts and the amount of change in the positions of school authorities they bring about.

All of the groups have given highest priority to economic welfare and next highest to working conditions. Still, they have differed in terms of the intensity of effort devoted to objectives in these areas. No organization has come close to rivaling the United Federation of Teachers in this regard. The New York union has constantly used pressure tactics to win higher salaries and to improve working conditions and prevent them from deteriorating, going so far as to threaten or employ the most forceful sanctions on an almost continual basis. Efforts by Boston and San Francisco groups have been much less intense. In both cities the usual practice has been for teachers to simply appeal to school authorities for improvements in salaries or working conditions. Seldom was there resort to direct pressure; instead, reliance was on reasoned argument or personal diplomacy.

On matters popularly referred to as educational policy, those we term "style" issues, organizational attention has been slight and efforts minimal. Until very recently, Boston teacher groups have not even offered proposals on questions such as these. They left things like the organization of the school system, curricula, and racial imbalance to the School Committee and administration to decide. In contrast, the San Francisco union has formulated and presented a variety of proposals along these lines, although until 1968 it never attempted more than advocacy to get them adopted. Only UFT has gone further on a number of problems— prodding, cajoling, bargaining, demonstrating, and finally prolonging an already lengthy strike in order to persuade school authorities of the educational merits and political wisdom of the union's approach to policy.

Influence does not depend on effort alone, although unless attempts are made it is extremely difficult to discover who prevails. The influence of a teacher organization also depends on whether and to what degree it can change the position or behavior of the school board, superintendent, and bureaucracy. Admittedly, it is no easy task to determine what the actual positions of different participants are, especially since initial positions often are taken with a view to bargaining and eventual compromise.[22] Nonetheless, it is possible to discern differences among teacher groups in this respect.

Boston teachers have not really succeeded in budging school authorities on issues where they refused to move. Generally, the School Committee and administration have gone along with the money demands of organizations, but the mayor has been the stumbling block, and pressures by teacher groups on him have been negligible. On other questions, teachers have occasionally overcome administrative objections because of the responsiveness of the School Committee to rank-and-file appeal. Organizational demands have been few, however, and impact on policy barely perceptible. The situation is approximately the same in San Francisco, but here teacher influence may possibly have been greater because of more frequent and varied attempts to initiate change. With a board and superintendent, who have tended to delay and evade, teacher groups have played a role as reminders and suggesters, if not actual persuaders. On a number of issues, school authorities acquiesced because they had no serious objection to spending moderate amounts to keep their employees content. But on others, where authority or prerogatives were at stake, teacher groups made little progress in pushing their employers from strongly held positions. Only when SFFT resorted to forceful action were significant gains achieved.

UFT stands out in terms of influence. This is due partly to the large size of its membership and the opportunities afforded by collective bargaining. It is due also to the Federation's resourceful leaders and their intense efforts on behalf of group objectives. Surely, there can be little doubt that real differences separated school authorities and the union in their repeated clashes. Allowing for extreme positions taken for purposes of negotiations, the two sides still stood far apart. Nor can there be much question that a good number of disputes were resolved more to the satisfaction of the union than to that of their opponents. Time and again, UFT attained higher salaries than the board of education was willing to provide. Time and again, it had written into its contract provisions which board and administration strenuously resisted. In more than one instance, it vetoed policies even after they had been publicly announced. On other occasions it pushed the school establishment, perhaps not very far but certainly in directions the union favored. From time to time, as illustrated by the battle over MES, its demands were

<hr>

[22] Cf., Robert A. Dahl, *Modern Political Analysis* (Englewood Cliffs, N.J.: Prentice-Hall, 1963), 41–3.

rejected, but even in these cases it was able to salvage something and regroup for subsequent campaigns. Exploiting its strength and skillfully practicing politics, the United Federation of Teachers was a force to be reckoned with in New York City. No other teacher organization wielded anything resembling its political clout in the government of public education.

VIII. Strength, Politics, and Power

Among the ways in which American teachers make known their views and attempt to shape their working environments, involvement in a teacher organization might be expected to offer the greatest opportunities. Teacher organizations, like other interest groups in American society, mediate on behalf of individual members, providing them with vehicles through which to collectively voice their complaints and gain some satisfaction for their demands. As recently as a few decades ago, however, the attention given organized teachers was scant. With only scattered exceptions, their demands were moderate, their activities undramatic, and their impact barely perceptible. Although effective in lobbying at Washington, D.C., and state capitols, teachers were politically immobile in local school districts throughout the nation. As community-based interest groups, teacher organizations were practically irrelevant to the decisional processes of local public education.

During the past decade, the transformation of teacher organizations has been startling. At varying rates and with varying degrees of intensity, teacher groups are mobilizing and beginning to wage battle in order to advance their interests. Higher salaries, better working conditions, and improved education command their energies as never before. The evidence is inescapable, as was brought out in Chapter I. Teacher attitudes are changing. Quiescence is giving way to militancy. Teacher participation is increasing. More and more local school districts provide for collective negotiations of one type or another. Conflict is on the rise. Threats and counter-threats, sanctions and reprisals are becoming standard practices in the resolution of disputes. Supported by new doctrine and forceful techniques, teacher organizations are now exerting demonstrable pressure on local governments of public education.

Changes over time should not be confused with the realities of the present. This study has focused on the current role of teacher organizations in several large cities. New York, Boston, Chicago, San Francisco, and Atlanta are by no means representative communities. They hardly constitute a sample of school districts from across the nation. But since the contemporary teachers movement is primarily an urban phenom-

174

enon, one might reasonably expect that teacher groups in cities like these would have made greater strides than those made by groups elsewhere. Chapters VI and VII have concentrated on the distribution and exercise of power by teacher organizations and selected participants in these cities. Our description, based upon the perceptions of teacher leaders and other materials, demonstrates the variability of influence from one issue area to another and from one city to the next.

Two sets of findings have emerged. First, there are patterned differences by issue domain. Municipal officials, such as mayors, chiefly intervene where finances are in question, specifically with regard to teacher salaries. Their involvement is less likely where decisions relate to school system personnel or organization, and unlikely on matters of educational curriculum. School boards and superintendents share control for the most part, with boards relatively more influential in salary and organization and superintendents strongest in personnel and curriculum. In most areas, administrative bureaucracies have a comparatively lesser voice and school principals have only a slight impact in policy-making for the entire educational system. Second, there are patterned differences by city. In New York and Boston, mayors play a much greater part than in other cities. In Chicago, the superintendent has clearly been stronger than anywhere else, whereas the school board in Boston has exercised greater influence than its counterparts in other places. Generally, power has been relatively concentrated in Chicago, San Francisco, and Atlanta and relatively dispersed in New York and Boston.

It is within this context that the influence of teacher organizations should be viewed. However significant their progress recently, the power of teachers is today less than overwhelming. Their impact is limited, if no longer negligible. No doubt, their increased agitation has resulted in benefits they might otherwise have been denied. Yet, in contrast to the established governors of public education, teacher groups have little to say about educational policies, with the possible exception of salaries and related matters. They are still far short of achieving a commanding position, controlling educational policy, or exercising major influence in the areas of school decision-making. The old regimes may be shaken, but they have not been toppled.

Our intention, however, has not been to exclusively describe the educational influence of teacher organizations. A good part of our effort has been devoted to an examination of the bases of group influence. In this respect, emphasis has been on trying to explain why some groups may be more influential than others. Work such as this can only be exploratory, since factors that potentially account for influence are innumerable and diverse. To treat all of them would be impossible. To deal with only one or two would be foolish. Therefore, we have selected some of the more important ones and examined them from different perspectives and with different techniques of analysis. The methods, and the results as well, are eclectic, but they underline the significance of three analytical dimensions in the study of interest groups. To better understand variations in group power, we have chosen to explore the dimensions of organizational strength, organizational opportunities, and organizational behavior.

Organizational strength involves a variety of factors or bases, all of which can conveniently be thought of as group resources. Size, wealth, legitimacy, access, cohesion, and leadership are a few examples of resources that have been examined in numerous studies of interest groups. Our own analysis has dwelt upon two resource categories: size, conceived of as group membership, and leadership, conceived of as leader motivations. In these terms, organizational strength is a function of membership size and leadership militancy.

Numbers are extremely relevant, as is evidenced by the efforts of teacher organizations to recruit more and more members. The principal energies of aspiring organizations are devoted to membership recruitment. This has been true in Boston, where the Teachers Union and the Teachers Alliance vied for the affiliation of public school pedagogues. It has also been the case in San Francisco, where competition for new members was the main focus for the Federation of Teachers and the Classroom Teachers Association. Even in New York, with the United Federation of Teachers einjoying the loyalty of two out of three teachers in the system, the drive for members continues to be conducted energetically.

The reasons for this amount of effort are obvious. The larger a group the greater its wealth, since income derives mainly from per capita dues. Wealth, in turn, is requisite for the support of group activities designed to increase cohesion, propagandize outsiders, develop programs, and wage combat with school authorities. Take the use of wealth by the UFT. Membership dues make it possible for the union to maintain a full-time leadership and a large professional staff, to finance public relations campaigns, and to risk the financial penalties of a teachers' strike. Discounting additional income, additional numbers would still matter. The more members, the more widespread the involvement in organizational activities and campaigns. As membership grows, participation may decrease proportionately. But, at least until a high level is reached, participation should increase absolutely as people join a group. Numbers are impressive to educational and municipal officials, and these people are the ones teacher organizations are trying hard to impress.

Yet, membership may not have exactly the same meaning in different places and under contrasting circumstances. A large membership does not necessarily mean that all or even most of those who affiliate will help promote a group's interests. Evidence for this point was presented at the beginning of Chapter II. Other things being equal, we would expect that in a competitive election a teacher organization with more members would defeat one with fewer members. This apparently holds where the local union has the membership advantage, as in Boston and Chicago. But it certainly is not true in each instance where the local association has an edge, as the outcomes of bargaining elections in New York, Philadelphia, and other school districts indicate.

What membership means seems to depend on motivations teachers have for joining one group or another. Some join because they are expected to, or sometimes are requested to do so by school administrators, or because certain fringe benefits accompany membership. These teachers are unlikely to bring much conviction or fervor to an affiliation which is primarily nominal. Others do so because they believe they can increase their power and advance their individual and collective interests through organizational membership.[1] These teachers are more likely to possess the qualities which may be converted by an organization into activism.

Membership in NEA and AFT generally appears to conform to these two patterns. Thus, a comparison between numbers of members in the affiliates of the two national organizations cannot tell enough about organizational influence or even organizational strength. Although the San Francisco Classroom Teachers Association has a much larger membership than its union challenger, it would be unwise to conclude from these data alone that the Association is stronger or more influential than the union. Nor is it sufficient simply to base a conclusion on the comparable memberships of one type of organization. In the period 1960–62, for example, the Chicago Teachers Union was far healthier in terms of numbers of members than the United Federation of Teachers. Yet it would be absurd to infer from this that the Chicago group was then stronger than the union in New York City.

Size is one component of group strength. But brute size is not likely to be of crucial account. As Harry Eckstein points out, ". . . we should speak of the politically effective size of a group: its ability to make its

---

[1] See, for example, Harmon Zeigler, *The Political Life of American Teachers* (Englewood Cliffs, N.J.: Prentice-Hall, 1967), 57–9.

quantitative weight felt."[2] Whether or not the number of organizational members counts effectively depends largely on the motivations of group leaders.

Our aim in Chapter III was to delineate and explore the orientations of teacher leaders of nine organizations in five cities. The unifying concept was militancy, of an attitudinal and not a behavioral sort. Discussion of the doctrines of NEA and AFT in Chapter I brought out three themes—participation, power, and combat—which characterize the contemporary teachers movement. Each one constitutes a significant dimension of attitudinal militancy.

It is intuitively evident that one motivational element of group strength is the desire to participate in determining educational policies for a school system. Unless a group wants to share in decision-making, its numbers, wealth, and other resources will remain stagnant. The more ambitious the participatory objectives, the greater the impetus a group will have to challenge the status-quo distribution of decisional authority. Organizations whose leaders seek a decisive rather than merely consultive role are more likely to mobilize resources, make demands, and attempt to exercise influence. Not only are goals critical, but strategies for achieving them are also important.

In view of the relative powerlessness of teacher organizations, it would seem natural for leaders to want to enhance group power at the expense of that of other participants. The greater the consensus, the more likely an organization will recognize that meaningful participation can be achieved only through substantial group power. In addition, there must also exist a disposition to engage in battle and employ forceful methods. The assumption here is that organizational strength depends partly on aggressive attitudes and the willingness to fight. Thus, the more combative a leadership, the more likely that teachers will actually press to achieve group power and participation in the domains of educational policy-making.

In Chapters II and III we inquired also into the bases of membership size and leadership militancy. Many factors have been suggested to account for the increased strength of teacher organizations today. We decided to concentrate on certain variables and exclude others. To some extent, our findings on membership and militancy vary by time, place, and attitudinal dimension. In several respects, however, they are clear and very much in accord with expectations. First, associations between sex and membership and sex and militancy prove strong. Men are more inclined to join unions than are women. Male leaders are

[2] *Pressure Group Politics* (Stanford: Stanford University Press, 1960), 34.

likelier to have militant orientations than female leaders. Second, associations between teaching level, and membership on the one hand, and membership and militancy, on the other, also are strong. Teachers in junior and senior high schools are more apt to join unions than those in elementary schools. Group leaders are likelier to be militant if they have taught at the secondary school level. Third, associations between dissatisfaction and membership and militancy appear strong as well. The more dissatisfied are teachers with one or another educational condition, the more likely they are to join a union and have militant attitudes as leaders.

Surely the most significant factor examined was the affiliation of the group itself. With regard to the militancy of leadership attitudes, affiliation explained more than any other factors. Despite the recent convergence of national doctrine, differences in attitudes toward participation, power, and tactics between leaders who belong to AFT locals and those who belong to NEA or independent associations are striking. Among the organizations surveyed, the four affiliated with AFT had considerably higher percentages of leaders possessing militant orientations than the five others. Union leaderships are much more inclined than others to want a decisive participatory role, seek a redistribution of educational power, and express a willingness to engage in hard combat.

But whatever the factors determining membership and militancy, a central question concerns the relationship between a group's strength and its actual influence. Group strength offers a potential for influence. In order to realize that potential, however, an organization must translate the statics of strength into purposeful behavior. *Organizational behavior,* in theory at least, should closely reflect the orientations of leaders and members. There is ample evidence in the literature of the social sciences to demonstrate such linkages. Therefore, we would naturally expect stronger groups, particularly those with militant leaderships, to expend greater effort and act more aggressively than weaker ones, particularly those with acquiescent leaderships. In one respect this expectation is confirmed. When other critical factors are held constant, motivations and behavior are related. AFT locals in Boston, Chicago, and San Francisco, for instance, are more vocal and more aggressive than their less militant rivals. Thus, differences between the behavior of unions and associations in the same cities appear to be a function of leadership and rank-and-file motivations.

But, controlling for the affiliation of local organizations, we must still account for differences in group behavior or influence from one community to the next. Why, in other words, does a union local in one city perform at a different level of effort and aggressiveness than a union local in another? Motivations cannot provide a completely satisfactory explanation. There is no simple one-way determination. Given attitudes do not invariably result in given behaviors. To answer the question, making comparisons among groups in several communities, it is necessary to probe further. This is what we have done in Chapters IV and V, in a closer examination of the behavior of a few organizations in three cities.

Any comparison of the New York City United Federation of Teachers, the Boston Teachers Union, and the San Francisco Federation of Teachers would produce a host of dissimilarities, especially since these groups had achieved contrasting stages of organizational development at the time of our study. UFT had won collective bargaining and grown in size and wealth. BTU had overtaken its competitor in membership and was on the verge of winning representational status in a bargaining election. SFFT was still a minority with no immediate prospects of representing all, or even a majority, of teachers in the city school system.

In terms of motivation, two of these groups are substantially the same. The leaderships of both the New York and San Francisco locals agree on the need for decisive participation, group power, and combative tactics. Leadership in Boston, by contrast, is less cohesive and decidedly less militant. It is more willing to settle for consultation as a participatory goal and less inclined to resort to forceful action. On the basis of attitudes alone, we might predict that the behaviors of UFT and SFFT would resemble one another, while that of BTU would be at a lower level of militancy. The data, however, contradict such a prediction. As far as behavior is concerned, UFT emerges as the only organization which has customarily made significant demands and perennially engaged in conflict to advance them. However divergent the motivations of their leaderships, BTU and SFFT have operated in generally similar manner, accommodating to the system or maneuvering for narrow advantage, but eschewing full-scale battle. Relations between attitudinal and behavioral militancy can be discerned in the simple diagram presented below.

BEHAVIORAL MILITANCY	ATTITUDINAL MILITANCY	
	Higher	Lower
Higher	UFT	
Lower	SFFT	BTU

Attitudes and behavior are congruent in the cases of the New York and Boston unions, but not in the case of the San Francisco union.

These contrasting patterns of behavior suggest that militant motivations may be requisite for militant action, but that other factors also count. Therefore, it is valuable to explore the conditions under which militant attitudes will lead to more militant behavior and those under which they will lead to more compliant behavior. We have referred to them as "opportunities for action" or, briefly, *organizational opportunities.* Although one's orientation affects how he perceives conditions, opportunities may also be thought of as objective features of the environment. The existence of opportunities may have no impact when motivations to exploit them are lacking. Where attitudes are favorable, their existence will facilitate militant behavior and their non-existence will impede it.

Factors which may denote group opportunities are too numerous to examine thoroughly. This study has touched on a few, such as state statutes or regulations, in different contexts. But our attention concentrated on three types of factors, which are primarily of local nature: the styles of the political community, the conduct of educational chieftains, and the dispositions of teachers and teacher activists. Their collective impact cannot be dismissed, since it provides an ingredient essential to any explanation of why the organizational behavior of UFT contrasts sharply with that of BTU and SFFT.

In New York City the style of politics is characterized by contradictory attachments, competing interests, and perpetual conflict. This tends to encourage aggressive behavior by the teacher organization here (and also may partially account for the militancy of leadership attitudes). By contrast, politics in Boston and San Francisco is based largely on widely shared attachments, complementary interests, and less marked conflict. This tends to discourage aggressive behavior by teacher organizations (and also may partially account for the lesser militancy of BTU leadership attitudes).[3]

More directly, the practices of educational authorities, particularly school boards, superintendents, and central headquarters administrators, have structured organizational opportunities. Perhaps because of the size, complexity, and fragmentation of New York's school system, the steadfast opposition by educational chieftains to UFT demands has proven ineffective. Resistance to alteration in the rules of the game did not stem union activity but only encouraged it. Without the kind

[3] Robert L. Crain also treats the relationship between community styles and school politics, in *The Politics of School Desegregation* (Chicago: Aldine, 1968), esp. 195–221.

of challenge expressed by the words and actions of school leaders, UFT might have proceeded at a slower and less insistent pace. In Boston and San Francisco, teacher unions have also encountered opposition, but school leaders in these cities have acted authoritatively, yet benevolently. By means of skillful tactics they have been able to evade confrontations, divert power aspirations, and provide inducements for cooperation.

Political styles and establishment practices are among the important factors which affect feelings within the teaching community. How teachers feel in turn helps to shape the types of activities a group will undertake. Thus, organizational behavior is determined in part by the opportunities which members and potential members establish by their attitudes. This is especially true where two or more groups compete for support or separate factions within one group vie for control.

Once again, contrasts between UFT on the one hand, and BTU and SFFT on the other, appear sharp. Despite the over-all conservatism of New York City teachers, feelings of resentment toward the educational establishment have been and continue to be widespread. This is evidenced by the support the union received first in a collective bargaining election and then in successive strikes. Comparatively speaking, UFT leaders have suffered few restraints because of the unwillingness of the city's teachers to further union participation and power through collective action. Teachers in Boston and San Francisco, however, serve to constrain militant behavior by union organizations. In Boston, where personalism prevails, teachers exhibit deference and loyalty to established educational authority and thereby discourage aggressiveness by the union. In San Francisco, where complacency prevails, teachers exhibit apathy and caution, similarly discouraging overly aggressive behavior by the union.

As a consequence, union behavior differs from one city to another. In New York leadership motivations and organizational opportunities promote conflict. In Boston they promote accommodation. In San Francisco the former factors impel the union to action, while the latter prevent it from acting forcefully. The result is maneuver, not battle, and behavior which closely resembled that of BTU until very recently. Combining militancy and opportunities in order to explain group behavior, it is convenient to view relationships in the simple diagram below. On the basis of clues suggested by the few cases examined we would venture the following: (1) if both leadership militancy and organizational opportunities exist, behavioral militancy will necessarily be comparatively high; (2) if neither exists, it will necessarily be comparatively low; and (3) if either one or the other exists, it may be higher or lower, depending upon additional circumstances.

BEHAVIORAL MILITANCY	ATTITUDINAL MILITANCY AND ORGANIZATIONAL OPPORTUNITIES COMBINED		
	Higher	Medium	Lower
Higher	UFT		▓▓▓▓▓
Lower	▓▓▓▓▓	SFFT	BTU

This exploration of organizational behavior is designed to further our understanding of group influence. Although we can imagine cases where passive organizations exercise power, group activity and group power would appear to be linked. Educational power still resides with mayors, school boards, and superintendents. So does formal authority to decide policy. Therefore, a teacher organization has power to the extent that it can get educational leaders to do something that they would not otherwise do. It is difficult in each instance, and especially in a large number of instances, to establish the degree of aversion by school authorities to teacher demands. As a result, it is not easy to specify how group pressure causes school policies to vary from what they otherwise might have been. The amount of teacher influence in each policy domain or with regard to each issue cannot be determined precisely.

Leadership perceptions give us some idea of differences in group power. Case materials from three cities, which were discussed in Chapter VII, take us further. They reveal that among several teacher unions, only the United Federation of Teachers wields a considerable amount of influence. Its impact on the resolution of position and style issues has been greater than that of either the Boston Teachers Union or the San Francisco Federation of Teachers. Its participation has covered a broader scope and its efforts have been more intense. Its challenge to educational power relationships has been a significant one.

Neither of UFT's sister organizations has achieved comparable power. Teacher gains in Boston have been modest in quality and limited in scope. Generally, they are granted according to the original intentions of educational authorities. Since teachers possess the ability to support or oppose candidates for elections that decide the composition of the School Committee, teachers do have some influence on policy-making. But the union, *qua* organization, has relatively little effect. In San Francisco, too, the union has made less than a fundamental difference. Though its efforts are instrumental in prodding the superintendent and board to fulfill their obligations to the teaching staff or improve educational conditions, its ability to prevail in a contest of wills is still slight.

It may be that teacher power is an artifact of conflictual situations. In other words, only when conflict occurs is the power of a teachers group visible. But an alternative explanation seems closer to the mark. Given their marginal roles in educational policy-making, it is probable that power by teacher groups can only be achieved through conflict at the present time. If this is so, then a relationship between militancy and influence takes distinctive shape. Our findings, limited though they are, suggest the linkage that is portrayed in the diagram below.

ORGANIZATIONAL INFLUENCE	BEHAVIORAL MILITANCY	
	Higher	Lower
Higher	UFT	
Lower		BTU SFFT

Higher behavioral militancy is associated with greater organizational influence, while lower militancy is associated with lesser influence.

Organizational strength, opportunities, and behavior all must be considered in an assessment of the influence of teacher groups today. While we have examined them separately and consecutively, they overlap in the spheres of actual school politics. Influence depends upon behavior. It shapes behavior as well. If militant tactics succeed in one instance, they are likely to be employed in others. Aggressive behavior depends upon opportunities created by feelings within a teacher community, but action, by altering the attitudes of teachers, produces new opportunities. Organizational choices and establishment policies depend upon the number of teachers belonging to a group, and the number who can be mobilized in participation or support. Conversely, decisions made by group leaders, and the practices of educational authorities, help to determine how many teachers will join and what they will bring to their membership.

To return to the starting point of this study, ideology is particularly significant to group behavior and influence. It is extremely unlikely that acquiescent leaderships will steer their groups to positions of power. It is quite likely that militant leaderships, and especially those who are insistent that teachers share in educational policy-making, will impel their organizations to more militant behavior and thereby increase group power. When they do, more than higher teacher salaries will be at stake. A lack of favorable opportunities may temporarily block their paths, but at some stage leaders will probably risk forceful action, as the 1968 strike in San Francisco demonstrates.

Organizational imperatives now impel teachers to behavioral militancy. Contests between unions and associations, the conduct of professional organizers assigned to local affiliates, intra-group competition, and the achievements of the union in New York City all encourage action. Militancy has begun to alter educational power relationships. The prospect is for teacher organizations in growing numbers of communities throughout urban and suburban America to participate more decisively than ever before. If the past and present, as explored in this study, serve as an indication, the years ahead should produce an even greater impact by teacher groups on local governments of public education.

Index

Action orientations, 54, 71–73, 178
Administrative doctrine, 2–5, 6, 9, 10
Affiliation: impact on militancy, 59–61, 66, 67, 179. *See also* Membership
AFL–CIO, 7, 14
Age: related to membership, 33, 34; impact on militancy, 63–65
Agger, Robert, 12n, 126n
Allen, Ivan, 134
Altomare, George, 78
American Association of School Administrators (AASA), 19
American Federation of Teachers (AFT): doctrine, 5–13, 59, 68, 69, 178; activities, 18, 19, membership, 22, 23, 24, 25, 177; representational elections, 25–28; militancy, 49–52, 59–61, 65–67, 69, 71–73, 116–17, 179
Anderson, Lee F., 119n
Atlanta: group militancy, 48, 49, 50, 59, 71, 72; power distribution, 127, 128, 129, 131, 175; mayoral control, 132, 133; professional control, 141–42; teacher influence, 154–55
Atlanta Teachers Association (ATA): militancy, 48, 49, 50, 59, 71, 72; power distribution, 127, 128, 129, 131

Banfield, Edward C., 55n, 114n, 126n
Barber, James D., 94n
Barstow, Robbins, 9n, 10n
Batchelder, Richard, 5, 11
Behavior: of teacher groups, xi, 179–81, 184
Bensman, Joseph, 126n
Berelson, Bernard, 156n
Blalock, Hubert M., 60n
Board of education: power of, 128, 129, 130, 131, 143, 153

Bobbitt, Franklin, 3
Boston: group membership, 28–41, 45–47, 176, 177; group militancy, 48, 49, 50, 59, 71, 72, 73, 94, 179, 180, 181, 184, 185; group behavior, 82–87, 121, 122, 180, 181, 182–85; group opportunities, 95, 96, 122, 181, 182; educational change, 97; school authorities, 103–106, 182; teacher attitudes, 114, 115, 182; intra-group competition, 119, 120; power distribution, 127, 128, 129, 131, 175; mayoral control, 132, 133, 135, 136; professional control, 141–43, 148–50; teacher influence, 154, 155, 157, 158, 160, 161, 162, 163, 166, 167, 171, 172, 183, 184
Boston Teachers Alliance (BTA): membership, 28–41, 45–47, 176, 177; militancy, 48, 49, 50, 59, 72, 73, 179; accommodation, 84–87, 122; opportunities, 95, 96, 122; school authorities, 103–106, 122; teacher attitudes, 114, 115; power distribution, 127, 128, 129, 131; welfare, 157, 158; working conditions, 160, 161, 163; educational policy, 166, 167, 171, 172
Boston Teachers Union (BTU): membership, 28–41, 45–47, 176, 177; militancy, 48, 49, 50, 59, 71, 72, 94, 179, 180, 181; accommodation, 84–87, 122, 180, 181, 182, 183; opportunities, 95, 96, 122, 181, 182; school authorities, 103–06, 122, 182; teacher attitudes, 114, 115, 122, 182; internal competition, 119, 120; power distribution, 127, 128, 129, 131, 183, 184; welfare, 157, 158; working conditions, 160, 161, 162, 163; educational policy, 166, 167, 171, 172

187

Breyer, Irving, 90
Bridges, Edwin M., 36n
Buckley, Kevin P., 134n, 152n
Buder, Leonard, 19
Budget, 133–38, 147, 148, 151, 152, 157, 160, 167n, 170n
Bundy, McGeorge, 139
Bureaucracy: power of, 128, 129, 130, 131, 143–46, 148, 150, 153
Button, H. Warren, 3n

California Teachers Association (CTA), 88, 90
Callahan, Raymond E., 3n
Campaigns: impact on membership, 41–45, 47
Campbell, Angus, 59n
Campbell, Roald F., 4n, 141n
Cannon, Mark W., 75n
Center for Urban Education, 169, 170
Charters, W. W., 3
Chicago: group membership, 24, 26, 177; group militancy, 48, 49, 50, 59, 71, 72, 73, 179; power distribution, 127–31 *passim*, 175; mayoral control, 132–35 *passim*; professional control, 141–43, 151–53; teacher influence, 154, 155
Chicago Education Association (CEA): membership, 177; militancy, 48, 49, 50, 59, 71, 72, 179; power distribution, 127–31 *passim*
Chicago Teachers Union (CTU): membership, 24, 26, 177; militancy, 48, 49, 50, 59, 72, 73, 179; power distribution, 127–31 *passim*
Christopher, George, 134
Citizens Coalition for an Adequate Education Budget, 167n
Citizens Committee for Effective Schools, 168
Citywide More Effective Schools Parents Association, 169
Clark, Terry N., 125n
Class size, 161–63
Cogen, Charles, 5, 15, 16, 43, 44, 51, 52, 78, 99, 117, 118
Cole, Stephen, 30, 34, 51n, 64n, 110

Collective bargaining, 7–9, 75–82, 85–87, 91, 92, 99–102, 106. *See also* Representation, elections
Collective negotiations, 7–9, 19, 20. *See also* Collective bargaining, Professional negotiation
Collins, John, 83, 135, 136
Combative orientations, 53, 54, 71–73, 178
Community control, 139, 145, 149, 150, 164, 165. *See also* Decentralization
Community political style, 73, 74, 82–84, 87, 88, 95, 122, 181
Competition: nationwide NEA vs. AFT, 2, 15–19, 22–28; intergroup, 96, 116, 117, 185; intragroup, 92, 93, 96, 117–22, 185
Condon-Wadlin Act, 95
Corwin, Ronald G., 51n, 98n
Cotton, Richard, 134n, 152n
Council of Supervisory Associations, 168
Crain, Robert L., 94n, 126n, 127n, 132n, 147n, 152n, 181n
Cronin, Joseph, 11n, 52
Cubberly, Ellwood, 3
Curriculum and instruction, 55, 57, 128, 129, 132, 141, 142, 145, 150, 152, 155, 167

Dahl, Robert A., 55n, 125n, 126n, 137n, 172n
Daley, Richard, 134, 135
D'Antonio, William V., 124n
Decentralization, 139, 145, 164, 165. *See also* Community control
Democratic administration, 2–5, 15
Diplomacy, 53, 84, 93
Disruptive children, 159, 160
Dissatisfaction: impact on militancy, 62, 63, 67, 68, 179; related to membership, 179
Doctrine: administrative, 2–5, 6, 9, 10; teacher group, 5–13, 59, 68, 69
Doherty, Robert E., 11n, 12n, 14, 15, 17n, 23n, 91n
Donovan, Bernard, 98, 99, 110, 139, 144

Duty-free lunch, 41, 160, 161

Easton, David, 124n
Eckstein, Harry, xi, 51n, 177, 178
Educational authorities, *See* School authorities
Educational change, 96–98
Eisenstadt, Thomas, 86
Eldersveld, Samuel J., xi
Elections, 105, 106, 166
Elementary School Principals Association, 138
Ellman, Mary, 134n, 153n
Empire State Federation of Teachers, 157n
Erickson, Eugene C., 124n

Faculty councils, 89, 108
Featherstone, Joseph, 165
Fiscal independence, 133
Flynn, Ralph, 91
Ford Foundation, 164
Fox, David J., 170n
Froman, Lewis A., 156n

Gans, Herbert J., 126n
Gartland, Arthur, 86
Giardino, Alfred, 101
Gillis, Frederick, 148
Gittell, Marilyn, 96, 97, 113, 126n, 127n, 137, 153n
Goal orientations, *See* Participatory orientations
Greenstone, J. David, 51n
Gregg, Russell T., 4n
Grievance procedures, 101
Griffiths, Daniel E., 154
Gross, Calvin, 6, 52, 53, 79, 98, 99, 101, 143, 144
Gross, Neal, 3n, 40n, 123

Hauser, Philip, 152
Hechinger, Fred, 111n
Herriott, Robert E., 40n
Hicks, Louise Day, 86, 104
High School Teachers Association, 74, 75
Hochberg, Samuel, 118

Hollander, T. Edward, 127n, 153n
Holman, Stephen R., 93

Ideology, *See* Doctrine, Militancy
Integration, 127, 146, 147, 148, 149, 152, 162n, 166
Interest groups, x, xi

Jackson, Dan, 92
Jaffe, Sol, 117
James, H. Thomas, 133n, 135n, 157n
Junior High School Principals Association, 138

Kaplan, Joel, 156n
Kaufman, Herbert, 55n, 74n, 126n, 143
Kennedy, John F., 14
Key, V. O., 59n
Kidd, Dick, 92
Kimbrough, Ralph B., 126n
Kleinmann, Jack H., 6n
Kozol, Jonathan, 84n, 104n, 105n

Leadership: militancy of, 51–54, 71–73; constraints on, 111–16; elections, 117, 118, 121
Lee, Joseph, 86
Lee, Robert D., 147n
Levin, Murray B., 83n
Lieberman, Myron, 6n, 14n, 22, 23n, 76n, 154n, 156n
Lindsay, John, 81, 137–39, 164, 167n
Lipset, Seymour Martin, 36n, 117n
Litt, Edgar, 83n
Local schools, 102, 108, 109
Logue, Edward, 83
Lowe, William T., 30n, 34, 35, 37

March, James G., 124n
Martin, Roscoe C., 55n, 140
Mason, Ward S., 30, 33n
Masotti, Louis H., 126n
Mayer, Martin, 144n, 164n
Mayor: power of, 75–81 *passim,* 128–31 *passim,* 131–40, 145n, 157, 158
Mazen, Ben, 117, 118
Membership: nationwide, 23–25; local factors influencing, 28–47; and strength, 176, 178. *See also* Affiliation

Mesirow, David, 24n
Militancy: explanations of, 13–15; concept, 47–54; dimensions, 55–58; correlates, 58–70; strength and behavior, 178, 180
Monsen, R. Joseph, 75n
More Effective Schools (MES), 81, 101, 113, 114, 168–71
Morphet, Edgar L., 4n
Moskow, Michael H., 6n, 7n, 14n, 17, 22, 23n, 25n, 39n, 76n, 156n
Munger, Frank J., 55n

National Education Association (NEA): doctrine, 5–11, 16, 17, 59, 68, 69, 178; activities, 18, 19; membership, 23, 24, 177; representational elections, 25–28; militancy, 49, 50, 59–61, 65–67, 69, 71–73, 116, 117
National School Boards Association, 20
Negotiating Council, 90, 91, 92
New York City: group membership, 23, 24, 26, 28–47, 176, 177; group militancy, 48, 49, 50, 54, 59, 64n, 65n, 71, 72, 73, 94, 180, 181, 184, 185; group behavior, 73–82, 121, 122, 180–85 *passim*; group opportunities, 95, 96, 122, 181, 182; educational change, 96, 97; school authorities, 98–103, 181, 182; teacher attitudes, 109–14, 182; intra-group competition, 117–19; power distribution, 126–31 *passim*, 175; mayoral control, 132–40; professional control, 141–43, 146; teacher influence, 154, 155, 156, 157, 159, 160, 162, 163–65, 166, 167–71, 172, 173, 183, 184
New York City Office of Education Liaison, 139
New York State Board of Regents, 164
New York State Department of Education, 4

Oberer, Walter E., 11n, 12n, 15n, 17n, 23n, 91n
Ocean Hill-Brownsville district, 164n, 165
O'Connor, William, 86, 105

Ohrenberger, William, 105, 148, 149
O'Neill, John, 77n
Opportunities: of teacher groups, xi, 94–96, 121, 122, 181–83, 184

Parente, Roger, 117, 118
Participants, 125, 126, 128
Participatory orientations, 51, 52, 55–58, 71–73, 178
Perry, Charles R., 11n
Personnel, 55, 57, 128, 129, 132, 141, 142, 145, 149, 152, 155, 163, 164
Peterson, Paul E., 51n
Pois, Joseph, 151, 152
Political culture, *See* Community political style
Polsby, Nelson W., 124n
Posey, Rollin B., 14n
Power orientations, 52, 53, 71–73, 178
Presthus, Robert, 124n
Principals: related to membership, 39–41, 47; power of, 102, 128–31 *passim*
Professional negotiation, 7–9. *See also* Representation, Elections
Public Education Association, 77n, 139, 143, 144, 166
Public employees, 14

Race, related to membership, 38n
Raskin, A. H., 82n, 103n
Redmond, James, 152n
Remsberg, Bonnie, 151n
Remsberg, Charles, 151n
Representation: elections, 23, 25–28, 76, 86, 87, 121
Rockefeller, Nelson, 77
Rogers, David, 126n, 142n, 145n
Rose, Arnold M., 124n
Rosenthal, Alan, 126n, 127n
Rubin, Max, 76, 144

Salary, 55, 57, 77–80 *passim*, 87, 104, 128, 129, 132, 138, 141, 142, 147, 155–59
San Francisco: group membership, 176, 177; group militancy, 48, 49, 50, 59, 71, 72, 73, 94, 179, 180, 181, 184, 185; group behavior, 87–91, 121, 122,

180, 181, 182–85; group opportunities, 95, 96, 122, 181, 182; educational change, 97, 98; school authorities, 106–109, 182; teacher attitudes, 115, 116, 182; intra-group competition, 120, 121; power distribution, 127–31 *passim,* 175; mayoral control, 132–35 *passim*; professional control, 141, 142, 146–48; teacher influence, 154, 155, 158, 159, 161, 162, 163, 166, 167, 171, 172, 183, 184

San Francisco Classroom Teachers Association (SFCTA): membership, 176, 177; militancy, 48, 49, 50, 59, 72, 73, 179; maneuver, 88–91, 122; opportunities, 95, 96, 122; school authorities, 106–109, 122; teacher attitudes, 115, 116; power distribution, 127–31 *passim*; welfare, 158, 159; working conditions, 161, 163; educational policy, 166, 167, 171, 172

San Francisco Federation of Teachers (SFFT): membership, 47n, 176, 177; militancy, 48, 49, 50, 59, 71, 72, 73, 94, 179, 180, 181, 184; maneuver, 88–93, 122, 180, 181, 182, 183; opportunities, 95, 96, 122, 181, 182; school authorities, 106–109, 122, 182; teacher attitudes, 115, 116, 122, 182; internal competition, 120, 121; power distribution, 127–31 *passim,* 183, 184; welfare, 158, 159; working conditions, 161, 162, 163; educational policy, 166, 167, 171, 172

Sayre, Wallace S., 55n, 74n, 126n, 143

School authorities: practices of, 95, 122, 181, 182; resistance, 96–103; benevolence, 104–106; diversion and delay, 107

School budget, *See* Budget

School decentralization, *See* Decentralization

School division: related to membership, 34–36, 46, 179; impact on militancy, 63–68 *passim,* 179

School elections, *See* Elections

School schedule, 163

School size, *See* Size of school

School organization, 55, 57, 128, 129, 132, 141, 142, 155, 164, 165

Schrag, Peter, 83, 84, 88n, 97, 98n, 103n, 104n, 106n, 127n, 148n, 150, 151

Selden, David, 12, 17n, 77, 162, 163

Seniority: related to membership, 33, 34; impact on militancy, 63–68 *passim*

Sex: related to membership, 30–33, 45, 46; impact on militancy, 13, 63–68 *passim,* 178, 179

Shanker, Albert, 12, 13, 20, 54, 79, 80, 82, 117, 118, 138n, 140, 164n

Shelley, John, 134, 135

Sick leave, 41, 158

Size of school: related to militancy, 13, 14; related to membership, 36, 37

Spears, Harold, 89, 98, 107, 108, 146–48

State legislation, 8, 76, 86, 90, 94, 95, 101, 108, 138, 157n

Steffensen, James P., 8n, 20n

Stinnett, T. M., 6n, 10, 14

Strategic orientations, *See* Power orientations

Street, David, 126n, 132n, 152n

Strength: of teacher groups, xi, 22, 176–79, 184

Strikes, 16–19 *passim,* 42–45, 65n, 75, 77, 80, 81, 93n, 121, 138

Superintendent: power of, 128–31 *passim,* 140–53

Swanson, Bert E., 74n, 126n

Tactical orientations, *See* Combative orientations, Action orientations

Taylor Act, 95, 138

Teachers: attitudes, 17, 95, 96, 109–16, 122, 181, 182; action, 17, 18; influence, 154, 155, 171–73, 175, 184, 185; assignment, 163, 164; recruitment, 168

Teachers Association of San Francisco (TASF): militancy, 48, 49, 50, 59, 72, 179; maneuver, 88–91; school authorities, 106–109; teacher attitudes, 115, 116; power distribution, 127–31 *passim*

Teachers Guild, 74, 75

Teaching experience, *See* Seniority
Teaching situation: related to membership, 37–39
Theobald, John, 98, 99, 143
Truman, David B., xi

United Federation of Teachers (UFT):
membership, 22n, 23, 24, 26, 28–47, 176, 177; militancy, 48, 49, 50, 54, 59, 64n, 65n, 71, 72, 94, 122, 180, 181, 184, 185; conflict, 73–82, 122, 180, 181, 182, 183; opportunities, 95, 96, 122, 181, 182; school authorities, 98–103, 122, 181, 182; teacher attitudes, 109–14, 122, 182; internal competition, 117–19, 122; power distribution, 126–31 *passim,* 183, 184; welfare, 156, 157; working conditions, 159, 160, 162, 163–65; educational policy, 166, 167–71, 172, 173
United Parents Association (UPA), 80, 166

Usdan, Michael D., 16n, 20n

Vanecko, James J., 126n
Vidich, Arthur J., 126n
von Hoffman, Nicholas, 83n

Wagner, Robert, 75, 77, 99, 100, 118, 134, 136, 137, 138
Webb, Harold, 20n
West, Allen M., 17n
Wildman, Wesley A., 11, 15, 154
Willis, Benjamin, 134, 151–53
Winick, Charles, 43, 64n
Winton Act, 90, 91, 108
Wolfinger, Raymond E., 124n
Wollett, Donald H., 9n
Working conditions: related to membership, 37–39; impact on militancy, 62, 63, 67, 68, 100

Zeigler, Harmon, 11n, 30, 177n